Wow! 365 Chicken Breast Recipes

(Wow! 365 Chicken Breast Recipes - Volume 1)

Laura Mueller

Copyright: Published in the United States by Laura Mueller/ © LAURA MUELLER

Published on December, 02 2020

All rights reserved. No part of this publication may be reproduced, stored in retrieval system, copied in any form or by any means, electronic, mechanical, photocopying, recording or otherwise transmitted without written permission from the publisher. Please do not participate in or encourage piracy of this material in any way. You must not circulate this book in any format. LAURA MUELLER does not control or direct users' actions and is not responsible for the information or content shared, harm and/or actions of the book readers.

In accordance with the U.S. Copyright Act of 1976, the scanning, uploading and electronic sharing of any part of this book without the permission of the publisher constitute unlawful piracy and theft of the author's intellectual property. If you would like to use material from the book (other than just simply for reviewing the book), prior permission must be obtained by contacting the author at author@friesrecipes.com

Thank you for your support of the author's rights.

Content

365 AWESOME CHICKEN BREAST RECIPES 9

1. "Chicken Noodle Soup" Casserole Recipe . 9
2. 7 Minute Cooked Dinner Recipe 9
3. A Good Easy Garlic Chicken Recipe 10
4. Adams Recipe For Unholy Chicken Recipe 10
5. Afghanistan Chicken Recipe 11
6. African Apricot Chicken On Skewers Recipe 11
7. Aji De Gallina Recipe 12
8. Alfredo Chicken With Cinnamon Recipe . 12
9. Almond Crusted Chicken Recipe 13
10. Aloha Chicken Recipe 13
11. Amish Chicken And Macaroni Casserole Recipe 13
12. Angel Hair Pasta With Chicken Recipe 14
13. Apple Chicken Quesadillas Recipe 14
14. Apricot Barbecue Chicken Recipe 14
15. Apricot Chicken Recipe 15
16. Aromatic Chicken In Coconut Cream Recipe 15
17. Artichoke Portobello Chicken In Cream Recipe 16
18. Articoke Chicken Recipe 16
19. Asparagus And Chicken Casserole Recipe 17
20. Autumn Noodle Bake Recipe 17
21. BBQ Chicken Pizza Recipe 17
22. Bacon Wrapped Chicken Recipe 18
23. Baked Chicken And Chorizo Paella Recipe 18
24. Baked Chicken Breasts With Cherry Tomato Sauce Recipe 19
25. Baked Chicken With Fire Roasted Tomato And Bacon Sauce Recipe 19
26. Baked Chicken With Artichokes And Mushrooms Recipe 20
27. Baked Chicken With Mushrooms And Artichokes Recipe 20
28. Baked Mexican Chicken Recipe 20
29. Balsamic Asian Italian Chicken Recipe 21
30. Balsamic Oregano Chicken Recipe 21
31. Beef Or Chicken Fajitas Recipe 22
32. Beer N Lime Grilled Chicken Recipe 22
33. Belgian Chicken And Leeks Casserole Recipe 22
34. Bell Pepper Chicken And Rice Recipe 23
35. Black And White Sesame Chicken Recipe 23
36. Bombay Chicken Recipe 23
37. Bourbon Laced Tipsy Chicken With Peaches Recipe 24
38. Bourbon Street Chicken Recipe 24
39. Bruschetta Stuffed Chicken Breasts Recipe 25
40. Buffalo Chicken Chili Recipe 25
41. Busy Moms Chicken And Dumplings Recipe 26
42. Buttermilk Country Fried Chicken Recipe 26
43. CAJUN STYLE PASTA Recipe 26
44. CHICKEN MARSALA SANDWICH Recipe 27
45. CHICKEN OR TURKEY PAD THAI Recipe 28
46. CHILI CHICKEN CORN N PASTA Recipe 28
47. CREAMY BASIL PASTA WITH CHICKEN Amp VEGETABLES Recipe 29
48. Cajun Chicken Ala King Recipe 29
49. Cajun Chicken Breasts In The Oven Recipe 30
50. Cajun Style Chicken Nuggets Recipe 30
51. Cap Cai Indonesian Vegetable Stir Fry Recipe 30
52. Cappellini Florentine Recipe 31
53. Caribbean Style Chicken With Tropical Salsa And Spicy Sweet Potato Sticks Recipe 31
54. Caribbean Salsa Chicken Recipe 32
55. Ceasar Chicken With Orzo Recipe 32
56. Cheap Fast And Easy General Tsos Chicken Recipe 33
57. Cheese Chicken Recipe 33
58. Cheese Herb Stuffed Chicken Breast Recipe 33
59. Cheese Chickena Dn Rice Recipe 34
60. Cheesy Chicken Recipe 34
61. Cheesy Chicken Spaghetti Bake Recipe 35
62. Cheesy Chicken And Potato Casserole Recipe 35
63. Cheesy Chicken And Rice Bake Recipe 35
64. Cheesy Crockpot Chicken Recipe 36

65. Cheezit Chicken Recipe 36
66. Chicken Rice Cheese Casserole Recipe 36
67. Chicken & Asparagus Bundles (italian) Recipe 37
68. Chicken & Cream Cheese Stuffed Peppers Recipe 37
69. Chicken & Sun Dried Tomato Orzo Recipe 38
70. Chicken Adobo Recipe 38
71. Chicken Alfredo Recipe 39
72. Chicken And Cheese Stuffed Avacado Recipe 39
73. Chicken And Rice In A Mug Recipe 39
74. Chicken And Shrimp Recipe 40
75. Chicken And Vegetable Pie Recipe 40
76. Chicken Asparagus Mushroom Bake Recipe 41
77. Chicken Athena Recipe 41
78. Chicken Breast Dijon Recipe 41
79. Chicken Breast Supreme Recipe 42
80. Chicken Breasts Diane Recipe 42
81. Chicken Breasts Pierre Recipe 43
82. Chicken Breasts With Garlic And Oil Recipe 43
83. Chicken Breasts With Ginger Orange Sauce Recipe 44
84. Chicken Breasts In Chutney Cream Recipe 44
85. Chicken Chasey Breaded Chicken Lasagna With Mozzerella Cheese Recipe 45
86. Chicken Chorizo Pasta With A Creamy Sauce Recipe 45
87. Chicken Cilantro Soup Recipe 46
88. Chicken Cordon Bleu Recipe 46
89. Chicken Dijon Pasta Salad Recipe 47
90. Chicken Elegante Recipe 47
91. Chicken Enchilada Casserole Recipe 47
92. Chicken Enchiladas Recipe 48
93. Chicken Enchiladas With Mole Sauce Recipe 48
94. Chicken Florentine Casserole Recipe 49
95. Chicken Florentine Recipe 49
96. Chicken Gorgonzola Pasta Recipe 50
97. Chicken Gyro Recipe 50
98. Chicken In Sour Cream Sauce Recipe 51
99. Chicken Italiano Recipe 51
100. Chicken Kabobs Recipe 52
101. Chicken Kiev Recipe 52
102. Chicken Lasagna Recipe 53
103. Chicken Makhani Curry Recipe 53
104. Chicken Marengo Recipe 54
105. Chicken Marsala Recipe 54
106. Chicken Neufetchel Recipe 54
107. Chicken Noodle Stir Fry Recipe 55
108. Chicken On A Stick Recipe 55
109. Chicken Oreganata Recipe 56
110. Chicken Paprika And Vegies Recipe 56
111. Chicken Pasta Provencale Recipe 57
112. Chicken Pasta Ricardo Recipe 57
113. Chicken Pecan And Cucumber Finger Sandwiches Recipe 58
114. Chicken Picatta Recipe 58
115. Chicken Pineapple Pizza Recipe 59
116. Chicken Pot Pie Recipe 59
117. Chicken Pot Pie With A Cornbread Top Recipe 60
118. Chicken Puffs Delight Recipe 60
119. Chicken Puttanesca Recipe 61
120. Chicken Reuben Casserole Recipe 62
121. Chicken Rice Skillet Recipe 62
122. Chicken Royce Recipe 62
123. Chicken Schnitzel Recipe 63
124. Chicken Schnitzel With Roquefort Gravy Recipe 63
125. Chicken Sfeeha Recipe 64
126. Chicken Skillet With Stuffing Recipe ... 65
127. Chicken Spagetti Recipe 65
128. Chicken Strips Recipe 66
129. Chicken Stroganoff Recipe 66
130. Chicken Tacos With Charred Salsa Recipe 66
131. Chicken Tamale Casserole Recipe 67
132. Chicken Tortellini With Asparagus Recipe 67
133. Chicken Vegetable Rice Dish Recipe 68
134. Chicken Vegetable Skillet Recipe 68
135. Chicken With Chipped Beef Recipe 69
136. Chicken With Ham And Cheese Recipe . 69
137. Chicken With Key Lime Glaze Recipe ... 69
138. Chicken With Lemon Caper Sauce Recipe 70
139. Chicken With Mushrooms And Grapes Recipe 70
140. Chicken With Portabella Mushrooms Recipe 71

141. Chicken With Potato, Green Pepper, Tomato Recipe 71
142. Chicken With Provencal Sauce Recipe 71
143. Chicken With Sherry Sauce Recipe 72
144. Chicken Amp Mushroom Tagliatelle Recipe 72
145. Chicken And Broccoli Casserole Recipe ... 72
146. Chicken And Goat Cheese Enchiladas With Black Bean Sauce Recipe 73
147. Chicken And Spinach Calzones Recipe 74
148. Chicken In Champagne And Mushroom Sauce Recipe 75
149. Chicken In Creamy Pesto Sauce Recipe.... 75
150. Chicken In White Cream Sauce With Garam Masala Recipe 75
151. Chicken With Creamy Cassis Sauce Recipe 76
152. Chicken Zucchini Alfredo Recipe 77
153. Chili Spiced Chicken Recipe 77
154. Chinese Almond Chicken Recipe 78
155. Chinese Chicken Balls Recipe 78
156. Chinese Fire Pot With Fish Balls Recipe .. 79
157. Chipotle Chicken And Noodles Recipe 79
158. Coco Ichibanya Cocos Style Chicken Cutlet Curry Recipe 80
159. Coconut Chicken Phase 1 Recipe 80
160. Copycat California Pizza Kitchens Chicken Tequila Fettuccine Recipe 81
161. Corn And Bell Pepper Chicken Bake Recipe 82
162. Country Captain Recipe 82
163. Cranberry Chicken Recipe 82
164. Crazy Coconut Chicken Recipe 83
165. Cream Of Green Chile Chicken Soup Recipe 83
166. Cream Of Mushroom Chicken Recipe 84
167. Creamed Smokey Chicken Recipe 84
168. Creamy Bacon And Mushroom Chicken Recipe 84
169. Creamy Chicken Curry Recipe 85
170. Creamy Pot Pie Recipe 85
171. Creole Chicken Bonne Femme Recipe 86
172. Creole Chicken Fried Chicken With Creole Ranch Dressing Recipe 86
173. Crisp And Creamy Baked Chicken Recipe 87
174. Crock Pot Italian Chicken Stew Recipe 87
175. Crock Pot Italian Chicken And Potatoes Recipe 88
176. Crockpot Bacon Ranch Chicken Recipe ... 88
177. Crockpot Chicken And Mushroom Gravy Recipe 89
178. Crunchy Chicken Chunks With Thai Peanut Sauce Recipe 89
179. Crunchy Chicken Fingers Recipe 89
180. Cumin Fried Chicken Recipe 90
181. Deep Fried Monte Cristo Sandwiches Recipe 90
182. Dotties Chicken And Broccoli Alfredo Recipe 91
183. EASY Crunchy Honey Chicken Nuggets Recipe 91
184. Easy Chicken Scampi Recipe 91
185. Easy Chicken Stir Fry Recipe 92
186. Easy Chicken And Noodles Recipe 92
187. Easy Elegant Cheesy Chicken Recipe 93
188. Easy Sunday Afternoon Chicken Recipe... 93
189. Electric Skillet Chicken Recipe 93
190. Elegant Chicken Recipe 94
191. Farmhouse Chicken And Dumplings Recipe 94
192. Focaccia Chicken Sandwich Recipe 95
193. Foil Baked Garden Chicken Recipe 96
194. Foil Pack Chicken Fajita Dinner Recipe 96
195. French Country Chicken Dinner Recipe... 97
196. Fried Lumpia Recipe 98
197. Garlic Chicken Breasts Recipe 99
198. Garlic Garlic Chicken Recipe 99
199. Garlic Pecan Fried Chicken Recipe 99
200. Garlic Smothered Chicken Recipe 100
201. Garlicky Chicken Pasta With Veggies Recipe 100
202. George Foreman Awesome Chicken Sandwich Recipe 101
203. Ginger Black Sesame Chicken Recipe 101
204. Glazed Chicken Recipe 102
205. Grandma's No Peek Chicken Casserole Recipe 102
206. Greek Chicken Breasts Recipe 102
207. Greek Chicken Recipe 103
208. Greek Chicken In The Crockpot Recipe 103
209. Greek Gods Pasta Salad With Marinated Chicken Breast Recipe 103
210. Green Curry Recipe 104
211. Grilled Almond Chicken With Savory Plum

Sauce Recipe 104
212. Grilled Bacon Wrapped Chicken Breast Recipe 105
213. Grilled Chicken Roller Recipe 105
214. Grilled Chicken With Curry Lime Sauce Recipe 106
215. Grilled Chicken With Portobello Mushroom Sauce Recipe 106
216. Grilled Chicken And Red Pepper Taco Recipe 106
217. Grilled Cumin Chicken With Fresh Tomatillo Sauce Recipe 107
218. Grilled Lemon Thyme Chicken Breasts Recipe 107
219. HAWAIIAN CHILI Recipe 108
220. Harissa Grilled Chicken And Vegetables Recipe 108
221. Hawaiian Chicken Parmigiana Recipe 109
222. Hawaiian Chicken Recipe 109
223. Home Made Enchiladas Recipe 110
224. Honey Orange Chicken Recipe 110
225. Idiot Chicken Recipe 111
226. Improved Chicken Divan Recipe 111
227. Indian Curry Chicken Recipe 112
228. Italian Baked Chicken And Rice Recipe .. 112
229. Italian Chicken Flat Bread Recipe 112
230. Italian Margarita Chicken Recipe 113
231. Italian Marinade Chicken Recipe 113
232. Jamaican Jerk Chicken Recipe 114
233. Jamaican Jerked Chicken Recipe 114
234. Japanese Chicken Katsu Recipe 115
235. Junes Chicken Florentine Recipe 115
236. Junes Chicken Parmigiana Recipe 116
237. Kai Sarap Crispy Chicken And Pork Adobo Flakes Recipe 116
238. Kane's Favorite Chicken Enchiladas Recipe 116
239. Kennedys Pub Chicken Vienne Recipe ... 117
240. Key West Chicken Recipe 117
241. Kickin Kitchen Sink Stir Fry Recipe 118
242. Kickin Pasta Recipe 118
243. Kung Pao Chicken Recipe 119
244. Kung Pow! Chicken Recipe 120
245. Lazy Roast Chicken Recipe 120
246. Lean Portola Valley Chicken Recipe 121
247. Lemon Cumin Grilled Chicken Breast Recipe 122
248. Lemon Apricot Chicken Recipe 122
249. Light Sesame Chicken Recipe 122
250. Lime Tequila Chicken Recipe 123
251. MY Butter Chicken Recipe 124
252. Mango Lime Chicken Recipe 124
253. Mediterranean Chicken And Village Salad Recipe 125
254. Mediterranean Chicken Breasts With Avocado Tapenade Recipe 125
255. Mexican Chicken Corn Chowder Recipe 126
256. Moms Easy Chicken Piccata Recipe 126
257. Monterey Chicken Recipe 126
258. More Kunfunky Chicken Really Fried This Time Recipe 127
259. Moroccan Chicken And Lentils Recipe .. 128
260. Moroccan Chicken Pie Recipe 128
261. Mos Chicken Salad Recipe 129
262. Mourgh Recipe 130
263. MozzaMustard Chicken Recipe 130
264. MrsLynams Cheater Pot Pie Chicken Recipe 130
265. Munster Chicken Recipe 131
266. Mushroom Chicken Bake Recipe 131
267. Naked Chicken With Broccolini Recipe . 132
268. New Delhi Spiced Chicken Recipe 132
269. One Skillet Spicy Chicken Italiano Recipe 133
270. One Step Creamy Chicken Breasts Recipe 133
271. Orange Amaretto Chicken Recipe 134
272. Orange Chicken Recipe 134
273. Orange Flavored Bourbon Grilled Chicken Recipe 135
274. Orange Glazed Ginger Chicken Recipe . 135
275. Outstanding Grilled Basil Chicken Burgers Recipe 136
276. Oven Fried Chicken Recipe 136
277. Oven Fried Chicken Tenders Recipe 136
278. Overnight Chicken Light Recipe 137
279. Parmesan Crusted Chicken Breasts Recipe 137
280. Parmesan Stuffed Chicken Breasts Recipe 137
281. Party Chicken Recipe 138
282. Peach Glazed Chicken Breasts Recipe 138
283. Pecan Crusted Chicken In Honey Mustard Sauce Recipe 138

284. Pecan Crusted Chicken And Shrimp Recipe 139
285. Pegs Chicken Enchiladas Recipe 139
286. Poached Italian Chicken With Rice Tabbouleh Recipe 140
287. Pollo Asado And Yellow Vegetable Rice Recipe 141
288. Pollo Con Crema Ala Donna Recipe 141
289. Polynesian Chicken Recipe 142
290. Popeye Recipe 142
291. Pretty In Pink Chicken Salad Recipe 143
292. Quick Chicken Cacciatore Recipe 143
293. Ranch Chicken Recipe 143
294. Ranch Chicken Wrap Recipe 144
295. Ranch Style Chicken Recipe 144
296. Ricotta Baked Chicken Recipe 145
297. Ritzy Chicken Casserole Recipe 145
298. Roasted Garlic Cream Pasta Recipe 145
299. Rosemary Chicken Recipe 146
300. Rotini With Chicken Asparagus And Tomatoes Recipe 147
301. Sausage Stuffed Chicken Breast Recipe .. 147
302. Sauted Boneless Breast Of Chicken With Mushroom Sauce Recipe 147
303. Shish Taouk Chicken Kebobs Recipe 148
304. Shredded Chicken Burritos With Cactus Pear Sauce Recipe 148
305. Simple Grilled Chicken Recipe 149
306. Skillet Chicken Parmesan Recipe 150
307. Slow Cooker Chicken Burritos Recipe 150
308. Slow Cooker Chicken Taco Stew Recipe 150
309. Sour Cream Southern Fried Chicken Recipe 151
310. Southern Marinated Maple Chicken Recipe 151
311. Southwest Chicken Kiev Recipe 152
312. Southwestern Chicken Casserole Recipe 152
313. Spice Rubbed Chicken Fingers With Cilantro Dipping Sauce (south Beach Diet Cookbook) Recipe 152
314. Spiced Pistachio Chicken Recipe 153
315. Spicy Braised Chicken With Mushrooms And Star Anise Recipe 154
316. Spicy Chicken Enchiladas Recipe 154
317. Spicy Chicken Pizza Recipe 155
318. Spicy Oat Crusted Chicken With Sunshine Salsa Recipe 155
319. Spicy Thai Rice And Chicken Wraps Dated 1962 Recipe 156
320. Spinach Chicken Pasta Recipe 156
321. Spinach Pasta With Alfredo And Chicken Breast Recipe 156
322. Stadium Salsa Chicken Rice Casserole Recipe 157
323. Steak Chicken And Vegetable Tacos Recipe 157
324. Stir Fry Chicken And Broccoli Recipe 158
325. Stroking Chicken Recipe 159
326. Stuffed Chicken Breast With Lemon Gravy Recipe 159
327. Stuffed Greek Chicken Recipe 159
328. Stuffed Santa Fe Chicken Recipe 160
329. Sunday Chicken And Rice Casserole Recipe 160
330. Super Easy Chicken Manicotti Recipe 160
331. Sweet And Sour Chicken Recipe 161
332. Szechuan Chicken Recipe 161
333. TEX MEX CHICKEN Recipe 162
334. Tasty Apricot Chicken Recipe 162
335. Teriyaki Chicken Salad Recipe 163
336. Thai Chicken Patties Recipe 163
337. Thai Green Curry With Chicken Winter Squash And Fresh Basil Recipe 163
338. The Best Homemade Sweet And Sour Chicken You'll Ever Have!! Recipe 164
339. Tippin Family Fajitas Recipe 164
340. Top Ka Gai Chicken Coconut Soup Recipe 165
341. Torikatsu Chicken Cutlets With Hot Sauce Recipe 166
342. Tortilla Crusted Chicken With Salsa Recipe 166
343. Turkish Rice Pilaf With Chicken Recipe 167
344. Tuscan Chicken Recipe 167
345. Twenty Minute Chicken Creole Recipe .. 167
346. Two Soup Chicken Recipe 168
347. Unbelievable Chicken Recipe 168
348. Utica Chicken Riggies Recipe 168
349. Velveeta Cheesy Pasta Casserole Recipe 169
350. Waikiki Beach Chicken Or Pork Recipe. 169
351. Way To Go Dad Chicken Recipe 170
352. Wheat Free Chicken Nuggets You Cant Stop Eating Recipe 170
353. Worcestershire And Lemon Baked Chicken

Recipe 171
354. Yakisoba Chicken Recipe 171
355. Zesty Apricot Chicken Recipe 171
356. Asian Spiced Chicken With Vanilla Apricot Sauce Recipe 172
357. Baked Chicken Breasts To Perfection Recipe 172
358. Creamy Baked Chicken Breast Recipe 173
359. Easy Baked Ranch Chicken Recipe 173
360. Fiesta Chicken Recipe 173
361. Lemon Chicken Recipe 174
362. Potato Chip Chicken Recipe 174
363. Sour Cream And White Wine Chicken Recipe 174
364. Tuscan Chicken Recipe 174
365. Zucchini Stuffed Chicken Breasts Recipe 175

INDEX 176

CONCLUSION 179

365 Awesome Chicken Breast Recipes

***

1. "Chicken Noodle Soup" Casserole Recipe

Serving: 6 | Prep: | Cook: 60mins | Ready in:

Ingredients

- 3-4 skinless, boneless chicken breast halves
- 6-8 ounces wide egg noodles
- 1 (10.75 ounce) can condensed cream of mushroom soup
- 1 (10.75 ounce) can condensed cream of chicken soup
- 1/4 cup low-sodium chicken broth
- 3-5 ribs celery, diced
- 1 cup sour cream
- 1 cup frozen peas
- 1 cup frozen broccoli florets, chopped
- 1 cup frozen carrots, cubed
- 1 lemon, juiced and zested
- salt to and fresh ground black pepper to taste
- 1/4 cup fresh Italian parsley, chopped
- 1 sleeve (40) Ritz or buttery round crackers
- 1/2 cup unsalted butter, melted

Direction

- Preheat oven to 350 F (175 C).
- Poach chicken in a large pot of simmering water for about 10-12 minutes. Remove chicken from pot and set aside to cool.
- Bring chicken cooking water to a boil and cook pasta to al dente, about 4-5 minutes. When the pasta has about a minute left of cooking time, add the diced celery.
- Drain pasta and celery and toss with olive or vegetable oil to prevent sticking. Set aside.
- Cut chicken into small pieces, about 1/2-inch cubes, and mix with noodles.
- In a small bowl, add the frozen peas, broccoli, carrots, and a tablespoon or two of water. Cover and microwave for 30-45 seconds. Drain any excess water.
- In a large bowl, gently mix together the peas, broccoli, and carrots; chicken and mushroom soup; chicken broth; onion and garlic powder; and sour cream. Season with salt and pepper to taste. If you'd like to cut down on the richness of the casserole and add a bit of dimension, add 1 tablespoon of lemon juice.
- Gently fold in the chicken, noodles, and celery with the soup and vegetable mixture in the large bowl.
- Pour the mixture into a 9 x 13 inch baking sheet and evenly spread with a spatula. Sprinkle with Italian parsley and lemon zest.
- In a food processor, add the Ritz or buttery round crackers and pulse 4-6 times. Add the melted butter to the cracker mixture and pulse 3-4 times. Sprinkle the cracker mixture evenly over the casserole.
- Bake for 30-35 minutes, or until heated and top is golden brown. Let rest for 10-15 minutes before serving.

2. 7 Minute Cooked Dinner Recipe

Serving: 2 | Prep: | Cook: 7mins | Ready in:

Ingredients

- 6 organic potatoes
- 1tsp grass fed butter or organic olive oil
- 1/4 minced organic onion
- 1 clove of minced organic garlic
- 1 tsp celtic sea salt

- 1/2 tsp fresh organic winter savory (optional)
- Organic cracked pepper to taste
- 1 tbs of organic grass fed butter or margarine
- 1/8 Cup grass fed milk or organic ric milk
- 2 cups organic frozen mixed vegetables
- 1 tbs organic flour (or corn starch for ceilac)
- 1 grass fed chicken breast sliced in two thin pieces (can be substutied for any other meat, mushrooms or tofu of the same size)

Direction

- First peel and cut into quarters 6 medium potatoes
- Put them on boil.
- In a frying pan add
- 1tsp butter 1/4 minced onion and 1 clove of minced garlic, 1 tsp sea salt and some cracked pepper. Sauté onions and garlic until caramelized add a tbs of water so it don't completely stick to pan then add your meat or mushrooms (this works well with any thin cuts of meat or a large Portobello mushroom cap) meat must be no thicker than an inch. Put a lid on the pan and cook for 3 minutes.
- During that 3 minutes steam 2 cups of your favorite frozen veggie medley and drain your potatoes.
- Mash cooked potatoes with a tbs of butter and 1/8C milk (or rice milk) whisk until creamy.
- Turn your meat over… the pan should be well caramelized but not burned and add 3/4 cup of water whisking with a fork to remove all caramel from the pan. In a jam jar add 1 heaping Tbs of flour a pinch of savory and 1/8c water…shake shake shake until there are no lumps…swiftly add this to the pan stirring constantly until gravy has thickened and add savory.
- Serve and enjoy.

3. A Good Easy Garlic Chicken Recipe

Serving: 4 | Prep: | Cook: 15mins | Ready in:

Ingredients

- 3 tablespoons butter
- 4 skinless, boneless chicken breast halves
- 2 teaspoons garlic powder
- 1 teaspoon seasoning salt
- 1 teaspoon onion powder

Direction

- Melt butter in a large skillet over medium high heat. Add chicken and sprinkle with garlic powder, seasoning salt and onion powder. Sauté about 10 to 15 minutes on each side, or until chicken is cooked through and juices run clear.

4. Adams Recipe For Unholy Chicken Recipe

Serving: 2 | Prep: | Cook: 25mins | Ready in:

Ingredients

- 2 boneless, skinless chicken breasts
- 4-5 slices of bacon, raw
- 3 garlic cloves, minced
- 1/2 cup chopped onion
- 1 cup cheddar cheese, shredded
- 1 jalapeno pepper, minced

Direction

- Either butterfly the chicken breasts or pound them flat between two pieces of plastic wrap. Marinate them overnight in the marinade of your choice. For this recipe, bold and savory marinades work the best.
- In a small skillet, sauté the onion, pepper, and garlic until soft.

- Set aside to cool.
- Load each chicken breast with half the onion, pepper, and cheese, being careful to not overfill.
- Roll up the chicken and wrap a couple of slices of bacon around it. Secure with toothpicks.
- This process is messy, but worth it.
- Grill over medium-low heat, turning often until done.
- Be warned, this may cause flare-ups and burnt cheese.
- You must tend the grill constantly for this.
- That's it! Enjoy!

5. Afghanistan Chicken Recipe

Serving: 4 | Prep: | Cook: 20mins | Ready in:

Ingredients

- 2 large cloves garlic minced
- 1/2 teaspoon salt
- 2 cups plain, yogurt
- 4 tablespoons juice and pulp of 1 large lemon
- 1/2 teaspoon black pepper
- 2 large whole chicken breasts
- 1 lemon cut into wedges

Direction

- Put the salt in a wide, shallow, non-reactive bowl.
- Add the garlic, and mash them together until you have paste.
- Add yogurt, lemon, and pepper.
- Skin the chicken breasts, remove all visible fat, and split the halves.
- Break the bones (by bending backward) so the pieces lie flat.
- Add to the yogurt and turn, so all surfaces are well-coated.
- Cover the bowl tightly, and refrigerate.
- Allow to marinate at least overnight and up to a day and a half, and turn occasionally.
- To cook, remove breasts from marinade, and wipe off all but a thin film.
- Broil or grill about 6 inches from the heat for 6 to 8 minutes

6. African Apricot Chicken On Skewers Recipe

Serving: 6 | Prep: | Cook: 20mins | Ready in:

Ingredients

- 3 pounds boneless chicken breasts cut into 4" chunks
- 2 cloves garlic minced
- 1/2 teaspoon salt
- 1 teaspoon freshly ground black pepper
- 4 medium onions finely chopped
- 2 tablespoons oil
- 1-1/2 teaspoons coriander
- 1/2 teaspoon cumin
- 1-1/2 teaspoons hot curry powder
- 1 tablespoon brown sugar
- 1/2 cup fresh lemon juice
- 4 tablespoons apricot jam
- 2 tablespoons flour
- 30 dried apricot halves
- 1 onion cut into 2" chunks
- 2 bay leaves

Direction

- In a large bowl combine chicken pieces, garlic, salt and pepper then set aside.
- Fry onions in oil until golden then stir in coriander, cumin and curry powder.
- Stir to coat onions then add brown sugar, lemon juice and jam.
- Add 1/2 cup water then bring to a boil stirring constantly then remove from heat.
- When cool pour over chicken then add bay leaves and refrigerate overnight.
- The next day thread meat with onions and apricots on skewers.

- Grill over coals for 7 minutes on each side.
- While meat grills remove bay leaves from marinade and transfer it to a heavy pot.
- Bring to a boil then serve over rice.
- Serve over potatoes or rice and garnish with grated Parmesan cheese, sliced hard-boiled eggs and black olives.
- *Available in the ethnic aisle of your supermarket or in specialty stores.

7. Aji De Gallina Recipe

Serving: 4 | Prep: | Cook: 20mins | Ready in:

Ingredients

- 2 cups water
- 2 Knorr® Reduced Sodium chicken flavor bouillon cubes, crumbled
- 2 boneless, skinless chicken breast halves
- 2 cups fresh white bread cubes
- 1/4 cup Skippy® Super Chunk® peanut butter
- 1 Tbsp. Bertolli® olive oil
- 1 medium sweet onion, chopped
- 2 cloves garlic, chopped
- 2 Tbsp. yellow pepper paste (aji amarillo)*
- 1 package 1 package Knorr® Sazon with coriander and Annatto

Direction

- Bring water and Knorr® Reduced Sodium Chicken flavor Bouillon Cubes to a boil in a medium saucepan. Add chicken and simmer about 10 minutes or until thoroughly cooked. Remove chicken and shred. Reserve cooking liquid.
- Process bread, peanut butter and 1-1/2 cups reserved cooking liquid in a blender or food processor until smooth.
- Heat olive oil in a large non-stick skillet over medium heat and cook onion about 4 minutes, stirring occasionally. Add shredded chicken and remaining ingredients and cook about 2 minutes, stirring occasionally. Add bread mixture and remaining cooking liquid and bring to a boil. Reduce heat and simmer about 2 minutes or until slightly thickened, stirring occasionally.

8. Alfredo Chicken With Cinnamon Recipe

Serving: 8 | Prep: | Cook: 20mins | Ready in:

Ingredients

- 2 lbs. chicken breast (I use tenders)
- 1 lb. box rotini
- 2 jars alfredo sauce (I use Classico)
- cinnamon
- parmesan
- pepper
- seasoning salt
- garlic salt

Direction

- Prepare pasta as directed on box, drain & set aside.
- Meanwhile season one side of chicken breast with seasoning salt & pepper.
- Place chicken in lightly oiled skillet seasoned side down and grill.
- Season top side with garlic salt.
- Grill until cooked. You may have to cook in batches. Keep warm in oven.
- Chop chicken into bite sized pieces.
- Warm sauce in large pot.
- Add pasta stirring well to coat.
- Stir in chicken.
- Season with cinnamon to taste. A few shakes. Stir well.
- Top with parmesan.
- Enjoy!

9. Almond Crusted Chicken Recipe

Serving: 4 | Prep: | Cook: 18mins | Ready in:

Ingredients

- 1/3 cup finely chopped almonds
- 1/4 cup brown sugar
- 1/2 teaspoon garlic salt
- 4 boneless, skinless chicken breast halves
- 2 teaspoons finely chopped fresh parsley for garnish (optional)

Direction

- Heat oven to 400 degrees F
- Combine almonds, brown sugar, and garlic salt in a bowl.
- Dredge chicken in the almond-brown sugar mixture
- Arrange chicken on a baking sheet.
- Firmly pat any remaining mixture on top of each chicken piece.
- Bake for 18 minutes, or until a thermometer inserted in the thickest part registers 180 degrees F.
- Garnish with parsley, if desired.

10. Aloha Chicken Recipe

Serving: 4 | Prep: | Cook: 45mins | Ready in:

Ingredients

- 2 skinless boneless chicken breast halves cut into bite size pieces
- 1 teaspoon ground ginger
- 1 teaspoon paprika
- 1 tablespoon onion powder
- 2 tablespoons garlic salt
- 3 tablespoons cider vinegar
- 1 cup ketchup
- 1/4 cup soy sauce
- 20 ounce can crushed pineapple with juice
- 1/4 cup packed brown sugar

Direction

- Preheat oven to 400.
- Arrange chicken pieces in a single layer in well-greased rectangular baking dish.
- In small bowl mix together ginger, paprika, onion powder and garlic salt.
- Add vinegar and mix well then divide this mixture.
- Brush 1/2 over the chicken pieces and bake 15 minutes.
- Turn chicken pieces then baste with remaining vinegar mixture and bake 15 minutes longer.
- Meanwhile in a medium bowl combine ketchup, soy sauce, pineapple and brown sugar.
- Spoon pineapple mixture over chicken and bake 30 minutes longer then serve immediately.

11. Amish Chicken And Macaroni Cassorole Recipe

Serving: 4 | Prep: | Cook: 60mins | Ready in:

Ingredients

- 1 cup cooked elbow macaroni
- 2 cups diced cooked chicken breast
- 1 1/2 tbsp. grated onion
- 2/3 cup chopped green pepper
- 1 cup cooked tiny baby carrots(I like ones in jar)
- 1/4 tsp. papricka
- fresh ground black pepper
- 1 1/2 tsp. salt
- 2 eggs lightly beaten
- 1 1/2 cups milk
- Also may add favorite cheese if desired(optional)

Direction

- Combine all the ingredients, except the eggs and milk
- Place into a greased 1 1/2 quart casserole.
- Combine the eggs and milk, pour over other ingredients
- Set into a large pan of hot water.
- Bake in a preheated oven 350 degrees, about one hour or until firm.
- Great with hot rolls and salad.

12. Angel Hair Pasta With Chicken Recipe

Serving: 4 | Prep: | Cook: 15mins | Ready in:

Ingredients

- 2 tablespoons olive oil, divided
- 2 skinless, boneless chicken breast halves, cut into 1-inch cubes
- 1 carrot, sliced diagonally into 1/4-inch pieces
- 1 (10-ounce) package frozen broccoli florets, thawed
- 2 cloves garlic, minced
- 12 ounces angel hair pasta
- 2/3 cup chicken broth
- 1 teaspoon dried basil
- 1/4 cup grated parmesan cheese

Direction

- Heat 1 tablespoon oil in a medium skillet over medium heat; add chicken. Cook, stirring, until chicken is cooked through, about 5 minutes. Remove from skillet and drain on paper towels.
- Heat remaining oil in same skillet. Begin heating water for pasta. Add carrot to skillet; cook, stirring, for 4 minutes. Add broccoli and garlic to skillet; cook, stirring, for 2 minutes longer.
- Cook pasta according to package directions. While pasta is cooking, add chicken broth, basil and Parmesan to skillet. Stir to combine.

Return chicken to skillet. Reduce heat and simmer for 4 minutes.
- Drain pasta. Place in a large serving bowl. Top with chicken and vegetable mixture. Serve immediately.

13. Apple Chicken Quesadillas Recipe

Serving: 6 | Prep: | Cook: 30mins | Ready in:

Ingredients

- 3 apples, peeled and sliced
- 2 cups cooked diced chicken breast
- 1 cup shredded cheddar cheese
- 1 cup shredded mozzarella cheese
- 1/2 cup corn
- 1/2 cup chopped tomatoes or salsa
- 1/2 cup chopped onion
- 1/4 teaspoon salt
- flour tortillas (2 per each quesadillas) make your own or bought I make my own
- toppings of your choice
- lettuce/salsa/sour cream

Direction

- 1. I also use quesadilla machine.
- 2. I place the first 8 ingredients in a bowl and mix together and when the machine is heated. I place a homemade tortilla and top with a cup of chicken mixture or a little more place another tortilla on top and close the machine until green light says it is done and then put on plate and cut the sections apart with a knife and then top with your favourite toppings

14. Apricot Barbecue Chicken Recipe

Serving: 8 | Prep: | Cook: 30mins | Ready in:

Ingredients

- 4 chicken breasts- bone in and split
- 4 drumsticks and thighs
- 1 bottle Teriyaki glaze
- 1 jar apricot preserves
- 1/4 cup hot water

Direction

- Prep time does not include 24 hour chilling
- Pour glaze into a zip lock bag.
- Add chicken and marinade in refrigerator for 24 hours
- Heat grill to medium
- Remove chicken from glaze, salt and grill to brown on both sides
- Remove chicken from grill and place in aluminum pan
- Place chicken in pan.
- Mix preserves with the water until a paste consistency.
- Brush over chicken.
- Cook chicken on grill in pan about 25 minutes or cooked through.
- Turn and baste occasionally

15. Apricot Chicken Recipe

Serving: 23 | Prep: | Cook: 15mins | Ready in:

Ingredients

- 500 grams sliced or four single chicken breasts
- 1 onion
- 1 tin of apricot nectar
- 200 grams of dried apricots
- 100 grams of flaked almonds
- 1 packet of dry French onion soup
- 1 tablespoon of olive oil

Direction

- Combine French onion soup and apricot nectar and set aside.
- Fry sliced onion in olive oil and add chicken and cook until just cooked...
- Add nectar and dried apricots and simmer for about 5 minutes.
- Add flaked almonds just prior to serving and serve with steamed rice.

16. Aromatic Chicken In Coconut Cream Recipe

Serving: 4 | Prep: | Cook: 30mins | Ready in:

Ingredients

- 500gr skinless chicken breast for healthier option (better with bone and skin)
- 1 pc medium size Indian red onion - roughly chopped
- 1 pc big red chili (best to use small red chilies...quantities to your desire...the spicier the dish the better it would turns out)
- 1/2 tsp garlic paste
- 1/2 tsp ginger paste
- 10 pcs canddlenuts, roasted (kemiri)
- 1/2 tsp turmeric powder
- 1 pc lemongrass - crushed
- 1 pc pandan leave - torn lenghtwise
- 1 pc tomato - roughly chopped
- 5 pcs lime leaves
- 2 pcs lime - for marinating the chicken
- 1 cup half cream milk (originally the recipe uses coconut milk)
- 1-2 cup water
- cooking oil
- salt
- 1 tbs lemon juice
- 1 pc onion leaves/ spring onion - slice 2cm
- About a fist of lemon basil leaves - take only the leaves and wash clean

Direction

- Cut the chicken to your liking, wash and marinate with lime juice and salt for 15

minutes. Afterwards, wash the chicken thoroughly and keep aside until it's needed
- Grind: red onion, chopped red chili and candlenuts with a bit of oil. Add to the mixture: ginger and garlic paste and turmeric powder
- Heat oil in a wok/ pan, put lime leaves, lemongrass and Pandan leaves. Sauté for about 1 minute, then add the tomato. Keep stirring until tomato gets soften
- Add the grinded red onion mixture, stir for about 3-5 minutes
- Add chicken pieces and 1/2 cup of water. Mix well and cover. Let it simmer for about 20 minutes
- Add the milk and let it simmer for another 5 minutes
- Before putting off the stove, add the 1 tbs lemon juice, lemon basil leaves and chopped onion leaves/ spring onion
- Add salt to taste
- Serve with steamed white rice
- *You may add potato into the dish, yummy...if you would like to add potato, add it on the 15th minutes when the chicken is simmering on the stove

17. Artichoke Portobello Chicken In Cream Recipe

Serving: 2 | Prep: | Cook: 15mins | Ready in:

Ingredients

- 1 whole chicken breast, cut in half pounded evenly
- 3 tbsp of unsalted butter
- 2 portobello mushrooms sliced 1/2 inch thick
- 1/2 onion sliced
- 1 can of artichoke halves, drained (not marinated, please)
- salt and pepper
- 2 tsp of mashed garlic
- 1/2 cup of heavy cream
- 1 tsp of drained capers

Direction

- Pound the chicken thin, salt and pepper very lightly, set aside in the refrigerator.
- In large skillet, heat the butter to just below browning point, you want it to foam, quickly add the mushroom pieces and onion slices.
- Cook on high heat and brown the mushrooms, you want them caramelized and toasty about 4 minutes each side on high.
- Sprinkle lightly with salt and pepper, remove to side plate.
- In pan drippings, over high heat sear the chicken 2 minutes per side till nicely browned add a touch more butter if necessary.
- Add the mushrooms, onion, artichoke pieces, garlic and heavy cream, turn heat to low and simmer 10 minutes and reduce the cream to near nothing.
- Sprinkle with capers and serve.

18. Articoke Chicken Recipe

Serving: 8 | Prep: | Cook: 60mins | Ready in:

Ingredients

- 8 boneless chicken breast halves
- 2 tablespoons butter
- 2 (6 ounce) jars marinated artichoke hearts
- 1 large can mushrooms, drained (Sauteed fresh mushrooms can be used as well.)
- 1/2 cup sweet onion, chopped
- 1/3 cup all-purpose flour
- 1 tablespoon fresh rosemary, chopped (or to taste)
- 1 teaspoon salt
- 1/4 teaspoon ground black pepper
- 1 cup chicken stock or broth
- 1 cup dry white wine
- Hot cooked pasta (I usually use angel hair)
- fresh parsley, chopped

Direction

- Drain one jar of artichoke marinade into skillet. Set artichokes aside.
- Add 1 tablespoon butter to skillet and heat over medium-high heat.
- Add 4 chicken breast halves and brown on both sides.
- Arrange in greased 13x9 inch baking dish.
- Repeat with remaining marinade, butter and chicken breasts.
- Coarsely chop artichokes and arrange on top of chicken.
- Sprinkle with mushrooms.
- Add onion to pan juices and sauté until softened.
- Whisk in flour, rosemary, salt and pepper. Add chicken broth and wine and cook until thickened and bubbly.
- Spoon over chicken.
- Cover and bake at 350 degrees for 50 to 60 minutes or until chicken is tender.
- Arrange pasta on large serving platter. Top with chicken and sauce.
- Sprinkle with fresh parsley.

19. Asparagus And Chicken Casserole Recipe

Serving: 6 | Prep: | Cook: 30mins | Ready in:

Ingredients

- 4 large chicken breasts, boiled and chopped
- 1 can asparagus, drained and chopped
- 1 cup mayonnaise
- 1 lemon, squeezed
- 1 10 3/4 ounce can of cream of chicken soup
- 1 roll of Ritz crackers
- 1/2 cup butter, melted

Direction

- Layer your chicken in your casserole dish
- Next layer your asparagus.
- Mix the mayonnaise, lemon juice, and chicken soup.
- Add this as your third layer
- Add the crushed crackers and drizzle with butter
- Bake at 350 for 30 minutes.

20. Autumn Noodle Bake Recipe

Serving: 4 | Prep: | Cook: 30mins | Ready in:

Ingredients

- 1 can cream of mushroom soup
- 1/2 cup milk
- 8 ounces chicken breast cooked and cubed
- 8 ounces canned carrots drained
- 8 ounces canned green beans drained
- 4 ounces egg noodles cooked and drained
- 1/2 teaspoon salt
- 1/2 cup cheddar cheese shredded

Direction

- Preheat oven to 350. Spray a square casserole dish with cooking spray then set aside. In mixing bowl combine soup and milk and mix well. Stir in noodles, chicken, vegetables and salt then mix well again. Spoon mixture into prepared dish. Sprinkle cheese on top and bake for 20 minutes.

21. BBQ Chicken Pizza Recipe

Serving: 6 | Prep: | Cook: 25mins | Ready in:

Ingredients

- pizza dough for 2 12" pizzas.
- 1-1 1/2 cups BBQ sauce, your favorite (we like the honey garlic kind, Bull's Eye has a nice smoky flavor or Diana Sauce honey garlic)

- approx 2 cups cooked chicken, roughly cut up or shredded. Hubby has even gone and BBQ'd some chicken breasts(2) ahead of time for even more flavor- this is when we have plenty of time. I really like picking up a couple of roasted chickens from the supermarket deli and using the meat for various dishes in the week. Great when you're pressed for time.
- red onion, chopped or thinly sliced, as much as you like, a handful for each pizza.
- green pepper, same as for red onion
- 1 tin pineapple chunks, drained
- 8-12oz mozzarella cheese, grated
- for extra flavor and decadence, fry up a few slices of bacon for crumbling. This is entirely optional, but it tastes amazing!
- cornmeal for dusting the pans

Direction

- Grease 2 12" pizza pans and dust with cornmeal.
- Press dough into each pan, pushing into edge for a nice rounded crust.
- Spread dough with about 1/3 cup BBQ sauce for each pizza or more if you like it saucy
- Pour a bit of sauce on the chicken, too, and stir to just coat.
- Sprinkle roughly 1/2 of the cheese on each pizza and top with the chicken.
- Next add the red onion, green pepper, pineapple, and bacon if using.
- Top with remaining cheese.
- Preheat the BBQ on one side only on high. You will be using the indirect cooking method.
- Put one pizza on the top warming tray, and the other on the side the heat is NOT on. Close the lid and give the pizza a quarter turn every 5-7 minutes. Switch the pizzas around after about 15 minutes (up goes down and vice versa)
- Should be done in about 25 - 30 minutes.
- Once you have had BBQ'd pizza you may never want to go back to the oven again. It is fabulous!

22. Bacon Wrapped Chicken Recipe

Serving: 4 | Prep: | Cook: 1hours | Ready in:

Ingredients

- •1 pound(s) uncooked boneless, skinless chicken breast, 4 boneless, skinless breast halves
- •8 oz fat-free cream cheese
- •1 tbsp Country Crock Shedd's Spread light margarine, divided
- •4 slice(s) uncooked turkey bacon
- •1 spray(s) cooking spray

Direction

- Spray cooking spray on baking pan.
- Flatten chicken to 1/2 in thickness. Spread 3tbsps cream cheese over each. Dot with butter and sprinkle w/salt; roll up. Wrap each with a bacon strip. Place, seam side down, on baking pan.
- Bake uncovered at 400 degrees for 35-40 min. or until juices run clear. Broil 6 in. from heat for 5 min or until bacon is crisp.

23. Baked Chicken And Chorizo Paella Recipe

Serving: 5 | Prep: | Cook: 20mins | Ready in:

Ingredients

- 4 tablespoon olive oil
- 1lbs chorizo
- 1 red bell pepper rough chopped
- 1 green bell pepper rough chopped
- 1 large onion rough chopped
- 1 cup sliced black olives
- 2 tablespoons minced garlic
- 2 pinches saffron threads
- 1 bay leaf

- 2 cups arborio rice
- 4 chicken breast cut in to 1/2 in. cubes
- 3 cups chicken stock
- 1 cup white wine
- 3/4 cup chopped cilantro
- salt & pepper to taste

Direction

- Heat oven to 400°F. Heat oil in a large sauté pan to med high heat
- Add chorizo, onion, bell peppers and garlic sauté till vegetables are tender crisp and chorizo is done 4-5 min.
- Then add rice, saffron, bay leaf sauté mixing well 3-5 min.
- Add chicken breast, chicken stock, white wine and the olives
- Add 1/2 of the chopped cilantro mixing well bring to a boil
- Add salt & pepper to taste
- Put in oven and bake till done 20-25 min.
- Serve and top with the rest of the cilantro

24. Baked Chicken Breasts With Cherry Tomato Sauce Recipe

Serving: 4 | Prep: | Cook: 50mins | Ready in:

Ingredients

- 4 chicken breasts
- 1 tablespoon olive oil
- 1 garlic clove minced
- 2 tablespoons minced shallot
- 1 cup halved cherry tomatoes
- 1/2 teaspoon minced fresh oregano
- 1/4 teaspoon salt
- 1/8 teaspoon pepper
- 1/8 teaspoon red pepper flakes
- 2 teaspoons red wine vinegar

Direction

- Place chicken breasts in small shallow roasting pan.
- Brush with olive oil then season with salt and pepper.
- Roast in oven at 350 for 45 minutes.
- Heat olive oil in small pan then add garlic and shallot and sauté 2 minutes.
- Add tomatoes, oregano, salt, pepper and red pepper flakes.
- Cook over high heat stirring frequently until tomatoes are pulpy about 5 minutes.
- Stir in vinegar.
- To serve arrange chicken on 2 plates then top each serving with a dollop of tomato sauce.

25. Baked Chicken With Fire Roasted Tomato And Bacon Sauce Recipe

Serving: 46 | Prep: | Cook: 20mins | Ready in:

Ingredients

- cooking spray
- 16 ounces fire roasted tomatoes, diced (canned)
- 4 to 6 slices turkey bacon
- 8 boneless, skinless chicken breasts or thighs (breasts are lower calorie and fat)
- 1 large onion, cut into round 1/4" slices
- salt and pepper

Direction

- Preheat oven to 350 degrees. Spray the bottom of a 13 x 9 inch pan with cooking spray.
- Cover the bottom of the pan with the tomatoes.
- Cook turkey bacon until crispy, saving any drippings. Remove bacon to paper towels.
- Add cooking spray or a teaspoon olive oil to skillet and salt and pepper both sides of chicken. Brown chicken, allowing it to absorb

bacon flavor. Turn to brown other side. Do not wash skillet.
- Place chicken on tomatoes in baking pan and place in oven. Cook until chicken is no longer pink inside, 10 to 20 minutes or until done.
- Meanwhile, cook onions in same skillet, sprinkle with 1/4 teaspoon salt and 1/4 teaspoon sugar. Allow the onions to caramelize.
- Serve with chicken on a bed of tomatoes, top with onions and crumbled bacon.

26. Baked Chicken With Artichokes And Mushrooms Recipe

Serving: 4 | Prep: | Cook: 45mins | Ready in:

Ingredients

- 4 split chicken breasts
- salt and pepper to taste
- 1 6oz. jar marinated artichoke hearts
- 8oz. sliced marinated mushrooms
- 1 large onion chopped
- 1Tbs chopped garlic
- 1c dry white wine

Direction

- Season chicken with salt and pepper and place skin side up in 9x13" baking dish
- Drain artichokes, reserving marinade. Cut artichokes in half and top chicken breasts with artichokes, mushrooms and marinade, garlic and onions. Pour reserved marinade and white wine over all.
- Bake uncovered until chicken is cooked through, about 35 to 45 mins.
- For extra moist chicken, marinate overnight in mixture.

27. Baked Chicken With Mushrooms And Artichokes Recipe

Serving: 4 | Prep: | Cook: 45mins | Ready in:

Ingredients

- 4 boneless chicken breast halves (can use up to 6 if desired)
- kosher salt and ground black pepper
- 1 (6 ounce) jar marinated artichoke hearts
- 12 ounces fresh mushrooms, sliced
- 6 green onions, thinly sliced
- 1 cup dry white wine

Direction

- Season chicken with salt and pepper to taste.
- Arrange in greased 13x9 inch baking pan.
- Drain artichoke hearts, reserving marinade.
- Cut artichoke hearts in half.
- Top chicken breasts with artichoke hearts, mushrooms and green onions.
- Combine reserved artichoke heart marinade and wine. Pour over chicken.
- Bake at 350 degrees for 35 to 45 minutes or until chicken juices run clear.

28. Baked Mexican Chicken Recipe

Serving: 6 | Prep: | Cook: 60mins | Ready in:

Ingredients

- 4 to 6 boneless, skinless chicken breasts
- 1 teaspoon taco seasoning mix
- 1 (10 oz) can enchilada sauce

Direction

- Place chicken in a pan that has been sprayed with a nonstick cooking spray. Sprinkle desired amount of taco seasoning mix over chicken. Pour enchilada sauce over chicken.

Bake at 350F for 1 hour or until tender. Serve with warmed corn tortillas.

29. Balsamic Asian Italian Chicken Recipe

Serving: 4 | Prep: | Cook: 35mins | Ready in:

Ingredients

- 2 Boneless, skinless chicken Breasts, trimmed and cubed
- 3 shallots, peeled and sliced
- 1/2 lb fresh green beans, trimmed and halved (Not sure about this measurement, use your judgement)
- 2 red bell peppers, seeded and cut into strips
- 1 1/2 cups balsamic vinegar
- 1 cup olive oil
- 1/2 Cup Worsestershire Sauce
- 1/3 cup soy sauce
- 1 tbspn garlic powder
- All-Purpose or rice flour (rice flour dissolves better)
- salt and Pepper to taste
- More balsamic vinegar, oil, Soy and Worsestershire Sauce to add if the sauce isn't strong enough. (Optional, for people with weak taste buds like me.)

Direction

- In a wok or large frying pan, sauté the shallots and peppers over high flame until slightly browned, 5-8 minutes.
- Turn flame down to medium and add the chicken.
- Add the sauces, oil and spices to taste.
- Sautee, stirring occasionally for 15 minutes, then add the green beans.
- Sautee an additional 15-20 minutes, or until chicken is cooked through.
- Stir flour with cold water in a separate bowl with a fork until smooth, then slowly add to the sauce to thicken. You may use corn starch or arrowroot instead, but flour is cheaper, and tastes better.
- Serve over rice or ramen noodles. It's Mmm-mm Good, bitch!

30. Balsamic Oregano Chicken Recipe

Serving: 0 | Prep: | Cook: 1hours | Ready in:

Ingredients

- 4 large bone-in chicken breasts, skin removed
- 1/4 cup balsamic vinegar
- 1 Tblsp olive oil
- 1 tsp dried oregano
- salt & freshly ground black pepper to taste

Direction

- Clean chicken and place in lightly greased baking dish (bone side down).
- Mix the balsamic vinegar and olive oil, evenly pour over the chicken.
- Sprinkle with oregano, salt, and pepper.
- *crushing the oregano (or any dried herb used in cooking) between your fingers before using will release additional flavor*
- Tightly cover with aluminum foil and bake 20 mins.
- Baste with juices; continue baking uncovered for about 20-30 more minutes (depending on the size and type of chicken you use).
- Most recipes say to cook until juices run clear, but it's safer to check it with a meat thermometer. My thermometer says to cook poultry to 180 degrees, I usually take it out of the oven at 175 and let it rest, covered, for about 5 minutes and it continues to cook internally.

31. Beef Or Chicken Fajitas Recipe

Serving: 4 | Prep: | Cook: 10mins | Ready in:

Ingredients

- 1 lb skirt steak (or 1 lb boneless skinless chicken breasts)
- juice of 1 lemon
- 1 small onion, sliced
- 2 cloves garlic, mashed
- 1/4 cup olive oil
- salt/pepper

Direction

- Place meat in a gallon-sized ziplock bag, and add lemon juice, onion, garlic, and oil. Marinate overnight or at least for a few hours.
- Remove meat from bag; discard marinade. Salt/pepper meat lightly.
- Grill for 5 minutes on each side (may need longer cooking time for chicken). Wrap in foil and let meat rest for at least 5 minutes before slicing.
- Slice into thin strips against the grain.

32. Beer N Lime Grilled Chicken Recipe

Serving: 4 | Prep: | Cook: 14mins | Ready in:

Ingredients

- 1 lime, juiced
- 1 (12 fluid oz) can light colored beer
- 1 tsp honey
- 2 cloves garlic, minced
- 2 Tbs chopped, fresh, cilantro
- salt and pepper
- 4 boneless, skinless, chicken breast halves

Direction

- In a bowl, mix the lime juice, beer, honey, garlic, cilantro, salt and pepper until honey dissolves. Pour the mixture over the chicken, cover and marinate for 30 minutes.
- Preheat an outdoor grill for medium heat and lightly oil grate.
- Remove chicken from marinade and shake off excess; discard remaining marinade. Grill chicken until tender and juices run clear, about 7 minutes per side.
- Enjoy!

33. Belgian Chicken And Leeks Casserole Recipe

Serving: 6 | Prep: | Cook: 45mins | Ready in:

Ingredients

- 2 large chicken breasts, halved
- 5 T. olive oil
- 1 leek, white and light green parts, chopped
- 1 celery stalk, chopped
- 10 oz. cremini (baby bello) mushrooms, halved if large
- 3 T. flour
- 3 T. sherry
- 2 1/4 c. chicken stock
- 3/4 c. whole milk
- 1 bay leaf
- 8 slices dense multi-grain bread, crusts removed, sliced into triangles
- 2 T. chopped parsley
- 1/3 c. grated Parmesan
- 5 Tbs vermouth (my variation)

Direction

- Preheat oven to 350 degrees. Season chicken with salt and pepper on both sides. Heat 2 T. oil in a medium frying pan over medium-high heat. Add chicken and cook on one side for approx. 3-4 mins. Until browned. Flip over, reduce heat and cook all the way through. Once finished, set aside on a plate.
- Heat remaining oil in pan on medium heat. Add leeks, mushrooms, celery and a pinch of

salt. Cook until golden brown and tender, about 10 mins.
- Stir in flour and cook, stirring often for about 2 mins. Add sherry, vermouth, stock, milk and bay leaf.
- Bring back to a boil, then turn heat down to a simmer. Cook for about 5 mins. Discard bay leaf.
- Arrange bread on bottom of large baking dish, overlapping slightly.
- Spoon half the veggies and sauce over bread. Slice chicken crosswise, 1/2 inch thick, and arrange on bread.
- Spread remaining veggies and sauce over chicken, topping with parsley and Parmesan.
- Bake until golden brown and bubbling, about 25-30 mins. Allow to sit for 15 minutes before serving.

34. Bell Pepper Chicken And Rice Recipe

Serving: 4 | Prep: | Cook: 120mins | Ready in:

Ingredients

- 4 boneless chicken breast, cut into 1/4 inch cubes
- 2 bell peppers, One Green, One Red or Yellow (for color)
- 5 or 6 roma tomatoes, diced
- 1/4 white onion
- 1/4 red onion
- 6 cloves garlic, chopped
- 1 tbsp white wine vinegar
- 2 tbsp fresh parsley, chopped
- 1 cube chicken bouillon (Knorr)
- 1/4 c butter
- 1 tbsp olive oil
- salt and pepper to taste
- 4 c brown rice, cooked

Direction

- Cut chicken and set aside
- Chop Peppers, Onions and Garlic
- In large pan, sautéed onions and garlic in olive oil
- Add Tomatoes and peppers, cook on low until softened but not mushy
- Add the rest of the ingredients, including the chicken, cover and cook until chicken is completely cooked
- Salt and Pepper to taste and serve over rice

35. Black And White Sesame Chicken Recipe

Serving: 4 | Prep: | Cook: 30mins | Ready in:

Ingredients

- 2 tablespoon sweet soy sauce
- 2 tablespoon Asian sesame oil
- 1/8 teaspoon hot red pepper sauce
- 1/8 teaspoon granulated sugar
- 1 teaspoon minced ginger root
- 1/3 cup coconut milk
- 4 boneless skinless chicken breast halves
- 1 tablespoon black sesame seeds
- 1 tablespoon white sesame seeds

Direction

- In shallow dish stir together soy sauce, oil, hot sauce, sugar, ginger and coconut milk.
- Add chicken then turn to coat and set aside for 30 minutes.
- Preheat grill or broiler then transfer chicken to plate discarding marinade.
- Sprinkle chicken on both sides with sesame seeds then grill or broil 5 minutes per side.
- Serve immediately.

36. Bombay Chicken Recipe

Serving: 4 | Prep: | Cook: 40mins | Ready in:

Ingredients

- 2 pound chicken breast
- salt/ black pepper
- 1/2 cup butter
- 2 onions
- 3 garlic cloves
- 4 tsp. curry paste
- 2 tsp. ginger minced
- ! tsp. cinnamon
- 1 can diced tomatoes
- 1/4 cup sour cream
- 1/4 tbl. coriander
- 1- 2 limes

Direction

- Melt 1/2 butter add onions and garlic, cook 5 min.
- Cut chicken in strips, salt and pepper, add to butter …till brown
- Stir in curry past, ginger, cinnamon cook for 30 sec. then add tomatoes with juice and left over butter.
- Cook for 20 minutes.
- Stir in sour cream and coriander

37. Bourbon Laced Tipsy Chicken With Peaches Recipe

Serving: 4 | Prep: | Cook: 30mins |Ready in:

Ingredients

- 4 chicken breast halves
- 1/2 teaspoon salt
- 1/8 teaspoon freshly ground black pepper
- 2 tablespoons butter
- 1 large onion finely chopped
- 1 teaspoon paprika
- 6 green onions chopped including green part
- 1/2 cup orange juice
- 2 tablespoons bourbon
- 1 cup chopped fresh peaches
- 1/4 teaspoon nutmeg

Direction

- Preheat oven to 400.
- Sprinkle chicken with salt and pepper then place in rectangular baking pan and set aside.
- In medium skillet melt butter over medium heat.
- Add chopped onion and cook stirring occasionally for 5 minutes.
- Add paprika and all but 1 tablespoon of the green onions.
- Continue to cook stirring occasionally for 4 minutes.
- Spread onion mixture evenly over chicken then spoon orange juice and bourbon over top.
- Bake for 30 minutes turning and basting occasionally.
- Remove chicken from oven and spoon peaches over top and sprinkle with nutmeg.
- Return to oven for 20 minutes longer.
- Remove chicken from pan and place on serving dish then pour juices over top.
- Garnish with the remaining green onions and serve immediately.

38. Bourbon Street Chicken Recipe

Serving: 4 | Prep: | Cook: 90mins |Ready in:

Ingredients

- bourbon Street chicken
- 4 chicken breasts
- 1 teaspoon ground ginger
- 4 ounces soy sauce
- 2 tablespoons dried onion flakes
- 1/2 cup brown sugar
- 3/8 cup bourbon whiskey
- 1/2 teaspoon garlic powder

Direction

- Place chicken breasts in a rectangular baking dish.

- In small bowl combine ginger, soy sauce, onion flakes, sugar, bourbon and garlic powder.
- Mix together and pour mixture over chicken then cover and place in refrigerator overnight.
- Preheat oven to 325 then remove dish from refrigerator and cover and bake for 1-1/2 hours.

39. Bruschetta Stuffed Chicken Breasts Recipe

Serving: 8 | Prep: | Cook: 45mins | Ready in:

Ingredients

- 1 can (14.5 oz) Italian-style tomaotes, undrained
- 1-1/4 cups shredded low-moisture part-skim mozzarella cheese, divided
- 1/4 cup chopped fresh basil
- 1 pkg (6 oz) Stove Top stuffing mix for chicken
- 8 small boneless skinless chicken breast halves (2 lb)
- 1/3 cup Kraft roasted red pepper Italian with Parmesan Dressing

Direction

- Heat oven to 350 degrees. Mix tomatoes, 1/2 cup cheese and basil in medium bowl. Add stuffing mix; stir just until moistened.
- Place 2 chicken breasts in large freezer-weight resealable plastic bag. Pound with meat mallet or side of heavy can until chicken is 1/4 inch thick. Remove from bag; place top sides down, on cutting board. Repeat with remaining chicken. Spread chicken with stuffing mixture. Starting at 1 narrow end, tightly roll up each breast. Place, seam-sides down, in 13X9-inch baking dish. Drizzle with dressing.
- Bake 40 minutes or until chicken is done. Sprinkle with remaining cheese; bake 5 minutes or until melted.

- VARIATION: Use dice tomatoes with bell or jalapeno peppers, Kraft Mexican Style shredded cheese instead of the mozzarella cheese and chopped cilantro instead of basil.
- When I made this I halved the recipe, so I had a little of the dressing mixture left over. I cut up some sun-dried tomatoes and added them to the mixture. I placed it in a ramekin and pressed it down. I baked them about 30 minutes (I had added about 2 tablespoons of tomato juice) and they came out perfect.

40. Buffalo Chicken Chili Recipe

Serving: 10 | Prep: | Cook: 75mins | Ready in:

Ingredients

- 1 tablespoon extra-virgin olive oil
- 2 tablespoons butter
- 2 pounds ground chicken breast
- 1 large carrot, peeled and finely chopped
- 1 large onion, chopped
- 3 stalks celery, finely chopped
- 5 cloves garlic, chopped
- 5 tablespoons chili powder
- 2 tablespoons ground cumin
- 1 tablespoon ground paprika
- salt and pepper to taste
- 1/2 cup hot buffalo wing sauce (such as Frank's® REDHOT buffalo wing sauce), or to taste
- 2 (15 ounce) cans tomato sauce
- 1 (15 ounce) can crushed tomatoes
- 1 (15 ounce) can white kidney or cannellini beans, drained
- 1 (19 ounce) can red kidney beans, drained

Direction

- Heat olive oil and butter in a large pot over medium-high heat.
- Place chicken in the pot. Cook and stir 7 to 10 minutes, until chicken is no longer pink.

- Stir in the carrot, onion, celery, garlic, chili powder, cumin, paprika, and salt and pepper, and cook and stir until the onion is translucent and the vegetables are beginning to soften, 3 to 4 more minutes.
- Stir in the hot sauce, tomato sauce, crushed tomatoes, and white and red kidney beans.
- Bring to a boil, and simmer over medium-low heat about 1 hour, until the vegetables are tender and the flavors have blended.

41. Busy Moms Chicken And Dumplings Recipe

Serving: 6 | Prep: | Cook: 330mins | Ready in:

Ingredients

- 4 skinless, boneless chicken breasts
- 2 T butter or margarine
- 2 cans of condensed cream of chicken soup, undiluted
- 1 small onion, diced
- 2 (8 count) cans refrigerated biscuits
- water to cover

Direction

- Place the chicken, butter, soup and onion in a slow cooker.
- Fill with water to cover chicken.
- Cook on high for 5-6 hours or until chicken is cooked through and no longer pink inside.
- Approximately 30 minutes before serving, tear biscuit dough into separate pieces and place in soup mixture in slow cooker. The biscuits will turn into your dumplings. Test readiness of dumplings by cutting one in half, if its center is cooked, the dumplings are ready to eat.

42. Buttermilk Country Fried Chicken Recipe

Serving: 8 | Prep: | Cook: 30mins | Ready in:

Ingredients

- marinade
- 1 cup buttermilk
- 1 tsp ground red pepper(cayenne)
- 1/2 tsp salt
- 1 garlic clove, minced
- chicken
- 2 lb boneless skinless chicken breasts/thighs
- 3/4 cup flour
- 2 tbsp cornstarch
- 1 tsp dried thyme leaves
- 1 tsp paprika
- oil for frying

Direction

- In large dish or resealable bag mix marinade ingredients. Add chicken pieces and turn to coat. Refrigerate 2 hours or overnight
- In small pan, mix flour and remaining chicken ingredients except oil.
- Heat 1/2 inch oil in skillet over medium high heat.
- Remove chicken from marinade and allow excess to drip off. Discard marinade
- Roll chicken in flour mixture until well coated and then add to skillet.
- Cover and cook on medium high heat 10 minutes
- Uncover skillet and turn chicken
- Cook 5-8 minutes longer until the chicken is fully cooked through. Drain on paper towels and serve warm or refrigerate and serve cold!

43. CAJUN STYLE PASTA Recipe

Serving: 4 | Prep: | Cook: 30mins | Ready in:

Ingredients

- 2 cups milk
- 1 tsp butter
- 2 Tbs sherry
- 12 oz linguine
- 1/4 tsp cayenne
- 1/2 cup frozen peas
- 2 garlic cloves minced
- 2 1/2 Tbs all purpose flour salt and black pepper to taste
- 1/2 lb chicken breast meat diced
- 1/4 cup grated parmesan cheese
- 4 plum tomatoes seeded and chopped
- 12 medium size shrimp peeled and deveined

Direction

- Prepare the linguine according to package directions. Drain and keep warm until ready to serve. Melt the butter in the center of a large non-stick skillet over medium high heat. Add the garlic and cook for 1 minute then add the shrimps and chicken. Pan-fry until the chicken is cooked through. In a bowl, whisk the flour, milk, sherry and parmesan cheese together. Pour into the skillet and bring to a boil while stirring then reduce heat to medium and continue to cook for about 5 minutes until the mixture has thickened stirring occasionally. Add the cayenne and fold in the tomatoes and peas and cook until heated through. Season to taste with salt and pepper. Arrange the linguine on individual plates and spoon the sauce over the top. Garnish the Cajun Style Pasta with chopped fresh parsley.

44. CHICKEN MARSALA SANDWICH Recipe

Serving: 413 | Prep: | Cook: 30mins | Ready in:

Ingredients

- 1/4 cup olive oil
- 3 cloves garlic, finely chopped
- 1/4 cup all-purpose flour
- salt and pepper, if desired
- 1 lb chicken breast cut for scaloppini by butcher (or 1 lb boneless skinless chicken breasts pounded to 1/8-inch thickness)
- 1 can (6 oz) Green Giant® B in B® sliced mushrooms, drained
- 1/2 cup marsala (sweet) wine or apple juice
- 1 can (18.5 oz) Progresso® vegetable Classics French onion soup
- 4 kaiser rolls
- 4 oz Fontina cheese, sliced, shaved or grated*
- 1 tablespoon parsley flakes, if desired

Direction

- In small microwavable bowl, mix oil and garlic. Microwave on High 1 minute; set aside. Place flour on plate; stir in salt and pepper. Coat chicken with flour, shaking off excess.
- In 12-inch non-stick skillet (1 1/2 inches deep), place 1 tablespoon of the heated oil without garlic pieces. Heat oil over medium-high heat 1 to 2 minutes or until hot but not smoking. Add chicken, cutting large pieces in half, if necessary, so all chicken fits in skillet; cook 4 to 6 minutes, turning once, until no longer pink in center and golden brown. Remove chicken from skillet; place on plate and cover to keep warm.
- In same skillet, cook mushrooms over medium-high heat 1 minute, stirring occasionally, until thoroughly heated. Stir in wine and soup with heatproof rubber spatula or wooden spoon to scrape up brown bits from bottom of skillet. Cook 5 to 7 minutes, stirring occasionally, until thoroughly heated.
- Meanwhile, set oven control to broil. Split rolls; place cut side up on large cookie sheet. Broil 6 to 8 inches from heat 1 to 2 minutes or until toasted and golden brown. Brush cut sides with remaining oil mixture with garlic pieces; top evenly with Fontina cheese. Broil 30 to 60 seconds or until cheese is melted.
- Return chicken to skillet. Reduce heat to medium-low; simmer uncovered 2 to 3 minutes, turning chicken occasionally, until chicken is coated with sauce. Divide chicken

evenly among rolls. With slotted spoon, divide mushrooms and onions over chicken. Pour wine sauce into 4 (4-oz) ramekins or dipping bowls. Sprinkle parsley on individual plates; place sandwiches and ramekins of sauce for dipping on plates.

45. CHICKEN OR TURKEY PAD THAI Recipe

Serving: 4 | Prep: | Cook: 12mins | Ready in:

Ingredients

- 8 ounces rice noodles(vietnemise bahn pho or thai sen-mee)
- 1/4 cup salted peanuts, finely chopped
- 1/2 teaspoon grated lime zest
- 3 tablespoons fish sauce
- 2 tablespoons fresh lime juice
- 2 tablespoons packed brown sugar
- 4 1/2 teaspoons rice vinegar
- 1 tablespoon asian chile sauce
- 3 tablespoons olive or vegetable oil
- 1 lb bnlss skinless chicken breast cut into strips(or 1 lb leftover turkey diced)
- 1 tablespoon finely chopped garlic
- 1 egg, lightly beaten
- 1 cup fresh bean sprouts
- 1/3 cup chopped green onion
- 2 tablespoons fresh cilantro, chopped

Direction

- 1. Place noodles in a large bowl. Add enough hot water to cover; let stand 10-15 minutes until pliable but not soft. Drain well.
- 2. Combine peanuts and lime zest, set aside.
- 3. In a small bowl, combine fish sauce, lime juice, brown sugar, rice vinegar, and chili sauce; stir until blended. Set aside.
- 4. In a 12 inch (or thereabouts) non-stick skillet heat 1 tablespoon oil over med-high heat. Add chicken and garlic. Cook and stir frequently for 6 minutes until no pink remains. (*If using cooked turkey, only sauté for about two minutes*) Then transfer to a bowl and set aside.
- 5. Add egg to the hot skillet and cook for 30 seconds. Turn egg with spatula and cook for 30-60 seconds more, until set. Chop egg then remove, set aside.
- 6. In same skillet heat remaining 2 tablespoons oil over high for 30 seconds. Add drained noodles and sprouts; stir fry for 2 minutes. Add fish sauce mixture and poultry; cook 1-2 minutes more until heated through. Divide noodle mixture among four plates. Sprinkle with egg and peanut topping. Garnish with green onions and cilantro.
- ENJOY!!!!

46. CHILI CHICKEN CORN N PASTA Recipe

Serving: 4 | Prep: | Cook: 20mins | Ready in:

Ingredients

- 6oz pkg angel hair pasta
- 3 ears of fresh corn
- 1/4 cup veg oil
- 4 small boneless skinless chicken breasts
- 1 1/2 tsp chili powder; divided
- 1/4 tsp salt
- 1/4 tsp pepper
- 2 sliced med tomatoes
- 3 tbsp lemon juice

Direction

- Cook pasta and ears of corn in salted boiling water about 8 minutes.
- Drain and rinse with cold water.
- Mix 1 tsp chili powder, salt & pepper in a bowl and sprinkle over chicken breasts.
- In a large skillet cook chicken in 1 tbsp. oil over med heat for 10-12 minutes or until chicken is no longer pink, turning once.

- While chicken is cooking, cut the kernels from the cobs.
- Combine the remaining oil and chili powder along with the lemon juice in a jar.
- Mix the chicken, corn, tomatoes and pasta
- Serve onto plates.
- Drizzle with prepared dressing (the jar of lemon juice oil & chili powder) and lightly sprinkle lightly with salt & pepper.

47. CREAMY BASIL PASTA WITH CHICKEN Amp VEGETABLES Recipe

Serving: 6 | Prep: | Cook: 11mins | Ready in:

Ingredients

- pasta Ingredients:
- 6 ounces dried uncooked penne pasta
- Sauce Ingredients:
- 1 1/2 cups Low Fat Half &Half
- 1 (1.2-ounce) package creamy pesto sauce mix
- 1 tablespoon olive oil
- 1 teaspoon dried basil
- chicken & vegetables Ingredients:
- 1 tablespoon butter
- 1 pound boneless skinless chicken breast halves, cut into 1/2-inch pieces
- 1 medium (1/2 cup) onion, chopped
- 1 teaspoon finely chopped garlic
- 1/2 teaspoon salt
- 1/4 teaspoon pepper
- 2 cups small broccoli florets
- 1/2 cup chicken broth or white wine
- 2 red, yellow and/or orange bell peppers, cut into 1-inch pieces
- Shredded parmesan cheese, if desired

Direction

- Cook pasta according to package directions. Drain.
- Meanwhile, combine half & half, sauce mix, olive oil and basil in small bowl. Stir with wire whisk until smooth; set aside.
- Melt butter in deep 12-inch non-stick skillet. Add chicken, onion, garlic, salt and pepper. Cook over medium heat until chicken is no longer pink (5 to 8 minutes). Add all remaining ingredients except Parmesan cheese. Cover; continue cooking until broccoli is crisply tender (4 to 6 minutes).
- Gradually stir in sauce mixture. Reduce heat to low; cook, stirring constantly, until mixture is thickened and heated through (2 to 3 minutes). Stir in cooked pasta. Continue cooking until heated through; 1 minute. Serve immediately. Sprinkle with Parmesan cheese.
- Recipe Tip:
- A variety of pasta sauce mixes are available in the dry sauce/gravy section of the supermarket. We also tested this recipe using creamy Alfredo sauce mix and the results were excellent.

48. Cajun Chicken Ala King Recipe

Serving: 8 | Prep: | Cook: 60mins | Ready in:

Ingredients

- 6-8 chicken breasts
- 8 chicken boullion cubes
- 8 cups water
- 1 medium onion, chopped
- 1 stalk celery, chopped
- 1 stick butter
- 1 cup flour
- 3-4 cups milk
- 1 cup sweet peas, frozen or canned
- Homemade biscuits

Direction

- Dissolve bouillon cubes in water. Add chopped onion, celery, and chicken breast. Boil

until tender. Remove chicken and chop into bite size pieces. Reserve broth.
- In separate pot, melt butter. Add flour, and cook mixture for 3-5 minutes. Slowly add 4 cups of the cooked chicken broth. ADD SLOWLY AND STIR CONTINUOUSLY to avoid lumping. Add milk until mixture resembles a thick soup. (You can thin by adding more liquid, either broth or milk, or thicken by adding a paste of milk and flour.)
- Salt and pepper to taste. Add cooked chicken and peas. Heat thoroughly.
- Serve over homemade biscuits sliced in half.

49. Cajun Chicken Breasts In The Oven Recipe

Serving: 4 | Prep: | Cook: 42mins | Ready in:

Ingredients

- 1-tspn salt
- 1-tspn cayenne pepper
- 1-tspn paprika
- 1/2-tspn white pepper
- 1/2-tspn black pepper
- 1/2-tspn oregano
- 1/4-tspn onion powder
- 1/4-tspn garlic powder
- 1/2-cup lemon juice
- 1/4-cup canola oil
- 4-skinless, boneless chicken breast halves

Direction

- Combine dry spices in small bowl.
- In a shallow glass dish large enough to hold chicken in a single layer, place lemon juice and oil.
- Add half of spice mix; stir to combine.
- Marinate for 1 hour at room temperature or for 3 hours to overnight in the fridge - covered.
- Drain chicken from marinate and sprinkle both side with remaining seasoning mix.
- Place breasts on an oven broiling rack and cook in preheat 475 degree oven for 22 minutes on one side and 20 minutes on the other.

50. Cajun Style Chicken Nuggets Recipe

Serving: 4 | Prep: | Cook: 10mins | Ready in:

Ingredients

- 1 envelope onion soup mix
- 1/2 cup plain dry bread crumbs
- 1-1/2 teaspoons chili powder
- 1 teaspoon ground cumin
- 1 teaspoon thyme leaves
- 1/4 teaspoon ground red pepper
- 2 pounds boneless chicken breasts cut into 1" pieces
- oil for frying

Direction

- In a large bowl combine soup mix, bread crumbs, chili powder, cumin, thyme and pepper.
- Dip chicken in bread crumb mixture coating well.
- In large skillet heat 1/2" oil and cook chicken over medium heat turning once until done.
- Drain well on paper towels then serve immediately.

51. Cap Cai Indonesian Vegetable Stir Fry Recipe

Serving: 2 | Prep: | Cook: 15mins | Ready in:

Ingredients

- cauliflower, cut into small florets

- 1/2 carrot, cut into 1/2 cms thick
- 4 meatballs cut into 1/2 cms thick
- 1 cup of chicken breast, cubed (optional)
- 1/2 onion, cut into cubes
- 1 spring onion, cut into 10 cms lenght
- 3 fresh shitake mushrooms
- 2 cloves of garlic, finely chopped
- 1/2 cup of chicken stock
- 1 chilli pepper
- salt and white pepper to taste
- 1/2 tsp corn flour / corn starch mixed with 4 tbs of water

Direction

- With a little oil and medium heat, sauté garlic until fragrant; add onion until soft, add meat balls, (add chicken, if you're using).
- Add cauliflower, carrot and mushrooms and chili pepper.
- Add chicken stock, stir, cover with lid; let it cook for 5 minutes.
- Add salt, pepper and spring onion, corn starch mixture, stir well; serve hot.

52. Cappellini Florentine Recipe

Serving: 4 | Prep: | Cook: 15mins | Ready in:

Ingredients

- 16 oz. package angel hair pasta
- 2 Tbsp olive oil
- 4 large cloves garlic, minced
- 1 8-oz package of sliced mushrooms
- 1 10-oz package of fresh spinach
- 2 Tbsp balsamic vinegar
- 1 Tbsp crushed red pepper (or to taste)
- 1/4 lemon
- 2 chicken breasts, cooked and shredded
- 4 oz. mozzarella cheese, cut into cubes
- salt and pepper to taste

Direction

- Put water for pasta to boil on stovetop.
- In a large skillet, sauté garlic in oil over medium heat until the garlic takes on a little color, but do not allow to turn golden.
- Add mushrooms. Sauté 3-4 minutes until cooked through.
- Add spinach, stirring frequently until cooked down and wilted.
- Add red pepper, vinegar, and salt and pepper to taste. Cook 1-2 minutes longer.
- Take the pan off heat and add lemon juice. Toss to distribute evenly.
- Add pasta to the water and cook. When the pasta is ready (2-3 minutes), drain. Return pasta to pot and mix in spinach-mushroom mixture, chicken, and mozzarella cubes. Serve immediately.

53. Caribbean Style Chicken With Tropical Salsa And Spicy Sweet Potato Sticks Recipe

Serving: 4 | Prep: | Cook: 27mins | Ready in:

Ingredients

- Salsa:
- 1 cup diced peeled papaya
- ½ cup pineapple chunks
- 2 tablespoons finely chopped red onion
- 2 tablespoons minced fresh cilantro
- 1 tablespoon minced fresh mint
- 1 tablespoon minced jalapeno
- 2 tablespoons fresh lime juice
- Dash of sugar
- Chicken:
- 4 (4-ounce) skinless, boneless chicken breast halves
- 1 tablespoon Jamaican jerk seasoning, divided
- cooking spray
- 4 lime wedges
- cilantro sprigs (garnish)
- Sweet Potato:

- 4 medium sweet potatoes each cut into 8 equal sticks
- 1 tablespoon vegetable oil
- 1 teaspoon paprika
- 1/2 teaspoon cayenne pepper
- 1/8 teaspoon salt

Direction

- 1. Prepare grill or grill pan to medium heat
- 2. Preheat oven to 375 degrees
- 3. To prepare salsa, combine all 8 ingredients in a bowl, mix well.
- 4. To prepare chicken, sprinkle breast halves evenly with Jamaican jerk seasoning. Coat each half with cooking spray. Place on grill rack; grill 4 ½ minutes on each side or until chicken is done. Cut each breast into ½-inch-thick slices. Serve with salsa and a lime wedge; garnish with cilantro sprigs, if desired.
- 5. To prepare sweet potatoes: mix together the oil and seasonings then toss with sweet potato sticks. Spread single-layered on a cookie sheet and bake for 25-28 minutes or until crispy.
- Yield: 4 servings (serving size: 1 chicken breast, ¼ cup salsa, 1 lime wedge and 8 sweet potato sticks)

54. Caribbean Salsa Chicken Recipe

Serving: 4 | Prep: | Cook: 20mins | Ready in:

Ingredients

- 2 to 3 cups hot cooked rice
- 4 boneless skinless chicken breast halves, cut into bite-sized pieces
- 1 cup thicke and chunky salsa
- ¼ cup orange marmalade
- 1 tablespoon brown sugar
- 2 tablespoons fresh lime juice
- ¼ to ½ teaspoon allspice
- ¼ cup chopped fresh cilantro
- Fresh lime wedges, if desired
- Fresh orange wedges, if desired

Direction

- While rice is cooking, heat oil in large skillet over medium-high heat until hot.
- Add chicken; cook and stir 7 minutes or until chicken is no longer pink.
- In medium bowl, combine salsa, marmalade, brown sugar, lime juice, and allspice; mix well.
- Add to chicken; mix well. Bring to a boil. Reduce heat to low; cover and simmer 5 to 10 minutes, stirring occasionally.
- Stir in cilantro.
- Serve over hot cooked rice. Garnish with lime and orange wedges.

55. Ceasar Chicken With Orzo Recipe

Serving: 4 | Prep: | Cook: 25mins | Ready in:

Ingredients

- 1 Tbsp vegetable oil
- 4 boneless skinless chicken breasts
- 1 can chicken broth
- 1 cup water
- 1 cup uncooked orzo pasta
- 1 lb frozen vegetables (carrots, green beans, asparagus or other combinations)
- 3 Tbsp Caesar dressing
- salt
- pepper

Direction

- Heat oil in skillet and salt & pepper chicken to taste.
- Cook chicken in oil about 10 minutes, turning once, until brown.
- Remove chicken from skillet & keep warm.
- Add broth and water to skillet; bring to boiling.
- Stir in pasta; bring to boil again. Cook uncovered for 8 to 10 minutes, stirring occasionally, until pasta is tender.

- Stir in frozen vegetables and dressing.
- Heat to boiling, reduce heat and simmer uncovered about 5 minutes or until vegetables are crisp-tender and juice from chicken is clear.
- Serve over rice.
- If you would like, you can fry the rice in a pan with oil and add one beaten egg and soy sauce for a cheap and easy variation of fried rice.

56. Cheap Fast And Easy General Tsos Chicken Recipe

Serving: 2 | Prep: | Cook: 25mins | Ready in:

Ingredients

- 2 or 3 large chicken breasts.
- 1 packet of general tso's sauce mix ($1.25 at Kroger).
- 1 bag of frozen mixed stir fry vegetables ($1 at Kroger).
- 1 1/2 cups cooked rice of your choice, I use jasmine rice.
- crushed red pepper flakes.
- 1 tbsp. soy sauce.
- 1/3 cup water.
- 1/4 cup sugar.
- 1/3 cup flour.
- 1 egg (optional)

Direction

- If frozen, thaw chicken breasts. Cut into chunks or strips, and roll in a bowl with flour until evenly coated.
- Heat oil in a medium sauce pan, and stir fry chicken until brown on all sides.
- Add mixed vegetables to the chicken, and maybe even add a little more oil so nothing burns.
- While the veggies and chicken are cooking, combine general Tso's mix, soy sauce, water, sugar and a bit of crushed red pepper flakes if you'd like.
- Add the sauce mix to the chicken and veggies, and add even MORE crushed red pepper flakes if you'd like. Stir fry until the sauce is thick.

57. Cheese Chicken Recipe

Serving: 4 | Prep: | Cook: 55mins | Ready in:

Ingredients

- 1 (3oz) pkg of sliced dried beef
- 5-6 boneless, skinless chicken breasts
- 5-6 slices of bacon, uncooked
- 1 can condensed cheddar cheese soup
- 1 c sour cream

Direction

- Run cold water over dried beef; drain and arrange in the bottom of the baking dish.
- Place chicken breasts over beef; top each with a slice of bacon. Bake uncovered for 30 min. at 350.
- Combine condensed soup and sour cream; pour over chicken. Bake for 25 more minutes.

58. Cheese Herb Stuffed Chicken Breast Recipe

Serving: 4 | Prep: | Cook: 45mins | Ready in:

Ingredients

- 4 - 6 boneless chicken breasts
- 1/2 cup feta cheese, crumbled
- 1/2 cup fresh parsley, chopped
- 1 Tbsp. olive oil
- 1 tsp. dried oregano
- 1 14-oz. can diced tomatoes
- 1/2 cup black olives, sliced
- 1 Tbsp. cornstarch

- Note: I often double up on the ingredients.

Direction

- Cut a 2 - 3 inch slit in each chicken breast.
- Combine feta cheese, parsley, olive oil and oregano and mix well.
- Stuff each chicken breast with an equal portion of cheese mixture.
- Place stuffed chicken breasts in a baking dish.
- Combine tomatoes, olives and cornstarch and mix.
- Pour over chicken and bake for 45 minutes at 350 degrees.
- To go along with the chicken, Wolfgang suggests the following...
- BROCCOLI AND CARROTS WITH ORANGE BUTTER
- Ingredients:
- 2 cups fresh baby carrots
- 2 cups fresh broccoli florets
- 1/3 cup butter
- 1 Tbsp. grated orange peel
- 1/4 cup orange juice
- 1 tsp. cornstarch
- Method:
- Place carrots in a steamer and steam for about 5 minutes.
- Add broccoli to the steamer and steam until both are crisp-tender.
- Remove from the steamer and place on a serving platter.
- Combine butter, orange peel, orange juice and cornstarch in a saucepan and simmer until thickened.
- Pour over vegetables and serve.

59. Cheese Chickena Dn Rice Recipe

Serving: 4 | Prep: | Cook: 55mins | Ready in:

Ingredients

- cheese chicken and rice

- 1 can cream of chicken soup
- 1 1/3-cups water
- 3/4-cup uncooked rice
- 2-cups frozen mixed vegetables
- ½-tspn onion powder
- 1/4-tspn black pepper
- a generous sprinkling of salt
- 4 chicken breasts
- 1/2-cup shredded cheddar cheese

Direction

- Stir together the soup, water, rice, vegetables, onion powder, and pepper and pour into an 11X8" (or I used a 12-1/2- "X7") baking dish. Season chicken and put on top of mixture. Bake at 375 degrees for 50 minutes.
- Top with cheese and put back into oven just long enough for cheese to melt (about 5 minutes)

60. Cheesy Chicken Recipe

Serving: 4 | Prep: | Cook: 360mins | Ready in:

Ingredients

- 1 can cream of chicken
- 1 can cheddar cheese soup
- 1/4 teaspoon garlic powder
- Mix together pour over 2lbs of chicken breasts

Direction

- Slow cook 6-8 hours.
- I seasoned my chicken breast with salt and pepper before.
- So simple and we served it over egg noodles.
- You can also add: green chilies
- Salsa

61. Cheesy Chicken Spaghetti Bake Recipe

Serving: 4 | Prep: | Cook: 30mins | Ready in:

Ingredients

- 8 ounces spaghetti
- 4 skinless boneless chicken breasts
- 2 cans condensed cream of chicken soup
- 5 ounce jar processed cheese spread
- 5 ounce bottle processed cheese spread with jalapenos

Direction

- Boil spaghetti as directed on package then drain well.
- Brown chicken breast until tender and done all the way through.
- Shred chicken into bite size pieces then melt cheese in microwave as directed on jar.
- Pour drained spaghetti in large baking dish then add melted cheese and soup and mix well.
- Stir in chicken and mix well then cover with foil and bake at 425 for 25 minutes.

62. Cheesy Chicken And Potato Casserole Recipe

Serving: 8 | Prep: | Cook: 35mins | Ready in:

Ingredients

- 3 teaspoons vegetable oil
- 3 skinless, boneless chicken breasts
- 1 (5.5 oz) package scalloped potato mix
- 4 potatoes, thinly sliced
- 2 cups cheddar cheese, shredded

Direction

- Preheat oven to 350 degrees F.
- Heat oil in a medium skillet over medium-high heat. Add chicken breasts and sauté until tender. Meanwhile, prepare potatoes according to package directions, adding 1 cup (instead of 2/3) of milk and sliced potatoes. When chicken is tender, remove from heat, let cool and shred. Add shredded chicken to potato mixture.
- Fold chicken/potato mixture into 9x13-inch baking dish. Cover and bake in a preheated oven for 25 to 35 minutes. Add cheese and bake for another 10 minutes.

63. Cheesy Chicken And Rice Bake Recipe

Serving: 4 | Prep: | Cook: 60mins | Ready in:

Ingredients

- 1 can (10-3/4 oz.) Campbell's Cream of Chicken Soup
- 1-1/3 cup water
- 3/4 cup uncooked regular long-grain white rice
- 1/2 tsp. onion powder
- 1/4 tsp. ground black pepper
- 1-1/2 lb. skinless chicken breast halves
- (about 4-6)
- 1 cup shredded cheddar cheese (nice if you use more - to taste)

Direction

- Mix soup, water, rice, onion powder and black pepper in 2qt shallow baking dish. You can use a glass 9x13 pan or whatever :-)
- Top with chicken.
- Sprinkle chicken with additional pepper. Use your taste buds :-)
- Cover and bake at 375 degrees for 45 minutes or until chicken is no longer pink and rice is done.
- Took about an hour for me.
- Uncover. Sprinkle cheese over chicken.

- Return to oven till it melts, I shut off the oven. It only takes a minute or so.
- Get Your Veggies:
- Stir 2 cups of fresh or frozen vegetables into soup mixture before topping with chicken.
- You can add a can of Veg-All, drained and frozen corn.
- ENJOY!

64. Cheesy Crockpot Chicken Recipe

Serving: 5 | Prep: | Cook: 32mins | Ready in:

Ingredients

- 3-5 boneless, skinless chicken breast
- 2 cans cream of chicken soup
- 1 can cheddar cheese soup
- salt n pepper to taste
- garlic powder enough to sprinkle on chicken

Direction

- Sprinkle chicken breast with salt, pepper and garlic powder.
- Add to crockpot add the 3 cans of soups.
- Cook on low all day (at least 8 hours).
- DO NOT LIFT LID
- Serve over cooked rice or noodle.

65. Cheezit Chicken Recipe

Serving: 6 | Prep: | Cook: 15mins | Ready in:

Ingredients

- 1/2 box of Cheezit's (or cheese Nips)
- (Get creative! They have buffalo chicken, bleu cheese, and sour cream and chive flavored ones too)
- 6 chicken breasts or 10-12 smaller tenders
- 1/2 stick of butter
- salt and pepper
- Pinch of dill

Direction

- Wash chicken breasts.
- Place Cheezits in a large Ziploc bag and crush them into a rough shake.
- Melt butter.
- Combine a pinch of salt, pepper, and dill with Cheezits. (This is a good place for some cayenne pepper too!)
- Brush butter over both sides of chicken breasts and drop them in the Ziploc also.
- SHAKE VIGOROUSLY!!! (And dance)
- Bake at 350 for 15-20 minutes depending on your oven and size of your chickens.

66. Chicken Rice Cheese Casserole Recipe

Serving: 6 | Prep: | Cook: 25mins | Ready in:

Ingredients

- 3 chicken breast
- 1 cup shredded casserole cheese
- 2 cups of rice or 2 boil in a bags
- 1 can of cream of chicken
- salt
- pepper
- 1/2 cup of shredded parmesan cheese or Mozzarella

Direction

- Boil chicken until it is no longer pink inside
- Boil rice until it is tender
- Preheat oven to 350 degrees
- Spray a baking pan with a little bit of canola oil (or your choice of non-stick spray)
- Shred chicken into pieces or chop into small chunks whatever you prefer

- Mix rice, cream of chicken soup, cheese and chicken together. Put into the baking pan and sprinkle a little bit of Parmesan cheese on top put in the oven for about 10 minutes or until the cheese is melted.
- Once it is done baking fix you a plate add a little salt & pepper and indulge into this delicious meal!

67. Chicken & Asparagus Bundles (italian) Recipe

Serving: 3 | Prep: | Cook: 90mins | Ready in:

Ingredients

- 3 boneless, skinless chicken breasts (large sized (6+oz or more))
- 9-to-12 pieces of Asparagus (larger size preferred)
- 8 oz Bella (brown) Mushrooms..sliced
- 1# mixed Italian cheeses
- 8+ oz of your fav Pasta Sauce
- Italian herded bread crumbs (add more herbs..as you see fit)
- Olive Oil, as needed
- Salt & Pepper & Garlic to taste

Direction

- slice each chicken breast in half (longways)...pound each piece to thinness, apply salt & pepper & garlic (to taste)
- Cover each piece of chicken in breadcrumbs, fry in olive oil, brown BOTH sides, remove to platter
- NOW...build your beautiful bundles...repeat 3x....bottom...a breast piece, lay-in 3-to-4 asparagus, cover w/ the sliced mushrooms, now add a layer of the cheeses & cover w/ some pasta sauce
- COVER ALL THIS with another piece of breast meat...adding a layer of the cheeses, topped with more pasta sauce

- ALL 3 'bundles' should fit into a glass pie plate. BAKE at 350 until the cheeses melt. Serve w/a nice salad, toasted 'garlicky' bread & wine/or/beer.
- NOTE: this recipe freezes well...try to avoid storage in anything metal as the acids in the pasta and metal don't agree.
- ENJOY!!

68. Chicken & Cream Cheese Stuffed Peppers Recipe

Serving: 2 | Prep: | Cook: 45mins | Ready in:

Ingredients

- 1 boneless, skinless chicken breast half seasoned with adobo seasoning, fresh lime juice and olive oil, grilled
- 4 ounces cream cheese, room temperature
- 4 ounces sharp white cheddar, grated plus extra for topping
- 1 seeded jalapeno pepper, finely diced
- 1 teaspoon cumin
- 1 ear fresh corn, brushed with olive oil, grilled
- 1/4 cup fresh salsa (tomato, onion, cilantro, sea salt, lime juice)
- 1/4 cup panko breadcrumbs
- 2 red (or any color) bell pepper, cut in half, seeds removed

Direction

- Cut grilled chicken into small cubes, set aside.
- In a bowl, combine cream cheese, cheddar cheese, jalapeno, cumin, grilled corn and fresh salsa. Mix in the grilled chicken and stuff each pepper half with mixture (you may have filling leftover).
- Press each half of red bell pepper into panko, filling side down. Bake on a parchment lined baking sheet, covered, for 25 minutes in a 350 degree oven. The peppers should be fairly tender and the filling heated through. Remove

foil, sprinkle with a little more cheese and pop back in oven to broil, until golden on top.
- Serve on top organic baby spring mix with a simple red wine vinaigrette seasoned with cumin. Enjoy!

69. Chicken & Sun Dried Tomato Orzo Recipe

Serving: 4 | Prep: | Cook: 30mins | Ready in:

Ingredients

- 8 ounces orzo, preferably whole-wheat
- 1 cup water
- 1/2 cup chopped sun-dried tomatoes, (not oil-packed), divided
- 1 plum tomato, diced
- 1 clove garlic, peeled
- 3 teaspoons chopped fresh marjoram, divided
- 1 tablespoon red-wine vinegar
- 2 teaspoons plus 1 tablespoon extra-virgin olive oil, divided
- 4 boneless, skinless chicken breasts, trimmed (1-1 1/4 pounds)
- 1/4 teaspoon salt
- 1/4 teaspoon freshly ground pepper
- 1 9-ounce package frozen artichoke hearts, thawed
- 1/2 cup finely shredded romano cheese, divided

Direction

- 1. Cook orzo in a large saucepan of boiling water until just tender, 8 to 10 minutes or according to package directions. Drain and rinse.
- 2. Meanwhile, place 1 cup water, 1/4 cup sun-dried tomatoes, plum tomato, garlic, 2 teaspoons marjoram, vinegar and 2 teaspoons oil in a blender. Blend until just a few chunks remain.
- 3. Season chicken with salt and pepper on both sides. Heat remaining 1 tablespoon oil in a large skillet over medium-high heat. Add the chicken and cook, adjusting the heat as necessary to prevent burning, until golden outside and no longer pink in the middle, 3 to 5 minutes per side. Transfer to a plate; tent with foil to keep warm.
- 4. Pour the tomato sauce into the pan and bring to a boil. Measure out 1/2 cup sauce to a small bowl. Add the remaining 1/4 cup sun-dried tomatoes to the pan along with the orzo, artichoke hearts and 6 tablespoons cheese. Cook, stirring, until heated through, 1 to 2 minutes. Divide among 4 plates.
- 5. Slice the chicken. Top each portion of pasta with sliced chicken, 2 tablespoons of the reserved tomato sauce and a sprinkling of the remaining cheese and marjoram.
- NUTRITION:
- Per serving: 457 calories; 12 g fat (3 g sat, 6 g mono); 68 mg cholesterol; 54 g carbohydrates; 0 g added sugars; 36 g protein; 10 g fiber; 372 mg sodium; 546 mg potassium.

70. Chicken Adobo Recipe

Serving: 0 | Prep: | Cook: 1hours | Ready in:

Ingredients

- main ingredients:
- 1 kg of thigh chicken/ breast(optional)
- 4 big pieces of rosit potato
- 3 pieces of carrot
- 2 green chili(optional)
- sauce:
- salt, black pepper
- 1 cup white vinegar
- 2 tbsp. black soy sauce
- 4 tbsp. light soy sauce
- 1tsp of sugar (optional)
- 4 cloves of garlic (chopped)
- 2 medium onions thinly sliced
- 5 tbsp of oil (preferably olive oil)
- 1 tbsp of corn flour (optional)

Direction

- 1. Wash chicken properly and pat to dry; there should be no excess water
- 2. Marinate all the ingredients with the sauce; leave the oil, and onion separately.
- 3. Sauté the onion in an oil
- 4. Put the chicken; taken out from the sauce and let it fry for 3 minutes
- 5, put the sauce over the chicken and simmer, cover for 15 minutes and turn it.
- 6. Meanwhile, heat 4 tbsp. of oil in a pan;
- 7. Put chicken one each time and fry it till it's brown and will give a good smell;
- 8. Separate it from sauce while cooking it at the same time let sauce boil until potato and carrots are soften;
- 9. Add extra cornflour to the sauce to thicken it;
- 10. Put all fried chicken in the sauce and boil it for 10 minutes to enhance the taste.
- 11. Serve with boil white rice

71. Chicken Alfredo Recipe

Serving: 8 | Prep: | Cook: 30mins |Ready in:

Ingredients

- Chicken:
- * 1 1/2 lbs. boneless chicken breast, cut into 3/4 inch chunks
- * 2 Tbsp. olive or vegetable oil
- * 1/2 tsp. minced garlic
- * salt and pepper
- Sauce:
- * 8 oz. cream cheese
- * 1/2 c. butter
- * 3/4 c. milk
- * 3/4 c. grated parmesan cheese
- * 1/2 tsp. white pepper (may also use black pepper)
- 16 oz. cooked spaghetti, linguine, fettuccini or angel hair pasta
- parsley

Direction

- Cook chicken in olive oil with garlic and salt and pepper.
- While chicken is cooking, melt cream cheese and butter together in saucepan. Stir until smooth. Stir in milk, Parmesan cheese and pepper.
- Pour chicken and juices over spaghetti in a serving dish, then top with sauce and sprinkle parsley on top.

72. Chicken And Cheese Stuffed Avacado Recipe

Serving: 2 | Prep: | Cook: 45mins |Ready in:

Ingredients

- 2 whole chicken breasts
- 2 avacados cut into slices
- 1 cup grated cheddar cheese
- 2 eggs beaten
- 2 cups panko breading

Direction

- Pound the chickens flat
- Roll avocado and cheese into chicken making a ball
- Coat with egg and roll into panko covering all surfaces
- Wrap into foil and bake at 350 for 45 min

73. Chicken And Rice In A Mug Recipe

Serving: 1 | Prep: | Cook: 5mins |Ready in:

Ingredients

- 2 Tbsp. water
- 1 Tsp. dried minced onion
- 1/4 Tsp. sodium-free chicken bouillon powder
- 1/4 Cup frozen peas
- 1/2 Can (4.5 oz.) chunk chicken breast, drained (1/4 cup)
- 1 Container (4.4 oz.) Ready to Serve Fully cooked brown rice (3/4 cup)
- 1 Weight Watchers® Original Swiss Flavored cheese Wedge, cut into small pieces

Direction

- Combine water, onion and bouillon powder in a large microwave-safe mug; stir to combine.
- Add peas, chicken, rice and cheese; stir gently to mix.
- Cover and microwave on HIGH 2 minutes.
- Let stand 3 minutes before serving.
- *Recipe may be doubled
- Microwave ovens vary so cooking times might be different.

74. Chicken And Shrimp Recipe

Serving: 4 | Prep: | Cook: 30mins | Ready in:

Ingredients

- 1/2 cup milk
- 2 tablespoons butter
- 1/2 cup cream (heavy)
- 1/4 teaspoon poultry seasoning
- 1/8 teaspoon cayenne
- 1/8 teaspoon white pepper
- 1/8 teaspoon onion powder
- 1/2 cup white wine
- 1 tablespoon garlic powder
- 1 lb. linguine noodles
- 4 chicken breasts, skinless
- 1 8-oz package shrimp (raw, medium-size)
- 1 tablespoon olive oil

Direction

- Mortar spices well. Put cream & milk in pan with butter and 1/2 spice mixture. Thicken and reduce, set aside. Cook noodles. Sauté chicken breasts with wine and remaining spices until done. Remove and set aside. Sauté shrimp in same pan, adding wine if necessary. Serve each breast on a bed of noodles with shrimp. Cover with sauce.

75. Chicken And Vegetable Pie Recipe

Serving: 6 | Prep: | Cook: 2hours | Ready in:

Ingredients

- 6 chicken breasts
- 1 onion
- 2 cloves garlic
- 2 sticks of celery
- 2 leeks
- Cup of fresh basil
- 200 ml milk
- 2 peppers
- 3 Tbsp of broccoli sprouts
- 100 g of sweetcorn
- 3 carrots
- 2 sweet potatoes
- Handful of cheddar cheese
- 2 tbsp of water
- 2 tbsp of flour

Direction

- Chop all fat from chicken and grill until half cooked.
- Place chicken in casserole dish.
- Peal all vegetables
- Put the milk, broccoli sprouts, leeks, basil and celery into a blender
- And blend completely.
- Pour into casserole dish.
- Chop the onion and garlic finely and fry in a teaspoon of butter.

- Add 2 tablespoons of water and flour to onions and garlic.
- Add onion and garlic paste to casserole dish.
- Chop carrots into chunks.
- Add carrots and sweetcorn to casserole dish.
- Stir all ingredients in casserole dish together.
- Slice sweet potatoes finely and lay them on top
- Sprinkle with cheese
- Chicken and vegetable pie.
- Bake in a preheated oven at 180¤c for 45 minutes covered with tin foil and for 15 minutes uncovered.
- Season to taste.

76. Chicken Asparagus Mushroom Bake Recipe

Serving: 6 | Prep: | Cook: 35mins | Ready in:

Ingredients

- 1 Tbs. butter
- 1 Tbs. olive oil
- 2 boneless chicken breast {cut into bite size peices
- 2 cloves garlic minced
- 1 cup {Large can mushroom peices}
- 2 cups sliced aspargus
- black pepper to taste
- 1 pkg. cornbread stuffing{^ oz}
- 1/4 cup dry white wine Optional
- 1 can {41 1/2 oz chicken broth
- 1 can {101/2 oz}cream asparagus or cream of chicken soup {Undiluted

Direction

- PREHEAT OVEN 350 heat butter and oil in skillet until butter is melted
- Cook chicken and Garlic 3 minutes over medium high heat until CHICKEN is no longer pink add mushrooms cook and stir 2 minutes Add Asparagus cook stir 5 minutes or until crisp tender season.

- Put in a 2 1/2 Quart casserole top with stuffing mix. Add wine to skillet, cook and stir 1 minute over medium high heat. Scrape up any brown bits from bottom of skillet. Add broth and soup, cook and stir till well blended pour into casserole mix. WELL bake 35 MINUTES OR UNTILL LIGHT BROWN

77. Chicken Athena Recipe

Serving: 6 | Prep: | Cook: 240mins | Ready in:

Ingredients

- 6 boneless,skinless chicken breast halves(about 6oz ea)
- 2 med. onions,chopped
- 1/3c sun-dried tomatoes(not packed in oil),chopped
- 1/3c pitted Greek olives,chopped
- 2Tbs lemon juice
- 1Tbs balsamic vinegar
- 3 garlic cloves,minced
- 1/2tsp salt

Direction

- Place chicken in a 3qt. slow cooker. Add remaining ingredients.
- Cover and cook on low for 4 hours or till meat thermometer reads 170.

78. Chicken Breast Dijon Recipe

Serving: 4 | Prep: | Cook: 20mins | Ready in:

Ingredients

- 1/3 cup fine dry breadcrumbs
- 1 tablespoon parmesan cheese
- 1 teaspoon dried Italian seasoning
- 1/2 teaspoon dried thyme
- 1/4 teaspoon salt

- 1/4 teaspoon freshly ground pepper
- 4 skinned, boned chicken breast halves
- 2 tablespoons Dijon mustard
- 1 teaspoon olive oil
- 1 teaspoon butter

Direction

- Combine first 6 ingredients in a small bowl; stirring well.
- Brush both sides of each chicken breast half with mustard; dredge in breadcrumbs mixture.
- Heat olive oil and butter in a nonstick skillet over medium high heat until butter melts.
- Add chicken breasts, and sauté 6 to 8 minutes on each side or until chicken is done.

79. Chicken Breast Supreme Recipe

Serving: 0 | Prep: | Cook: 5hours | Ready in:

Ingredients

- 2 to 3 slices of bacon
- 4 to 6 boneless skinless chicken breast halves
- 1 jar of sliced mushrooms, drained. if desired
- 1 can of condensed cream of chicken soup
- 2 tbl dry sherry, if desired
- 3 to 4 slices of swiss cheese

Direction

- Cook bacon in large skillet over med. heat until crisp
- Remove and drain on paper towel, refrigerate until needed
- Keep bacon drippings in skillet
- Add chicken breast to bacon drippings
- Cook over med high heat until brown on both sides
- Transfer chicken to slow cooker
- Top with mushrooms
- Stir together soup and sherry
- Spoon over mushrooms
- Cover and cook 3-4 hours
- Top mixture in slow cooker with cheese crumble bacon over cheese
- Increase setting to high cover and cook for 10 to 15 min until cheese is melted
- With slotted spoon remove chicken ingredients from cooker serve with cooking juices from cooker.
- Enjoy!!!!

80. Chicken Breasts Diane Recipe

Serving: 4 | Prep: | Cook: 64mins | Ready in:

Ingredients

- 4 large boneless chicken breast halves or 8 small
- 1/2 tsp. salt
- 1/4-1/2 tsp. black pepper
- 2 Tbsp. olive oil or salad oil
- 2 Tbsp. butter or margarine
- 3 Tbsp. chopped fresh chives or green onions
- juice of 1/2 lemon or lime
- 2 Tbsp. brandy or cognac (optional)
- 3 Tbsp. chopped parsley
- 2 Tbsp. Dijion-style mustard
- 1/4 cup chicken broth

Direction

- Place chicken breast halves between sheets of waxed paper or plastic wrap. Pound slightly with mallet. Sprinkle with salt and black pepper.
- Heat 1 tablespoon each of oil and butter in large skillet
- Cook chicken over high heat for 4 min. on each side. Do not cook longer or they will be overcooked and dry. Transfer to warm serving platter.
- Add chives or green onion, lime juice and brandy, if used, parley and mustard to pan. Cook 15 seconds, whisking constantly.

- Whisk in broth. Stir until sauce is smooth. Whish in remaining butter and oil.
- Pour sauce over chicken. Serve immediately.
- Tip:
- You can pound chicken flat and leave flattened between sheets of plastic wrap. Wrap them airtight in one package and freeze for later use.
- This Meal Is Good With:
- Noodles with tomato sauce, steamed broccoli, and a fresh salad.

81. Chicken Breasts Pierre Recipe

Serving: 6 | Prep: | Cook: 40mins | Ready in:

Ingredients

- 6 boneless chicken breasts
- 1/4 c flour
- 1/2 t salt
- 3 T butter
- 2 T worcestershire sauce
- 1 t salt
- 2 t chili powder
- 1 t dry mustard
- 14.5 oz can stewed tomatoes, with liquid
- 1/2 c water
- 1 1/2 T brown sugar
- 2 T white vineger
- 1/2 t celery seed
- 1 garlic clove, minced
- 1/8 t hot sauce. or a littl more.

Direction

- Combine flour and salt. Coat chicken.
- Melt butter over med heat, and brown meat all over
- Drain on paper towels
- In same skillet, add all the rest of the ingredients. Bring to a boil, reduce heat, and put in the chicken. Cover, simmer about 35-40 min
- I usually uncover the last few min.

82. Chicken Breasts With Garlic And Oil Recipe

Serving: 6 | Prep: | Cook: 35mins | Ready in:

Ingredients

- 6 skinless, boneless chicken breast halves (about 2 lbs)
- 3/4 tsp. salt, plus more as needed
- 1/2 c. all-purpose flour
- 1/4 c. extra-vigin olive oil
- 2 tbsp. butter
- 8 or more large cloves garlic, sliced
- 1/4 tsp. red pepper flakes
- 3 tbsp. tiny capers in brine, drained
- 2 tbsp. red wine vinegar
- 1 c. chicken broth, turkey broth, or vegetable broth
- 1 tbsp. fine dry bread crumbs
- 3 tbsp. chopped fresh Italian parsley leaves

Direction

- Trim the chicken of all fat, skin and connective tissue.
- Flatten the small, loose flap on the underside of each half against the larger piece to form a neat oval.
- Sprinkle both sides of each breast with salt, using about 1/2 tsp. in all. Spread the flour on a piece of waxed paper and press and toss each breast to coat lightly on all surfaces; shake off excess.
- In a 14-inch skillet or sauté pan, heat 2 tbsp. of the oil and the butter over medium heat.
- When the butter is almost melted, lay the breasts in the pan, with space between them. Let them cook until sizzling without moving. After 2 minutes or so, lift the first breast you put in the pan and check the underside.
- You want it to be lightly tinged with brown. Cook longer if needed, turning each over when just beginning to color.

- Quickly scatter the garlic slices in between the chicken pieces, turn the heat up slightly, shake the pan, and stir the garlic slices to separate. When the garlic has begun to sizzle, sprinkle the hot pepper flakes in a hot spot, toast for a minute; then sprinkle capers in several hot spots around the pan. Give the skillet a few good shakes to distribute the seasonings, and run the hot juices all around the breast.
- Raise the heat another notch. When everything's sizzling hard, pour the vinegar into open spaces and shake the pan to spread it. Let the vinegar sizzle and reduce for 30 seconds or so, then pour in the broth.
- Turn temperature up to high, quickly bringing the liquid to a boil; drizzle with the remaining 2 tbsp. oil, and sprinkle on 1/4 tsp. salt. Let the sauce bubble and reduce for a couple of minutes, shaking the skillet frequently,
- Check doneness of chicken then sprinkle the bread crumbs into the sauce (not on the chicken) and stir and shake to mix. Cook, shaking the skillet, until the sauce has the consistency you like.
- Turn off the heat, sprinkle with parsley, and shake the skillet again.
- Serve just as it is or over spaghetti or orzo

83. Chicken Breasts With Ginger Orange Sauce Recipe

Serving: 2 | Prep: | Cook: 15mins | Ready in:

Ingredients

- 4 boneless, skinless chicken breasts
- 2 tbs lemon juice
- olive oil
- Sauce
- 1 tbs freshly grated ginger root
- 1 tsp minced garlic
- 1/4 cup soy sauce
- 1/4 cup orange juice
- 4 tsp water
- 2 tsp white vinegar

Direction

- Brush chicken breasts with lemon juice. Grill, or bake chicken. If grilling, brush olive oil to keep chicken moist. You can also sauté chicken in olive oil until browned and place in oven until finished. Nap chicken with clean sauce and serve over cooked soba noodles or jasmine or basmati rice.
- Sauce
- Combine all ingredients in pint jar and shake to mix well. Heat on high for one or two minutes. Makes one-half cup, enough for 4 chicken breasts. Recipe can be multiplied.

84. Chicken Breasts In Chutney Cream Recipe

Serving: 6 | Prep: | Cook: 20mins | Ready in:

Ingredients

- 6 boneless, skinless chicken breasts
- 1/4 cup of flour
- 6 TBSP. butter
- 2 green onions, finely chopped
- 1/2 tsp. minced fresh ginger
- 3 TBSP. chutney (Major Grey's)
- 1/3 cup of Madeira
- 3/4 cup of chicken broth
- 3/4 cup of whipping cream
- 2 TBSP. chopped, crystalized ginger

Direction

- Pound each chicken breast between plastic wrap until 1/4 inch thick.
- Dust each breast lightly with flour and shake off excess.
- Fry breasts in 3 TBSP. of butter on medium high until golden brown (about 4-6 minute).
- Add more butter if necessary.

- Transfer chicken on a warm plate to a 200 degree oven.
- To the pan add the onions, ginger, chutney, Madeira and broth.
- Boil on high heat, stirring, about 5 minutes.
- Add the cream and boil, stirring until reduced to about 1 and 1/4 cups.
- Pour the sauce over the chicken to serve and sprinkle with the crystalized ginger.
- Serve with curried rice.

85. Chicken Chasey Breaded Chicken Lasagna With Mozzerella Cheese Recipe

Serving: 4 | Prep: | Cook: 60mins | Ready in:

Ingredients

- 4 chicken breasts -- Beaten flat with pounder
- 2 Whole eggs or egg whites
- 1 C bread crumbs --Italian herb crumbs may be used for extra flavor
- 1/2 C Finely grated parmesan cheese --extra for topping
- 1 Can spaghetti sauce (your brand/flavor preference) I always like to have spare sauce and buy two just in case
- 3-4 large Mozzerella balls packaged in water -- drained and sliced thin
- garlic salt and pepper to taste
- 1Package spaghetti noodles- your preference although regular pasta noodles work best. Angelhair okay
- olive oil
- Food snobs may sub organic ingredients for all and use Ezekiel pasta noodles instead.

Direction

- Preheat oven to 350
- Set up three plates side-by-side. One bowl, one deep plate and one flat plate layered with paper towel sheets.
- In the 1st bowl beat eggs/ egg whites
- In the 2nd deep dish, mix bread crumbs with parmesan cheese
- The third bowl is for the finished chicken.
- Pound all chicken breasts with a pounder until as thin as possible without them falling apart. A helpful hint is to lay a piece of saran-wrap over the chicken to prevent the pounder from sticking to the chicken.
- Dip the breasts individually into one dish at a time, first covering the chicken completely in eggs. Dip immediately into dish two and cover completely with bread crumbs and parmesan cheese, and then set chicken aside. Chicken is ready to fry.
- Heat small amount of olive oil in pan and fry chicken breasts until a slight golden brown. Be careful not to burn the crust. Chicken is done when inside is white.
- When chicken is done, place in dish three, wrapping each breast in paper towel to soak up any excess oil. Set Chicken aside.
- Layer the bottom of a 9" lasagna dish.
- Layer one: 1/2 can spaghetti sauce. (Rest will be used for dressing)
- Layer two: Prepared chicken breasts spaced side-by side
- Layer three: Mozzarella cheese slices on top of chicken
- Place in oven for approx. 30 min or until all cheese is melted. Garlic salt may be added for extra flavor directly over chicken.
- During this time, cook pasta according to directions on box and drain.
- To serve:
- Dish out pasta onto plates and top them with chicken lasagna out of the oven. Salt, parmesan cheese and pepper to taste

86. Chicken Chorizo Pasta With A Creamy Sauce Recipe

Serving: 6 | Prep: | Cook: 20mins | Ready in:

Ingredients

- 2 single chicken breast
- 3x chorizo sausage – sliced
- 400g penne pasta
- 50g butter
- 150g parmesan cheese – grated
- 50g extra parmesan cheese – grated
- 150ml milk
- 150ml Cream
- 3x tomatoes – deseeded & diced
- baby spinach
- salt & pepper
- parsley - chopped

Direction

- Char grill chicken & sausages. (Slice chicken before serving)
- Cook pasta as packet directions
- Place butter, milk & cream in a pan over low heat until butter is melted & well combined, remove from heat add parmesan cheese, salt & pepper stir until blended & smooth.
- Drain pasta, toss with baby spinach leaves & chorizo sausage mix through creamy sauce.
- Add tomato, Plate up pasta, top with sliced chicken, sprinkle with extra parmesan & parsley.

87. Chicken Cilantro Soup Recipe

Serving: 6 | Prep: | Cook: 30mins | Ready in:

Ingredients

- cooked chicken carcass
- 3 carrots
- 3 celery stalks
- one whole onion cut into chunks
- 10 black peppercorns
- 3 chicken breast, cooked and chopped
- salt and pepper
- 1 can (28 ounce) Italian plum tomatoes, with juice
- 1 teaspoon dried or 2 tsp. fresh oregano
- cilantro

Direction

- Place carcass in a soup pot and cover with water. Add carrots, celery onion and peppercorns and salt to taste. Heat to boil, then lower heat and simmer 3 hours.
- Strain broth and discard vegies. Refrigerate broth about 4 hours and skim off fat. Return to stove over medium heat.
- Roughly chop tomatoes and add to the broth with their juice. Add oregano, cooked chicken and any additional salt and pepper. Cook over medium heat for 30 minutes them serve with a sprinkle of cilantro.

88. Chicken Cordon Bleu Recipe

Serving: 6 | Prep: | Cook: 50mins | Ready in:

Ingredients

- 6 flat chicken breasts, skinned and boned
- 1 package swiss cheese slices (8 oz)
- 1 package sliced cooked ham (8 oz)
- 3 Tablespoons flour
- 1 Teaspoon paprika
- 6 Tablespoons butter
- 1/2 cup dry white wine
- 1 chicken flavored bouillon cube
- 1 Tablespoon cornstarch
- 1 cup heavy or whipping cream

Direction

- Spread chicken breasts flat; fold cheese and ham slices to fit on top.
- Fold breasts over filling and fasten edges with toothpicks.
- On waxed paper; mix flour and paprika; use to coat chicken.

- In a 12 inch skillet over medium heat, in hot butter, cook chicken until browned on all sides.
- Add wine and bouillon.
- Reduce heat to low; cover and simmer 30 minutes or until fork tender; remove toothpicks.
- Remove chicken to platter.
- In a cup, blend cornstarch and cream until smooth; gradually stir into skillet.
- Cook, stirring constantly and scraping bottom, until thickened.
- Serve over chicken.

89. Chicken Dijon Pasta Salad Recipe

Serving: 2 | Prep: | Cook: 10mins | Ready in:

Ingredients

- 4 ounces pasta swirls uncooked
- 8 ounces plain yogurt
- 1/3 cup wheat germ
- 3 tablespoons white wine vinegar
- 1 tablespoon Dijon mustard
- 1/8 teaspoon freshly ground black pepper
- 1 cup boneless skinless chicken breasts cooked and diced
- 3/4 cup broccoli florets diced
- 1/2 cup tomato chopped and seeded
- 1/3 cup red onion chopped

Direction

- Cook pasta according to package directions.
- In medium bowl combine yogurt, wheat germ, vinegar, mustard and pepper then mix well.
- Add pasta and remaining ingredients then toss to coat.
- Serve immediately or chill before serving.

90. Chicken Elegante Recipe

Serving: 4 | Prep: | Cook: 120mins | Ready in:

Ingredients

- 4 ounces dried beef (See Notes)
- 10 each chicken breasts, cut lengthwise into halves
- 10 slices bacon
- 1 cup sour cream
- 1 cup mushroom soup
- 1/2 cup sliced mushroom

Direction

- Soak the dried beef if required.
- Arrange beef slices in the bottom of a 13 x 9 baking dish.
- Wrap each chicken breast half in a slice of bacon.
- Place on dried beef.
- Combine sour cream, mushroom soup and sliced mushrooms, pour over chicken.
- Cover and bake at 350 for 1-1/2 to 2 hours. Uncover for the last 1/2 hour.

91. Chicken Enchilada Casserole Recipe

Serving: 4 | Prep: | Cook: 60mins | Ready in:

Ingredients

- 4 chicken breasts, cooked and cubed
- 1-14.75 oz can cream of chicken soup (larger can than normal)
- 2-4 oz cans of diced green chili (more to taste)
- 2-3 c. shredded cheddar (sharper the better)
- 4-8oz sour cream
- 8-12 small corn tortillas

Direction

- 1. Preheat oven to 350 degrees

- 2. Combine chicken, soup, and green chiles.
- 3. Cover bottom of casserole dish (9"X9") with corn tortillas, place about 1 c of chicken mix, and then cover with 1 c. cheese.
- 4. Repeat until out of chicken mix.
- 5. Bake at 350 for 30-45 minutes, or until bubbly hot and yummy.
- 6. Serve on plate covered with sour cream.

92. Chicken Enchiladas Recipe

Serving: 6 | Prep: | Cook: 60mins | Ready in:

Ingredients

- 3 reg. sized cans of cream of chicken soup
- 1 small tub of sour cream
- 2 cups mozzarella cheese
- 1 small can mild diced chilies
- 2 chicken breasts
- 1 Package Large tortillas
- 1 More cup of mozzarella cheese for topping.

Direction

- Chicken Prep.
- Pre heat oven to 350
- Cook Chicken for 35-40 min.
- Cut into small cubes.
- Enchiladas
- Pre Heat oven to 350
- Mix together all ingredients and cubed chicken except for the 1 cup of cheese.
- With a small spoon, about 4 tbs into each tortilla and roll. Leave enough filling to spread over top of all the finished tortillas. When pan is full, spread the rest of the filling evenly over top and then add the left over cheese on top of that.
- Cook for 20-25 min.
- Let 'em cool off a bit before you give them to the kids, then dig in and enjoy! Yum Yum!

93. Chicken Enchiladas With Mole Sauce Recipe

Serving: 4 | Prep: | Cook: 25mins | Ready in:

Ingredients

- 3 tablespoons vegetable oil
- 1 1/2 pounds skinless boneless chicken breast
- salt and pepper
- 2 teaspoons cumin powder
- 2 teaspoons garlic powder
- 1 teaspoon Mexican spice Blend
- 1 red onion, chopped
- 2 cloves garlic, minced
- 1 cup frozen corn, thawed
- 5 canned whole green chiles, seeded and coarsely chopped
- 4 canned chipotle chiles, seeded and minced
- 1 (28-ounce) can stewed tomatoes
- 1/2 teaspoon all-purpose flour
- 16 corn tortillas
- 1 cup enchilada sauce, canned
- 1 cup shredded cheddar & jack cheese
- Garnish: Chopped cilantro leaves, scallions, sourcream, tomatoes.
- Mole Sauce:
- 2 teaspoons vegetable oil
- 1/4 cup finely chopped onion
- 1 tablespoon unsweetened cocoa powder
- 1 teaspoon ground cumin
- 1 teaspoon dried cilantro
- 1/8 tablespoon dried minced garlic
- 1 (10.75 ounce) can condensed tomato soup
- 1 (4 ounce) can diced green chile peppers

Direction

- Coat large sauté pan with oil. Season chicken with salt and pepper. Brown chicken over medium heat, allow 7 minutes each side or until no longer pink. Sprinkle chicken with cumin, garlic powder and Mexican spices before turning. Remove chicken to a platter, allow to cool.
- Sauté onion and garlic in chicken drippings until tender. Add corn and chilies. Stir well to

combine. Add canned tomatoes, sauté 1 minute.
- Pull chicken breasts apart by hand into shredded strips. Add shredded chicken to sauté pan, combine with vegetables. Dust the mixture with flour to help set.
- Microwave tortillas on high for 30 seconds. This softens them and makes them more pliable. Coat the bottom of 2 (13 by 9-inch) pans with a ladle of enchilada sauce. Spoon 1/4 cup chicken mixture in each tortilla. Fold over filling, place 8 enchiladas in each pan with seam side down. Top with mole sauce and cheese.
- Bake for 15 minutes in a preheated 350 degree F oven until cheese melts. Garnish with cilantro, scallion, sour cream and chopped tomatoes before serving. Serve with Spanish rice and beans.
- Mole Sauce: Heat the oil in a medium saucepan over medium heat, and cook the onion until tender. Mix in cocoa powder, cumin, cilantro, and garlic. Stir in the tomato soup and green chili peppers. Bring to a boil, reduce heat to low, cover, and simmer 10 minutes. Transfer to a gravy boat or pour directly over food to serve.

94. Chicken Florentine Casserole Recipe

Serving: 6 | Prep: | Cook: | Ready in:

Ingredients

- 4 x 3 oz boneless, skinless chicken breasts, pre-cooked, cut into cubes
- 1/2 box frozen spinach, thawed & squeezed to remove access liquid
- 1/8 to 1/4 tsp. garlic powder
- 1 Tbsp olive oil
- 2 Tbsp flour
- 1 Tbsp lemon juice
- 1 1/2 cups chicken broth
- pinch nutmeg
- 1 tsp dried oregano
- 1/2 tsp black pepper
- 1 cup low fat cottage cheese, blended to make smooth consistency
- 2/3 cup parmesan cheese
- 1/2 pound spiral pasta (or whatever pasta you wish to use)

Direction

- Preheat oven to 375 degrees F.
- Mist a 9 x 11 baking dish with oil.
- Cook pasta according to package directions.
- In a large pot, heat olive oil to medium-low and add garlic powder.
- Add flour and whisk for 30 seconds.
- Add chicken broth and stir until thickened.
- Add lemon juice, nutmeg, oregano & pepper.
- Bring to simmer.
- Remove from heat and add blended cottage cheese, spinach, chicken, Parmesan cheese & pasta.
- Stir to combine.
- Place in casserole dish.
- Bake for 30 minutes or until golden & bubbly.

95. Chicken Florentine Recipe

Serving: 4 | Prep: | Cook: 10mins | Ready in:

Ingredients

- 1/2 cup Italian salad dressing
- 1 tsp. dried Italian seasoning mix
- 4 boneless, skinless chicken breasts
- 10 oz. container refrigerated alfredo sauce
- 2 cups frozen chopped spinach, thawed and well drained
- 2 Tbsp. olive oil
- 12 oz. cooked fettuccine
- 1/2 cup grated parmesan cheese

Direction

- Mix dressing and Italian seasoning in large glass bowl. Add chicken breasts, turning to coat, and cover. Refrigerate 30 minutes.
- Combine Alfredo sauce with spinach in medium bowl. Heat oil in large non-stick skillet over medium heat.
- Remove chicken from marinade, and cook chicken in oil 7-10 minutes, turning once, until thoroughly cooked. Add Alfredo sauce mixture. Cook until bubbly.
- Serve over cooked and drained fettuccine and sprinkle with Parmesan cheese.

96. Chicken Gorgonzola Pasta Recipe

Serving: 4 | Prep: | Cook: 20mins | Ready in:

Ingredients

- 2 large boneless, skinless, chicken breasts, cut into 1" cubes
- salt
- pepper
- 1 T olive oil
- 3 tablespoons unsalted butter
- 3 shallots, minced
- 1 lb. farfalle, fusilli, or penne pasta
- 1/2 cup chicken stock
- 1/2 lb. gorgonzola cheese, rind removed, cut into small pieces
- 3/4 cup heavy (double) cream
- Grated zest of 1 lemon
- salt and freshly ground pepper
- 6 fresh sage leaves, coarsely chopped

Direction

- Season cubed chicken with salt and pepper
- In a large frying pan, heat olive oil. Sauté chicken breasts until cooked through. Set aside.
- Bring a large pot of water to a boil.
- Meanwhile, in the same pan used for chicken breasts, melt the butter. Add the shallots and sauté until soft, about 4 minutes.
- Generously salt the boiling water, add the pasta, and cook until al dente, 9-11 minutes.
- Reduce the heat under the frying pan to low and add the stock, cheese, cream, and lemon zest. Season with salt and pepper to taste and stir until all the ingredients are smooth and melted, about 4 minutes.
- Drain the pasta and add it to the frying pan. Remove from the heat. Add the chicken and sage; toss briefly until the pasta is well coated with the sauce. If the sauce seems too thick, add a bit more chicken stock or a splash of hot water. Pour into a large, shallow bowl. Serve immediately.

97. Chicken Gyro Recipe

Serving: 4 | Prep: | Cook: 30mins | Ready in:

Ingredients

- Marinade:
- 1/6 cup olive oil
- 1/8 cup fresh lemon juice
- 2 tsp garlic, pressed or minced
- 1/3 tablespoon dried mint
- 1/3 tablespoon dried oregano
- 1/3 tablespoon black pepper
- 1/6 tablespoon salt
- chicken Gryos:
- 1 2/3 pound boneless, skinless chicken breasts, cut into bite-sized pieces
- 4 pitas
- 2 ounces feta, crumbled
- yogurt-Dill Sauce:
- 1/4 pound cream cheese, softened (can use low fat cream cheese)
- 2/3 cup natural plain yogurt (can use low or non fat yogurt)
- 2 tsp fresh lemon juice
- 1/3 teaspoon garlic, pressed or minced

- 1/6 tablespoon dried dill
- 1/3 teaspoon salt

Direction

- In a medium bowl, whisk together all marinade ingredients. Set aside 3/4 cup marinade.
- Pour remaining marinade over chicken pieces and stir to combine. Marinate, refrigerated, 2 hours.
- In a large skillet over medium-high heat, add chicken and sauté until cooked through. Work in batches as necessary.
- Transfer chicken to large bowl, removing batches from skillet with a slotted spoon. Cool.
- Divide evenly among one-quart size freezer bags. Divide reserved marinade evenly among chicken, shaking to distribute (1/2 tablespoon per serving).
- Seal bag, pressing out excess air. Refrigerate.
- Wrap pitas in foil (1 per serving).
- Package cheese in snack bags (1/2 ounce per serving).
- Place a package of chicken, a pita, and a package of cheese in each of one-gallon size freezer bags.
- Seal bag, pressing out excess air. Freeze.
- Yogurt-Dill Sauce: If substituting low-fat or non-fat yogurt for natural yogurt, strain overnight in refrigerator in a coffee filter-lined sieve.
- Combine all ingredients in a mixing bowl or processor.
- Beat or process until smooth. Divide evenly among small freezer containers.
- Cover with a sheet of plastic wrap, pressing down to cling to food. Apply lid. Freeze.
- Preheat oven to 350F. Warm foil-wrapped pitas in oven 10 minutes. Warm chicken in oven or microwave until heated through. Stir Yogurt-Dill Sauce and transform into Tzatziki by adding 1/2 large cucumber which has been peeled, seeded, finely diced or shredded, and drained.
- Top pita rounds with chicken, Yogurt-Dill Sauce, and crumbled feta. Add fresh, sliced tomato if desired.

98. Chicken In Sour Cream Sauce Recipe

Serving: 6 | Prep: | Cook: 300mins | Ready in:

Ingredients

- 1 1/2 teaspoon salt
- 1/4 teaspoon pepper
- 1/4 teaspoon paprika
- 1/4 teaspoon lemon pepper seasoning
- 6 bone-in-chicken breast halves, skin removed
- 1 can (10 3/4 oz.) cream of mushroom soup, undiluted
- 1 cup sour cream
- 1/2 cup dry white wine or chicken broth
- 1/2 pound fresh mushrooms, sliced

Direction

- Combine the first 4 ingredients; rub over chicken. Place in a slow cooker. In a bowl, combine the soup, sour cream, and wine or broth; stir in mushrooms. Pour over chicken. Cover and cook on LOW for 6-8 hrs. or until chicken juices run clear. Thicken the sauce if desired

99. Chicken Italiano Recipe

Serving: 4 | Prep: | Cook: 30mins | Ready in:

Ingredients

- 8 boneless chicken breast halves
- seasoned breadcrumbs
- fresh mozzarella sliced in thin rounds
- fresh basil leaves
- ricotta cheese

- red tomato sauce (cooked)

Direction

- Wash chicken halves
- Coat chicken with seasoned bread crumbs and lay on a surface with skin side down
- Place a basil leaf, a slice of mozzarella cheese and a spat of ricotta on top of each piece of chicken
- Roll chicken as tight as possible and place in a baking dish
- Bake in preheated 350 degree oven for 30 mins
- ****would be best to serve straight from oven because the cheese is melted just right****
- After plating chicken, pour red sauce on top
- ENJOY!!

100. Chicken Kabobs Recipe

Serving: 5 | Prep: | Cook: 4hours | Ready in:

Ingredients

- 3lbs chicken breasts cut into 1 inch cubes
- 1/4 cup soy (china lily is best)
- 1/4 cup cider vinegar
- 2 Tbsp honey and canola oil
- 3 green onions
- 3 cloves garlic
- 1 pkg bacon
- 1 lb mushrooms
- Veggies of choice for kabobs.

Direction

- Dice chicken
- Mix all other ingredients together except for Vegetables and bacon
- Add chicken and mushrooms to marinade and let sit MINIMUM 5 hours or overnight if possible. (Save marinade for a later step)
- Cut Veg for kabobs into 1 inch cubes
- Cut 1 slice bacon in half and wrap around a chicken cube.
- Place on skewer and alternate with vegetables until you have used everything up
- BBQ on med heat until bacon is cooked and chicken juices run clear. I usually start them on the top rack and then move them down.
- If you want you can reduce the leftover marinade on the stove and use to baste kabobs 1/2 way through cooking.
- Goes great with curried cuscus and a cucumber dill yogurt mix.

101. Chicken Kiev Recipe

Serving: 0 | Prep: | Cook: 15mins | Ready in:

Ingredients

- 1/2 cup butter
- 1/2 tablespoon chopped fresh parsley
- 1/2 tablespoon chopped fresh chives
- 1 tablespoon lemon juice
- 6 skinless, boneless chicken breast halves
- salt and pepper to taste
- 2 cups dried bread crumbs
- 3 eggs, lightly beaten
- 3 tablespoons water
- Ajinomoto mami super seasoning
- vegetable oil for frying
- toothpicks
- Sauce:
- sour cream
- parsley, chopped

Direction

- 1. In a small bowl, combine the butter/margarine, parsley, chives and lemon juice. Add Ajinomoto Umami super seasoning. Blend all together and refrigerate.
- 2. Place chicken breasts between 2 pieces of wax paper and pound well to flatten. Remove paper and season breasts with salt and pepper to taste.
- 3. Remove seasoned butter from refrigerator and divide it into 6 portions. Place one portion

in the center of each chicken breast. Fold the short ends of the breasts into the center, then fold in the sides. Secure each breast with a wooden toothpick.
- 4. Add the water to the eggs and beat together. Coat each rolled breast with bread crumbs, dip into egg/water mixture, then into bread crumbs again, coating well.
- 5. In a deep fryer, heat oil. Carefully lower breasts into hot oil. Fry for 8 minutes or until golden brown. Drain on paper toweling and serve with sauce.

102. Chicken Lasagna Recipe

Serving: 8 | Prep: | Cook: 40mins | Ready in:

Ingredients

- 6 Tbs butter, divided
- 1-1/2 pounds of chicken breast cut into 1-inch cubes
- 2 garlic cloves, minced
- 3/4 tps. dried thyme
- 1/3 cup cup all-purpose flour
- 1/2 tps. salt
- 1-1/2 cups chicken broth
- 1 cup heavy whipping cream
- 8 ounces lasagna noodles, cooked and drained
- 2 cups (8 ounces) shredded swiss cheese
- Minced fresh parsley

Direction

- In a large skillet over medium heat, melt 2 Tbs. butter. Add chicken, garlic and thyme. Cook for about 10 minutes. Remove and set aside. Add the remaining butter to the skillet. Stir in flour and salt until smooth; cook and stir until golden brown. Gradually add broth and cream. Bring to a boil; cook and stir for 2 minutes or until thickened. In a greased 13-in. x9-in. x2-in. baking dish, layer half of the noodles, chicken, white sauce and cheese. Repeat layers. Cover and bake at 350F. for 20 minutes. Uncover; bake 20 minutes longer or until bubbly. Let stand 15 minutes before serving. Sprinkle with parsley.

103. Chicken Makhani Curry Recipe

Serving: 4 | Prep: | Cook: 30mins | Ready in:

Ingredients

- 4 large skinned chicken breasts
- 2 large red chillies
- 4 cloves of garlic, finely chopped
- 1 c. double cream
- 1 c. natural yogurt
- 1 fresh lemon
- 1 tsp garam masala
- 2 tsp ground cumin
- 2 tblsp coriander leaves
- 1/2 c. butter
- 1/2 tsp salt
- 6 fresh ripe tomatos

Direction

- Core and deseed the chilies, chop them up fine.
- Add the chilies, fine chopped garlic, cumin and masala to a blender.
- Blend add the juice of the lemon, coriander leaves and the yogurt to create the marinade.
- Chop up the chicken into small pieces and put into a glass bowl
- Mix in the marinade with the chicken, cover and put in the fridge for 3 hours.
- Quarter the tomatoes and put into a pan with nothing else. Warm for 20mins on a low to medium heat
- Strain the tomatoes into a clean pan using a fine sieve. Throw away the skins and pulp left over.
- Tomato sauce should be thick, heat this for 50 mins until reduced to a nice thick sauce. You

- may need to skim off any yellow stuff off the top as it is heating.
- Add in 1/2 c. of butter and salt then stir and heat for another 20 minutes.
- Add in 1 c. heavy whipping cream, heat through thoroughly and set aside.
- Heat a pan with 3 tbl spoons of vegetable oil and add all the chicken.
- Cook for 15 minutes on a medium heat.
- Add in the tomato sauce and stir and heat for 5 minutes.
- Serve with basmati rice.

104. Chicken Marengo Recipe

Serving: 4 | Prep: | Cook: 40mins | Ready in:

Ingredients

- 4 small whole chicken breasts
- salt and papper
- 1/4 C butter or oil
- 2 onions, thinly sliced
- 1 garlic clove, mashed
- 2 large tomatoes, peeled and chopped
- paprika
- 3/4 C good white wine
- 1 C sliced mushroom caps

Direction

- Wash chicken and pat dry
- Sprinkle with salt and pepper
- Sauté chicken in oil until golden on both sides (medium heat)
- Remove to platter
- Sauté onion and garlic until onions are tender
- Add tomatoes and cook until mushy
- Return chicken breasts to skillet
- Season again with salt, pepper and paprika to taste
- Pour in wine and cook, covered for 30 minutes, adding more wine if necessary (medium low heat or simmer)
- Add mushrooms to mixture and cook for 7 to 10 minutes longer (simmer)

105. Chicken Marsala Recipe

Serving: 4 | Prep: | Cook: 30mins | Ready in:

Ingredients

- 1/4 cup all-purpose flour for coating
- 1/2 teaspoon salt
- 1/4 teaspoon ground black pepper
- 1/2 teaspoon dried oregano
- 4 skinless, boneless chicken breast halves - pounded 1/4 inch thick
- 4 tablespoons butter
- 4 tablespoons olive oil
- 1 cup sliced mushrooms
- 1/2 cup marsala wine
- 1/4 cup cooking sherry

Direction

- 1. In a shallow dish or bowl, mix together the flour, salt, pepper and oregano. Coat chicken pieces in flour mixture.
- 2. In a large skillet, melt butter in oil over medium heat. Place chicken in the pan, and lightly brown. Turn over chicken pieces, and add mushrooms. Pour in wine and sherry. Cover skillet; simmer chicken 10 minutes, turning once, until no longer pink and juices run clear.

106. Chicken Neufetchel Recipe

Serving: 18 | Prep: | Cook: 30mins | Ready in:

Ingredients

- 1 chicken breast cooked and diced
- 1 lb turkey bacon Cooked and Crumbled

- 1 block neufetchel or cream cheese
- 1 cup cheddar cheese shredded
- 2 tablespoons parmesan cheese
- 1 green onion
- 1 cup Italian bread crumbs
- 1/2 tsp cayenne pepper
- 1 tsp sea salt
- 1/2 tsp white pepper
- 1 tsp garlic powder
- 1 can whole corn drained
- 2 eggs
- 1 can cream of chicken soup
- 1 pkg country style gravy mix
- 1 ready made pie crust

Direction

- Line 18 cup muffin pan with paper liners.
- In stand mixing bowl, add block Neufchatel cheese
- Cheddar cheese
- Parmesan cheese
- Green onion
- Bread crumbs
- Cayenne pepper
- Sea salt
- White pepper
- Garlic powder
- Corn
- Eggs
- Blend these ingredients until fully mixed.
- Then, with a spoon, add in the diced chicken breast, and cooked Bacon and fold in.
- Spoon ingredients into muffin pan filling each tin to the top.
- Cut the readymade Pie Crust into 1/2 inch squares and place 4 square atop each muffin cup covering the chicken filling.
- Bake at 375 degrees for 25 minutes or until golden brown on top.
- In separate pan, prepare country style gravy mix according to directions on package. Stir in cream of chicken soup.
- When Chicken Neufchatel is completely prepared, remove from muffin paper and place in a small puddle of soup mixture. Then drizzle soup on top of the Chicken Neufchatel. Enjoy!

107. Chicken Noodle Stir Fry Recipe

Serving: 46 | Prep: | Cook: 10mins | Ready in:

Ingredients

- 1 package (3 ounces) chicken ramen noodles
- 1 pound boneless skinless chicken breasts, cut into strips
- 1 tablespoon canola oil
- 1 cup fresh broccoli florets
- 1 cup fresh cauliflowerets
- 1 cup sliced celery
- 1 cup coarsely chopped cabbage
- 2 medium carrots, thinly sliced
- 1 medium onion, thinly sliced
- 1/2 cup canned bean sprouts
- 1/2 cup teriyaki or soy sauce

Direction

- Set aside seasoning packet from noodles. Cook noodles according to package directions. Meanwhile, in a large skillet or wok, stir-fry chicken in oil for 5-6 minutes or until no longer pink. Add vegetables; stir-fry for 3-4 minutes or until crisp-tender.
- Drain noodles. Stir the noodles, contents of seasoning packet and teriyaki sauce into the chicken mixture until well combined.

108. Chicken On A Stick Recipe

Serving: 6 | Prep: | Cook: 5mins | Ready in:

Ingredients

- Bonless skinless chicken Breasts
- onions
- bell peppers
- wooden skewers
- Batter:
- 4 cups all purpose flour
- 1 tsp paprika
- 1 tbs baking powder
- 3 cans beer
- 2 tsp grandulated garlic
- 2 tsp salt
- 2 tsp black pepper
- 4 dashes louisiana hot sauce
- oil for deep frying

Direction

- Cut chicken breast into cubes about 1 1/2 inches
- Peel and quarter onions. Separate into layers of about 3 rings
- Cut bell pepper into pieces about same size as chicken
- Skewer piece of chicken, onion, bell pepper and repeat about two more times.
- Heat oil to 350 - 360 degrees
- Combine all ingredients for batter.
- Dip skewered chicken, onions, peppers into batter and fry 3 or 4 minutes, until light golden.

109. Chicken Oreganata Recipe

Serving: 4 | Prep: | Cook: 45mins | Ready in:

Ingredients

- 1/2 cup lemon juice
- 2 tablespoons white vinegar
- 1 1/2 tablespoons dried oregano
- 1 tsp honey
- 1 tablespoon canola or olive oil
- 1 teaspoon paprika
- 1/4 teaspoon ground black pepper
- 1 tsp dried onion flakes
- 4 skinless, boneless chicken breast halves

Direction

- Mix the lemon juice, vinegar, oregano, honey, oil, paprika, pepper, and onion. Place chicken in a Ziploc bag, pour the marinade over the chicken, and marinate in the refrigerator at least 4 hours or overnight.
- Remove chicken from marinade and brown.
- Add 1/4 cup chicken broth to the skillet, cover, and simmer 10-12 minutes or until the chicken is done.
- Pour the remaining marinade in a small saucepan and reduce to a sauce consistency. Serve the reduced marinade sauce drizzled over the chicken, if desired.

110. Chicken Paprika And Vegies Recipe

Serving: 0 | Prep: | Cook: 90mins | Ready in:

Ingredients

- 4 pounds frozen chicken breast fillets, defrosted
- 2 large heads of broccoli, cut into bite-size pieces
- 1 large red onion. sliced
- 4 cloves of garlic, crushed
- 2 jalapeno peppers, seeded and sliced
- 1 green pepper, seeded and sliced into strips
- 1 red pepper, not the hot variety.
- 1 tablespoon paprika
- red pepper flakes
- ground black pepper
- 4 cups of vegetable broth or chicken broth
- sesame oil or bacon grease, your preference
- soy sauce
- noodles or rice

Direction

- Heat the sesame oil or grease in a large frying pan over medium high heat.
- Wash and dry the defrosted chicken breasts, pepper them, and place them in the pan.
- Sauté and turn until browned on both sides.
- Remove and place aside.
- Turn the pan up to high heat and add all the vegies, except the broccoli, at once.
- Sauté until still the onion starts to brown and caramelize. Most of the vegies should still be crisp.
- Remove the vegies to a plate.
- Return the chicken to the pan, along with 2 or 3 cups of water or broth, the paprika and the red pepper flakes.
- Cover and simmer until done. A fork should come out clean, with no visible pink or blood, and the chicken pieces should fall apart when pierced with a fork.
- Add the vegies and raw broccoli on top and cover the pan again.
- Simmer until the broccoli is done, but still crisp.
- Remove all and place in a warm covered dish.
- Cook the rice or noodles in the broth.
- Place portions of the rice, vegetables and chicken into serving bowls. I broke the chicken into bite-size pieces when I did this step.
- Pour some broth over each, and serve with soy sauce on the side.

111. Chicken Pasta Provencale Recipe

Serving: 4 | Prep: | Cook: 25mins | Ready in:

Ingredients

- 1 1/2 Cups dried pasta Shapes
- 4 Tbs. Dressing (recipe follows)
- 2 Tbs. olive oil
- 12 ounces skinless, boneless chicken breast, cut into strips
- 2 zucchini, sliced
- 1 red bell pepper, seeded and sliced
- 2 garlic cloves, sliced
- 4 tomatoes, cut into wedges
- 2 ounces anchovies, drained and chopped
- 1/4 Cup pitted black olives, halved
- Sprig of fresh parsley, to garnish
- Dressing:
- 3 Tbs. olive oil
- 1 Tbs. wine vinegar
- 1 garlic Clove crushed
- 1/2 tsp. Dijon mustard
- 1 tsp. honey
- salt and pepper

Direction

- Cook pasta in boiling lightly salted water for 10-12 minutes, until tender, but still firm to the bite. Drain thoroughly.
- Whisk all the dressing ingredients together until blended.
- Put the pasta into a bowl with the dressing and mix together.
- Heat the oil in a skillet.
- Add the chicken and stir-fry for 4-5 minutes, until cooked.
- Remove from pan.
- Add the zucchini, bell pepper and garlic to the skillet. Fry, stirring frequently, for about 10 minutes.
- Add the tomatoes, anchovies and olives to the pasta with chicken and vegetables. Mix thoroughly.
- Transfer to a serving dish and serve immediately while still warm.

112. Chicken Pasta Ricardo Recipe

Serving: 4 | Prep: | Cook: 15mins | Ready in:

Ingredients

- 6 tablespoons clarified butter

- flour
- 1 tablespoon fresh garlic, minced
- 1 teaspoon salt
- 1 teaspoon white pepper
- 1/2 cup white wine
- 1 cup heavy cream
- 1/2 box fettuccine, cooked
- 1lb. chicken breast, thin sliced
- 4 ounces mushrooms, sliced
- 8 ounces zucchini, julienned
- 4 ounces parmesan cheese, shredded

Direction

- Start the pasta according to directions on the box
- Heat a sauté pan to hot and add clarified butter
- To clarify butter: Melt butter over very low heat. Skim off what comes to the surface. It will "burp" and bubble a bit. Slowly pour off the oil part into another container or strain through doubled cheesecloth. Discard the solids. (Or see my recipe for Ghee)
- Put the chicken pieces and the flour into a one gallon zip lock bag and shake up until all pieces are well-coated, shake off excess and add to the pan along with the garlic, salt, white pepper and mushrooms
- Sauté until garlic turns white, approximately 5 minutes, stirring occasionally.
- Deglaze the pan with white wine (pour wine into skillet around edges) and sauté one minute longer to thicken the sauce
- Add zucchini, cooked fettuccine noodles and heavy cream
- Sauté, stirring occasionally, until heated through and cream sauce is reduced to a thick consistency, approximately 5 minutes.
- Add a generous amount of salt and pepper and stir.
- Turn onto plates or into pasta bowls and garnish with Parmesan cheese!

113. Chicken Pecan And Cucumber Finger Sandwiches Recipe

Serving: 24 | Prep: | Cook: | Ready in:

Ingredients

- 1½ cups cooked, diced chicken breast (I like to use a cooked rotisserie chicken to speed things up a bit)
- 2 hard-boiled eggs
- 1 cup mayonnaise (do not substitute)
- ½ cup onion, finely chopped
- 4 tablespoons pecans, finely chopped
- salt and pepper, to your taste
- McCormick's Montreal chicken seasoning, to your taste
- 1 loaf party rye bread, or any bread of your choice (I like to remove the crusts if using bread other than the party rye bread)
- softened butter
- 2 cucumbers, peeled and thinly sliced
- pecan halves

Direction

- Mix first 5 ingredients and add seasonings to your taste; chill mixture several hours.
- When ready to serve, butter bread very lightly on one side; top with a few slices of cucumbers, then the chicken mixture. Top each little open-faced sandwich with a pecan half. Serve immediately.

114. Chicken Picatta Recipe

Serving: 2 | Prep: | Cook: 15mins | Ready in:

Ingredients

- 3 boneless chicken breast halves
- 1/2 cup flour
- 4 Tb canola oil
- 2 Tb butter

- 1 large shallot, chopped
- 1/2 cup chopped yellow onion
- 3 cloves garlic, chopped
- lemon pepper
- 2 Tb chopped fresh parsley
- 1 Tb capers, mashed
- squirt of lemon juice (technically, the juice from one lemon)
- 1/2 cup sweet vermouth
- hot, buttered, broad noodles

Direction

- Lightly sprinkle the chicken breasts with lemon pepper, and perhaps a bit of additional plain pepper. Dredge them in a bowl containing 1/2 cup flour.
- Melt 2 Tb butter in a skillet along with 4 Tb canola oil. When hot, add the shallots, onion, and garlic. Cook until some of the bits begin to brown. Remove from skillet and place in a finger bowl for later addition back to the chicken.
- Add the chicken breasts to the oil and very lightly brown on both sides. Turn the breasts with a fork so that you do not disturb the crust and seasoning.
- Return the onions and shallots to the skillet. Add the vermouth, capers and parsley. Allow the vermouth to concentrate and the onions to caramelize.
- Remove and serve over hot buttered noodles. Scrape the caramelized onion mixture from the bottom of the skillet and use like gravy.

115. Chicken Pineapple Pizza Recipe

Serving: 4 | Prep: | Cook: 20mins | Ready in:

Ingredients

- 1 lb of boneless, skinless chicken breasts (best)
- or
- 2 cans of premium chunk chicken breast packed in water
- 1 Boboli Wheat pizza crust
- 2 Tbsp of olive oil
- 1 jar of Ragu or any type pizza/spaghetti sauce
- 1 1/2 Cups of Fat Free or Low Fat Shredded Mozzerella cheese
- 1 can of pineapple chunks in own juice
- 4 Tbsp of light brown sugar
- 1 tsp of garlic
- 1 Tbsp of crushed red pepper
- 1 Tbsp of dried minced onion

Direction

- Add olive oil to non-stick pan, brown chicken and cut into cubes cook until no longer pink.
- Add entire can of pineapple juice, brown sugar, garlic, red pepper and onion to pan.
- On medium high heat, boil the ingredients down until you caramelize the chicken then remove from heat.
- Put sauce on pizza crust.
- Spread chicken mixture evenly on pizza, place pineapple bits sparingly on top of chicken mixture then top with cheese.
- Cook pizza per Boboli Pizza Crust directions.

116. Chicken Pot Pie Recipe

Serving: 4 | Prep: | Cook: 30mins | Ready in:

Ingredients

- 4 boneless/skinless chicken breasts (to save some time, you can also get the chicken cutlets)
- 1 can (15oz) Veg-All
- 1 can cream of mushroom soup
- 1 can cream of chicken soup
- 2 pie-crusts
- salt and pepper to taste

Direction

- Boil chicken in water until done then pull apart or cut into bite sized pieces
- Mix together chicken, soups, veg-all, salt and pepper
- Place one pie crust into lightly greased pie pan
- Pour mixture into crust and top with the other pie crust
- Cut a few slits into the top crust to let steam escape
- (You may also brush with an egg wash if you like to get that extra golden color)
- Bake at 350 for about 25-30 minutes or until golden brown

117. Chicken Pot Pie With A Cornbread Top Recipe

Serving: 0 | Prep: | Cook: | Ready in:

Ingredients

- (12 ½") oven proof fry-pan
- 1 tablespoon olive oil
- 1 teaspoon butter
- 4 cups chopped carrots
- 2 cups chopped celery
- 3 cups chopped onion
- 1 tsp chili flakes
- 750g (1 1/2 lbs) chicken breasts or thighs, cubed
- 1 tablespoon flour
- 2 tablespoons barbecue sauce
- 4 cups chicken stock
- 1 teaspoon fresh thyme leaves
- salt and black pepper to taste.
- For the cornbread :
- 1 ¼ cups flour
- 1 ¼ cups cornmeal
- 1 tablespoon sugar
- ½ teaspoon salt
- 2 teaspoons baking powder
- ¼ cup butter
- 2 eggs, whisked
- 1 cup milk
- ¼ cup crumbly blue cheese, grated cheddar or monterey jack cheese

Direction

- Heat oil and butter over medium heat in a large, oven-proof fry pan. Add carrots, celery and onion. Sweat, stirring occasionally, until vegetables are slightly tender, about 10 minutes. Stir in chili flakes and chicken. Sauté until chicken is just cooked. Meanwhile, stir flour and barbecue sauce together in a small bowl. Stir into chicken and vegetables. Add stock and thyme leaves and simmer for 5 minutes. Mixture should be liquidy. If not, add a little more water. Set aside.
- Preheat oven to 350°F/180°C
- To make the cornbread, combine flour, cornmeal, sugar, salt and baking powder in a bowl. Stir well. Add butter, cutting it through the flour mixture with two knives until butter is pea-sized and well coated in flour. Add whisked eggs, milk and cheese. Stir just to combine.
- Spoon cornbread mixture over the top of chicken mixture. Transfer to oven and bake until cornbread is golden and liquid is bubbling beneath, about 10-15 minutes.
- Serve immediately.
- If you don't have an oven proof fry-pan, transfer the chicken mixture to a lasagna dish (36cmx28cm / 14"x11" at most) top with corn bread mixture and bake as above

118. Chicken Puffs Delight Recipe

Serving: 4 | Prep: | Cook: 25mins | Ready in:

Ingredients

- * 1/2 pound puff pastry squares
- * 1 tablespoon butter
- * 2 diced chicken breast halves
- * 6 chopped mushrooms

- * 4 ounces herb cream cheese
- * 1/4 cup chopped parsley
- * 1 beaten egg
- * salt
- * pepper

Direction

- Combine the Chicken and Mushrooms
- First, melt the butter on a skillet under medium-high heat. Add the chicken and the mushrooms. Season the pan with salt and pepper.
- Once the chicken is cooked through, and the mushrooms have released their juices, remove the mixture from the pan and put it to cool in the refrigerator for at least 15 minutes.
- Cut the Pastry Dough into Squares
- Preheat the oven to 400 degrees.
- Next pull out a layer of pastry dough and roll it into a 14-inch square. Cut it into four squares.
- Add the Chicken Puff Filling
- Spread 1-2 tablespoons of the cheese onto the square. Then top it off with a tablespoon of parsley and next, a spoonful of chicken and mushrooms.
- Now, brush the edges of the square with the beaten egg. This will help seal the edges of the pastry together.
- Bake the Chicken Puffs
- Pick up the corners, and fold into the center over the filling. Place the puff seam side down onto a parchment lined baking sheet.
- Do this for all of the squares. Brush the top of the puffs with the egg mixture so they will turn a nice golden brown.
- Bake for 25 minutes, until they are puffed and golden. Serve warm and enjoy.

119. Chicken Puttanesca Recipe

Serving: 6 | Prep: | Cook: 50mins | Ready in:

Ingredients

- 3 tbsp. olive or vegetable oil
- 8 chicken pieces (like thighs and legs), or can use chicken breast
- 1 onion, chopped
- 12 cloves garlic, roughly chopped
- 2 cans (14 oz. each) fire roasted tomatoes, undrained
- 1 can (2 oz.) anchovies, drained and chopped
- 1 cup pitted black olives, chopped
- 1/3 cup capers, drained
- 3 tbsp. coarsely chopped sun-dried tomatoes (packed in oil kind)
- 1 tsp. dried oregano
- 1 tsp. dried thyme
- 1 tbsp. balsamic vinegar
- pinch red pepper flakes, or pinch cayenne pepper
- a small handful freash parsley leaves, chopped (optional)
- salt and pepper to taste
- Note*: go easy on the salt, becuase of salty capers, olives and anchovies in the sauce. You may not need to add any salt at all. Taste the end sauce first, before adding any.

Direction

- Heat the oil in a large skillet or Dutch oven. Add the chicken and brown on all sides. Remove from pan and set aside.
- Add the onion and garlic to the same pan and sauté until the onion is soft and translucent (about 5 minutes).
- Stir in undrained tomatoes, anchovies, olives, capers, sun-dried tomatoes, herbs, vinegar, red pepper flakes and black pepper. Return chicken to the pan and coat with sauce. Cover the pan and simmer until the chicken is tender, about 45 minutes. Taste for salt, and sprinkle with salt if desired. Garnish with fresh chopped parsley (optional).
- Serve hot with pasta or rice.

120. Chicken Reuben Casserole Recipe

Serving: 6 | Prep: | Cook: 300mins | Ready in:

Ingredients

- 32 oz sauerkraut (jar or bag) rinsed and drained
- 1 cup russian dressing
- 6 boneless chicken breast halves, skinless
- 2 tbsp prepared mustard
- 1 cup swiss cheese, shredded

Direction

- Layer half the sauerkraut in the bottom of the crockpot.
- Pour 1/3 of the dressing over it; place 3 chicken breasts on top and spread with 1 tbsp. of the mustard.
- Top with remaining sauerkraut, chicken breasts and mustard; pour another 1/3 of the dressing over all. Reserve the remaining 1/3 of dressing for serving.
- Cover and cook on low for about 5 hours, or until chicken is cooked through and tender. Sprinkle Swiss cheese and cook until cheese is melted. Serve with reserved dressing.

121. Chicken Rice Skillet Recipe

Serving: 4 | Prep: | Cook: 30mins | Ready in:

Ingredients

- 1/2 cup flour
- 1 teaspoon kosher salt
- 1/2 teaspoon freshly ground pepper
- 2 tablespoons peanut oil or vegetable oil
- 2 boneless, skinless chicken breasts (about 1 pound total)
- 2 1/2 cups chicken stock
- 1 cup rice - your choice - I personally like basmati rice for this recipe
- 2 medium carrots, thinly sliced or well diced
- 1/2 medium onion, diced
- 1/3 large Bay leaf
- 1/2 teaspoon crushed red pepper
- 1/2 teaspoon garlic powder
- 1/2 teaspoon dried thyme
- 5-6 ounces green peas (frozen peas are fine)

Direction

- Combine flour, salt and pepper in a pie pan or plastic bag
- Lightly flour chicken, shaking off excess flour
- Heat a skillet over medium heat until a drop of water sizzles, then add oil to the skillet and when hot, add the chicken breasts
- Cook the chicken approximately 4 minutes or until white juices begin to appear on the top of the chicken breasts
- Turn the breast over (use your tongs) and cook another 3-4 minutes
- Remove the chicken from the pan and place on a cutting board
- Use a mallet on the chicken to break the breasts into pieces (using a mallet tenderizes the chicken at the same time)
- In a Dutch oven or heavy sauté pan place the chicken broth (or can of soup as mentioned above), rice, carrots and onions and seasonings
- Bring to a boil over medium heat and stir, cover and reduce heat to low and cook 25 minutes or until rice is nearly done
- Add the chicken pieces and green peas, stirring well
- Cover and cook a few minutes more until the peas are done and the chicken is hot
- Use a spoon to portion onto plates and serve immediately.

122. Chicken Royce Recipe

Serving: 8 | Prep: | Cook: 60mins | Ready in:

Ingredients

- 8 chicken breasts, boneless, skinless
- 1 cup flour
- 1/2 tsp. pepper
- 1 tsp. salt
- 4 tsp. paprika
- 2 cups diced celery
- 1 stick butter
- 1 (10.5-oz.) can cream of chicken soup
- 1/2 cup half and half
- 3 cups shredded sharp cheddar cheese
- 2 Tbsp. diced pimiento
- 2 oz. slivered almonds

Direction

- Shake chicken in bag with flour, salt, pepper and paprika.
- Melt butter in frying pan and brown chicken.
- Spread celery in the bottom of baking pan.
- Lay chicken in a single layer on top of celery.
- Combine soup, cream, cheese and pimiento and spoon over chicken.
- Top with slivered almonds and bake uncovered at 350 degrees for 1 hour.

123. Chicken Schnitzel Recipe

Serving: 4 | Prep: | Cook: 10mins | Ready in:

Ingredients

- 4 boneless, skinless chicken breast halves
- Note: You can follow this recipe for veal or pork.
- 2/3 cup all-purpose flour
- 1/2 tsp. garlic or onion powder
- 1/2 tsp. salt
- fresh ground pepper
- 1 tsp. paprika
- 2 large eggs, beaten
- 1 cup seasoned bread crumbs
- 1/4 cup vegetable oil
- 2 Tbsp. butter
- *Note: I always add butter to the cooking oil.
- 1 lemon, cut into wedges

Direction

- Place the chicken breasts between 2 pieces of cling wrap and pound to a desired texture and thickness.
- In a shallow pie plate or dish, mix together flour, garlic or onion powder, salt, pepper and paprika.
- In second shallow bowl, beat eggs.
- In third shallow dish or plate, place seasoned breadcrumbs.
- One at a time, dip each pounded chicken breast first into the seasoned flour mixture, coating thoroughly and shake to dust off excess.
- Next, dip chicken breast in well beaten eggs, covering completely.
- Then coat chicken with bread crumbs.
- Place each breaded chicken breast on a plate or a small cooking sheet pan.
- In a large non-stick skillet, place vegetable oil and butter.
- Heat over a medium element.
- Place chicken in the skillet, and brown for about 5 minutes per side.
- Make sure the chicken is cooked thoroughly before transferring it to a plate that has been lined with about 4 sheets of paper towel.
- Serve with boiled, baked or mashed potatoes and your favorite vegetables.
- Garnish with lemon wedges.
- Serves 4

124. Chicken Schnitzel With Roquefort Gravy Recipe

Serving: 4 | Prep: | Cook: 45mins | Ready in:

Ingredients

- For Chicken:

- 4 fresh chicken breasts, 1/4" maximum thickness (pound each breast between waxed paper with mallet into thin cutlets)
- 1/2 c. flour
- 2 eggs, slightly beaten
- 1/2 c. Dry bread crumbs
- vegetable oil
- For Sauce:
- 4 tablespoons (1/2 stick) butter
- 1/3 c. finely chopped shallots
- 2 teaspoons all purpose flour
- 1/3 c. dry white wine
- 2/3 c. crumbled Roquefort cheese (about 3 ounces)
- 1/3 c. (or more) whipping cream
- 8 oz. mushrooms, chopped (I prefer crimini but white button will do)

Direction

- For Chicken:
- Dredge meat in flour, dip into eggs and coat on both sides with bread crumbs. Set aside to dry.
- Pour oil into a fry pan to fill about 1/4 inch and heat on medium-high heat.
- Fry schnitzel to a golden brown, turning only once.
- For Sauce:
- Melt 2 tablespoons butter in heavy medium saucepan over medium heat. Add shallots and sauté until just beginning to brown, about 5 minutes. Add flour and stir 1 minute. Gradually mix in wine. Boil until liquid is reduced to 1/4 cup, stirring frequently, about 5 minutes. Reduce heat to low. Gradually add Roquefort and stir until melted and smooth. Add 1/4 c. whipping cream and simmer until thickened to sauce consistency, about 2 minutes. Season sauce to taste with salt and pepper. (Can be prepared 1 day ahead, cover and refrigerate).
- I recommend serving chicken and sauce with Spätzle, German potato dumplings, which might be found at your favorite grocer (at mine it's near the instant potatoes).

125. Chicken Sfeeha Recipe

Serving: 0 | Prep: | Cook: 2hours | Ready in:

Ingredients

- for the dough
- 2 & 3/4 cups all-purpose flour
- 1 packet active dry yeast (or 1/2 oz fresh yeast)
- 1/2 tsp sugar
- 1/2 tsp salt
- 2/3 cup water
- 4 tbsp butter
- for the topping
- 2 large chicken breasts, thawed
- 1/4 cup finely chopped almonds
- 1 medium onion, diced
- 2 garlic cloves, minced
- 1/2 cup plain yogurt
- juice of 1/2 lemon
- 1 sprig fresh rosemary, minced
- 1 tsp ground: cinnamon, nutmeg, cloves, ginger
- 1/4 tsp black pepper, kosher salt
- olive oil

Direction

- For the dough
- Dissolve yeast & sugar in 1/2 cup of the water; let sit until foamy (about 10 minutes).
- Combine the flour, salt, & butter. Use your fingers to rub the butter into the flour, until it resembles coarse bread crumbs. Pour in the yeast mixture and mix until it forms a firm dough, adding more water if necessary.
- Knead dough on a lightly floured cutting board, until smooth and pliable (if it is dry, add a bit more water; if it is too sticky, and add a bit more flour). Form dough into a ball and transfer to a lightly oiled bowl. Cover with a clean towel and let it rise for 1 hour (should double in size).

- Preheat oven to 350 degrees Fahrenheit. Line two baking sheet with parchment paper, set aside.
- Punch down your dough, and form it into little balls (think golf-ball size). Space the balls out on the baking sheets, and cover with towels for 15 minutes.
- For the topping
- Cover the bottom of a large pan with olive oil and heat on medium high. Sprinkle chicken with the rosemary & spices, and brown on both sides. Cook for about 20 minutes, or until no longer pink in the middle. Deglaze your pan with the lemon juice, and remove the chicken to a cutting board. Let it rest for at least 5 minutes, then chop up very finely.
- Right after you have deglazed your pan with lemon juice, add in the onion. Let it become translucent; about 5 minutes. Turn to medium and stir in the garlic & almonds, cooking about 10 minutes. Remove pan from heat and stir in the chopped chicken and yogurt.
- When the dough formed into balls has rested, press each ball into 1/2 inch-thick disks. Spread each disk with the chicken topping, gently pressing down.
- Bake for 25-30 minutes, or until edges are golden.

126. Chicken Skillet With Stuffing Recipe

Serving: 6 | Prep: | Cook: 27mins | Ready in:

Ingredients

- 1 (16 oz) pkg stuffing mix for chicken
- 6 small boneless, skinless chicken breast halves
- 3 C frozen mixed vegetables
- 1 (10 3/4 oz) can cream of broccoli soup

Direction

- Prepare stuffing mix and set aside
- Heat a large non-stick skillet on medium high heat
- Add chicken; cover and cook for 5 to 7 minutes in each side or until done
- Remove chicken from skillet
- Add vegetables, soup and 1/2 C water to skillet; stir and cover
- Reduce heat to medium
- Cook 6 minutes or until heated through; stirring often
- Return chicken to skillet; cook 1 minute or until hot
- Serve with stuffing

127. Chicken Spagetti Recipe

Serving: 8 | Prep: | Cook: 20mins | Ready in:

Ingredients

- 4 boneless chicken breasts
- 1 can cream of chicken soup
- 1 can cream of mushroom soup
- 1 can Rotel tomatoes
- 1 1lb Mexican velveeta
- 1 16oz. pkg. spagetti noodles
- lemon/pepper seasoning to taste
- Dried onion to taste

Direction

- Boil chicken breast in water with dried onions, remove chicken and cool.
- Add spaghetti noodles to water chicken boiled in
- Shred chicken while spaghetti cooks.
- When noodles are done do not drain, the spaghetti will have a little water left, not a lot.
- Add all other ingredients and chicken to pot
- Cook until Velveeta is melted and enjoy.

128. Chicken Strips Recipe

Serving: 0 | Prep: | Cook: 10mins | Ready in:

Ingredients

- 1 cup mayonnaise
- 2 teaspoons dried minced onion
- 2 teaspoons dry mustard
- 2 cups Panko crumbs
- 1/2 cup sesame seeds
- 2 pounds of boneless, skinless chicken breasts cut into strips or you can use the all ready prepped chicken strips
- Sauce
- 1 cup mayonnaise
- 2 tablespoons honey

Direction

- 1. Preheat oven to 425 degrees F/ 220 degrees c
- 2. Combine in a shallow dish 1 cup mayonnaise, onion and mustard and mix together and set aside.
- 3. In a separate dish combine the panko crumbs and sesame seeds.
- 4. Dip the chicken in the mayonnaise mixture and then into the crumb mixture to coat.
- 5. Place the coated strips in a single layer on a lightly greased baking sheet.
- 6. Bake in the preheated oven for 15-18 minutes, or until juices run clear.
- 7. Mix 1 cup of mayonnaise and the honey together in a small bowl and serve with the chicken strips to dip.

129. Chicken Stroganoff Recipe

Serving: 4 | Prep: | Cook: 30mins | Ready in:

Ingredients

- 1 pound bonless chicken breast
- 1/2 cup onion chopped
- 1 cup mushrooms sliced thin
- 2 cloves garlic
- 2 tablespoons butter
- 1/2 cup warm water
- 2 teaspoons instant chicken bouillon granules
- 2 tablespoons flour
- 8 oz. sour cream
- 12 oz. bag egg noodles
- salt and pepper to taste

Direction

- Cut chicken into bite size pieces
- In a large skillet melt butter and add onions and garlic cook until tender.
- Add chicken and salt and pepper, cook until chicken is brown
- Add mushrooms and cook until they are tender
- With warm water dissolve chicken bouillon, add to skillet
- Stir flour into sour cream then whisk into skillet, cook until all is incorporated.
- Serve over egg noodles

130. Chicken Tacos With Charred Salsa Recipe

Serving: 4 | Prep: | Cook: 35mins | Ready in:

Ingredients

- marinade
- 1/4 cup orange juice
- 2 tbsp. olive oil
- 3 cloves garlic, finely chopped
- 1/2 tsp. salt
- 4 boneless, skinless chicken breasts
- Charred salsa
- 8 ripe roma tomatoes
- 2 jalapeno peppers
- 2 small red onions, halved
- 1/2 tsp. salt

- 2 tbsp. lime juice
- zest of 1 orange
- 1/4 cup chopped cilantro
- 8(6") flour or corn tortillas

Direction

- Have coals or grill ready with hot flames.
- In medium bowl stir together juice, oil, garlic and 1/2 tsp. salt. Marinate chicken for 15 minutes. Meanwhile; grill tomatoes, peppers, onions on grill rack. Grill, turning occasionally, for 5 minutes until charred. Set aside.
- Grill chicken breasts, turning once for 12 to 15 minutes. Meanwhile, chop tomatoes, seeded jalapeno peppers and onion. Season with 1/2 tsp. salt, lime, orange zest and cilantro.
- Serve chicken breasts with warm tortillas and salsa.

131. Chicken Tamale Casserole Recipe

Serving: 8 | Prep: | Cook: 30mins | Ready in:

Ingredients

- 1 1/4 cups (6 oz.) preshredded Mexican blend cheese
- 1 large egg
- 1/3 cup milk
- 1 teaspoon ground cumin
- 1 (14 3/4 oz.) can creamed corn
- 1 (8.5 oz.) box corn muffin mix (I use Jiffy)
- 1 (4 oz.) can chopped green chiles, drained
- cooking spray
- 1 (10 oz.) can red enchilada sauce (I use Old El Paso)
- 2 cups shredded cooked chicken breast
- sour cream, fresh diced tomatoes, diced avocado for garnish

Direction

- Preheat oven to 400
- Combine 1/4 cup of the cheese and the next 6 ingredients (through chilies) in a large bowl, stirring just until moist. Pour mixture into a 13x9-inch baking dish coated with cooking spray.
- Bake at 400 for 15 minutes or until set. Pierce entire surface liberally with a fork; pour about 2/3 of the enchilada sauce over top. Top with chicken, drizzle remaining sauce over chicken and sprinkle with remaining 1 cup of cheese.
- Return to 400 degree oven and bake for 15 minutes or until bubbly and cheese has melted. Remove from oven and let stand 5 minutes.
- Cut into 8 squares and top with sour cream, tomatoes and avocado!

132. Chicken Tortellini With Asparagus Recipe

Serving: 4 | Prep: | Cook: 10mins | Ready in:

Ingredients

- 3 cups Fresh tortellini
- 2 chicken breasts,1/4 inch cubed
- dash of cayene
- 1 cup asparagus
- 1 tablespoon dried chives
- white sauce
- 2 tablespoons butter
- 2 tablespoons flour
- 1 cup milk
- 1 teaspoon sour cream and chives powder
- dash of cayenne
- dash of salt
- dash of black pepper

Direction

- Start and complete all of the following at the same time:
- TORTELLINI

- Start pot of water to boil. Add Buitoni Three Cheese Tortellini when bubbles first start to appear. Set timer for 8 minutes
- ASPARAGUS
- Add to Tortellini pot, 4 minutes into timer.
- WHITE SAUCE:
- In small sauce pan, melt butter, add seasonings
- When all melted, add flour.
- Stir well
- Add milk
- Stir quickly
- Lower heat, stirring occasionally
- CHICKEN
- Dice into 1/4-inch pieces
- Add splash of olive oil to pan
- Toss in chicken
- Quickly stir fry
- Dash of cayenne
- When chicken is white, add dried chives.
- When all parts are finished, drain tortellini and asparagus, top with white sauce and chicken. Serve with bread and a touch of parmesan.
- LUNCH TIME!! (In less than 10 minutes!!)

133. Chicken Vegetable Rice Dish Recipe

Serving: 2 | Prep: | Cook: 20mins | Ready in:

Ingredients

- 1/2 cup brown rice
- 1 1/2 Cups water
- 1 Teaspoon cooking oil
- 3/4 Cup chicken broth
- 1 Boneless, skinless chicken Breast
- 2 Small or 1 Large carrot
- 1 Bunch green onions
- 1 Small apple
- 1 Teaspoon whole cumin seed
- 1 Teaspoon ground coriander seed
- 1 Pinch cayenne pepper

Direction

- In a sauce pan place 1/2 cup brown rice in 1 1/2 cups of water and bring to a boil. Reduce to simmer and cook for 30 min. or until water is absorbed and rice is done.
- While rice is cooking, cut boneless skinless chicken breast into small bite size pieces.
- Place 1 teaspoon cooking oil in a wok or frying pan and stir-fry chicken until no longer pink.
- Remove chicken and set aside.
- Peel and slice carrot into 1/4 inch coins and set aside.
- Slice the white part of the green onions up to the green part into coins and set aside.
- Peel and core small apple and chop fine. Set aside.
- In the same wok or fry pan place cooked rice, carrots, green onions apple and cooked chicken.
- Add 3/4 cup chicken broth and spices. Mix well.
- Bring to a boil and turn down heat and simmer for 15 to 20 min... or until carrots are desired doneness.
- If mixture is looking like it is dry add more chicken broth a little at a time.
- You might also want to check the seasonings and add more to your taste.
- You may also want to add more cayenne pepper to your taste.

134. Chicken Vegetable Skillet Recipe

Serving: 4 | Prep: | Cook: 10mins | Ready in:

Ingredients

- 1 Tbsp. olive oil
- 1 lb. boneless skinless chicken breasts, cut into 1" pieces
- 1 onion, chopped
- 9 oz. pkg. frozen asparagus cuts, thawed

- 1 tomato, chopped
- 1/4 cup zesty Italian salad dressing

Direction

- Heat olive oil in heavy skillet over medium heat. Add chicken; cook and stir for 3-4 minutes.
- Add remaining ingredients except salad dressing; cook and stir for 2-3 minutes.
- Then add salad dressing, bring to a boil, cook for 2-3 minutes until vegetables are crisp tender and chicken is thoroughly cooked, stir well and serve.

135. Chicken With Chipped Beef Recipe

Serving: 6 | Prep: | Cook: 120mins | Ready in:

Ingredients

- 1 small jar chipped beef
- 6 slices of bacon
- 1 3 oz package cream cheese
- 1 pint sour cream
- 1 can sliced mushrooms, drained
- 1 can mushroom soup
- 6 boneless chicken breasts
- salt and pepper to taste

Direction

- Place crumbled chipped beef in bottom of buttered casserole dish
- Wrap bacon around each chicken breast and sprinkle with pepper
- Lay in casserole
- Blend soup, sour cream, cream cheese
- Stir in mushrooms and blend well
- Pour this mixture over the chicken
- Cover with foil and bake for 2 hours at 300 degrees

136. Chicken With Ham And Cheese Recipe

Serving: 4 | Prep: | Cook: 20mins | Ready in:

Ingredients

- 2 T. butter
- 4 chicken breasts, boneless, skinless
- 2 cloves garlic, minced
- ½ C. mushrooms, sliced
- ½ C. onion, chopped
- 1 can cream of mushroom soup
- ¾ C. grated swiss cheese
- ¾ C. chopped ham
- ¼ C. white wine
- ½ C. sour cream

Direction

- Melt butter in a large skillet.
- Add chicken and cook until browned, about 10 min. Remove from pan and set aside.
- Add garlic, mushrooms and onion to skillet. Cook until tender.
- Add soup, cheese, ham, and wine to the pan. Cook and stir until it comes to a boil.
- Stir in sour cream. Reduce heat to low.
- Add chicken to pan, cover and simmer for about 5 min.

137. Chicken With Key Lime Glaze Recipe

Serving: 4 | Prep: | Cook: 25mins | Ready in:

Ingredients

- 1 small shallot, chopped
- 2 tsp. ginger, grated
- 2 tbls. butter
- 1 cup key lime juice
- 1/4 cup white wine

- 1 oz. honey
- 1/2 tsp. red pepper flakes
- salt and pepper to taste
- 1 chicken, cut up or 4 chicken breasts, or even chicken wings

Direction

- Melt butter over med low heat in sauté pan
- Add shallots and ginger and sauté until shallots are tender
- Add key lime juice, white wine, honey, salt, and pepper
- Reduce mixture by 50 %
- Remove from heat
- Brush glaze over chicken
- Cook over medium heat until done basting occasionally

138. Chicken With Lemon Caper Sauce Recipe

Serving: 4 | Prep: | Cook: 20mins | Ready in:

Ingredients

- 4 (6 oz) skinless, boneless chicken breasts
- 1/4 tsp salt
- 1/4 tsp black pepper
- 3 Tbsp all-purpose flour
- 2 Tbsp butter
- 1/2 cup fat-free, less-sodium chicken broth
- 1/4 cup fresh lemon juice
- 2 Tbsp capers, drained
- 3 Tbsp minced flat-leaf parsley

Direction

- Place chicken between two sheets of plastic wrap and pound to an even thickness using a meat mallet or small heavy skillet.
- Sprinkle chicken evenly with salt and pepper.
- Place flour is a shallow dish.
- Dredge chicken in flour, shake off any excess.
- Melt butter in a large nonstick skillet over medium-high heat.
- Add chicken to pan.
- Cook three minutes.
- Turn chicken over and cook another three minutes.
- Add broth, juice and capers.
- Reduce heat to medium and simmer three minutes, basting chicken occasionally with sauce.
- Sprinkle with parsley and cook for one minute.
- Remove chicken from pan and keep warm.
- Bring sauce to a boil and cook two minutes or until thick.
- Serve over chicken.
- 267 calories, 7.9g fat, 0.6g fiber

139. Chicken With Mushrooms And Grapes Recipe

Serving: 4 | Prep: | Cook: 40mins | Ready in:

Ingredients

- 2 chicken breasts split
- 1 cup fresh mushrooms quartered
- 2 tablespoons butter
- 10-3/4 ounce can condensed cream of chicken soup undiluted
- 1 clove garlic minced
- 2 tablespoons dry white wine
- 1/2 cup seedless grapes halved

Direction

- In skillet brown chicken and mushrooms in butter then add remaining ingredients except grapes.
- Cover and cook over low heat 30 minutes or until done stirring occasionally.
- Add grapes then heat through and serve over cooked rice.

140. Chicken With Portabella Mushrooms Recipe

Serving: 4 | Prep: | Cook: 15mins | Ready in:

Ingredients

- 1-1/2 pounds boneless skinless chicken breasts
- 1/4 pound portabella mushrooms sliced
- 1 tablespoon flour
- 1/2 cup chicken stock
- 1/3 cup heavy cream
- 1/8 teaspoon nutmeg
- olive oil

Direction

- In skillet sauté' chicken for 5 minutes in olive oil.
- Turn chicken then salt and pepper cooked sauce and sauté 5 minutes longer.
- Remove to plate and cover with foil to keep warm.
- Sprinkle mushrooms with flour and toss to coat.
- Add mushrooms to pan then add chicken broth and cook 1 minute.
- When sauce thickens add cream, nutmeg, salt and pepper to taste.
- Remove from heat and spoon over the chicken then serve immediately.

141. Chicken With Potato, Green Pepper, Tomato Recipe

Serving: 4 | Prep: | Cook: 30mins | Ready in:

Ingredients

- 3 chicken breasts
- 6 potato
- 2 clove garlic
- 1 can diced tomato
- green pepper
- 1 cup chicken broth
- 1 onion

Direction

- Chop up onion, potato, garlic and green pepper add to pan. Cook till tender. In another pan cook chicken after its done then put with potato and add the tomatoes and broth. Let cook together 15 or so min.

142. Chicken With Provencal Sauce Recipe

Serving: 4 | Prep: | Cook: 20mins | Ready in:

Ingredients

- 4 (6 oz.) boneless, skinless chicken breasts
- 1/4 tsp salt
- 1/4 tsp freshly ground pepper
- 1 1/2 tsp olive oil
- 1 garlic clove, minced
- 1 C fat-free, less sodium chicken broth
- 1 1/2 tsp dried herbs de Provence
- 1 tsp butter
- 1 tsp fresh lemon juice
- fresh thyme sprigs, optional

Direction

- Place chicken breast halves between 2 sheets of plastic wrap and pound to 1/2 thickness
- Sprinkle chicken evenly with salt and fresh ground pepper
- Heat oil in a large skillet over medium heat
- Add chicken to pan and cook approximately 6 minutes on each side or until juices run clear. Remove from pan and keep warm.
- Add garlic to pan; cook 1 minute, stirring constantly
- Add broth and herbs de Provence; bring to a boil, scraping pan to remove any browned bits

- Cook until broth mixture is reduced to 1/2 C about 3 minutes
- Remove from heat; add butter and lemon juice to pan, stirring until butter melts
- Serve sauce over chicken, garnishing with thyme sprigs, if desired
- 248 calories a serving

143. Chicken With Sherry Sauce Recipe

Serving: 4 | Prep: | Cook: 15mins | Ready in:

Ingredients

- 4 skinless, boneless chicken breasts
- 2 tomatoes, chopped
- 1 leek cut in half length wise. Rinsed then chopped coarsely
- 1/4 cup fresh dill - chopped. If none on hand you can use 1 tsp dried dillweed
- 2 tsp bottled chopped garlic
- 1 tbsp butter. Or if you prefer extra virgin olive oil
- salt to taste. Added slowly
- 1/2 cup dry sherry. If you like this can be substituted with port, red or white wine, or chicken broth

Direction

- Sprinkle the chicken breasts with salt
- Melt the butter in a large frying pan or wok over med heat
- Add the chicken and cook it until golden brown. Approx. 3 mins per side
- When this is achieved, add the tomatoes, leek, garlic, sherry and dill.
- Stir the mixture with a wooden spoon, making sure to scrape up and stir in any browned bits from the pan
- Reduce heat, cover and simmer for approx. 6 - 8 mins, turning the chicken often.
- Remove the chicken and place onto plates.

- Return the sauce to a gentle boil for about 3 - 4 minutes, stirring occasionally.
- Pour the sauce over chicken
- Serve with brown rice

144. Chicken Amp Mushroom Tagliatelle Recipe

Serving: 1 | Prep: | Cook: 15mins | Ready in:

Ingredients

- 1 chicken breast, cut into strips
- 5 mushrooms, sliced
- 1 handfull of ready cooked Tagliatelle
- 1 garlic clove, chopped
- 200 ml thick cream
- 10 ml olive oil
- Parmesan for serving
- salt and pepper to taste

Direction

- If pasta isn't cooked, cook it first.
- Cook the chicken and mushrooms in olive oil until ready.
- Add the garlic and cream.
- Cook until mixture thickens.
- Add salt and pepper to taste.
- Drain the pasta and throw in a serving bowl.
- Take the chicken and mushroom mixture and throw over.
- Top with as much parmesan your heart desires!!!!!
- Enjoy :)

145. Chicken And Broccoli Casserole Recipe

Serving: 8 | Prep: | Cook: 50mins | Ready in:

Ingredients

- 3 quarts water
- 1 (12-ounce) package broccoli florets
- 4 (6-ounce) skinless, boneless chicken breast halves
- 1 (12-ounce) can evaporated fat-free milk
- 1/4 cup all-purpose flour (about 1 ounce)
- 1/4 teaspoon salt
- 1/4 teaspoon freshly ground black pepper
- Dash of nutmeg
- 1 cup fat-free mayonnaise
- 1/2 cup fat-free sour cream
- 1/4 cup dry sherry
- 1 teaspoon worcestershire sauce
- 1 (10.75-ounce) can condensed 30% reduced-sodium 98% fat-free cream of mushroom soup, undiluted
- 1 cup (4 ounces) grated fresh parmesan cheese, divided
- cooking spray

Direction

- Preheat oven to 400°.
- Bring water to a boil in a large Dutch oven over medium-high heat. Add broccoli, and cook 5 minutes or until crisp-tender. Transfer broccoli to a large bowl with a slotted spoon. Add chicken to boiling water; reduce heat, and simmer 15 minutes or until done. Transfer chicken to a cutting board; cool slightly. Cut chicken into bite-sized pieces, and add chicken to bowl with broccoli.
- Combine evaporated milk, flour, salt, pepper, and nutmeg in a saucepan, stirring with a whisk until smooth. Bring to a boil over medium-high heat; cook 1 minute, stirring constantly. Remove from heat. Add mayonnaise, next 4 ingredients (through soup), and 1/2 cup cheese, stirring until well combined. Add mayonnaise mixture to broccoli mixture; stir gently until combined.
- Spoon mixture into a 13 x 9-inch baking dish coated with cooking spray. Sprinkle with remaining 1/2 cup cheese. Bake at 400° for 50 minutes or until mixture bubbles at the edges and cheese begins to brown. Remove from oven; let cool on a wire rack 5 minutes.

146. Chicken And Goat Cheese Enchiladas With Black Bean Sauce Recipe

Serving: 4 | Prep: | Cook: 150mins | Ready in:

Ingredients

- Sauce:
- 1 cup dried black beans
- 4 cups chicken broth, or slightly more
- 1/2 purple onion, chopped
- 2 cloves garlic, chopped
- 2 jalapeno chiles, cut in half, stems and seeds removed
- 2 tbs vegetable oil
- 2 tbs dry sherry
- 1 tbs lime juice
- 2 tsp orange zest
- Filling:
- 1 tbs ground red New Mexican chile
- 1 tsp garlic powder
- 1/2 tsp ground cumin
- 1.2 tsp dried oregano
- 1 lb boneless, skinless chicken breasts, cooked and cut into 3/4-inch pieces or shredded
- 1/2 purple onion, chopped
- 2 tbs vegetable oil
- 1 medium tomato, chopped
- 1/2 lb goat cheese, crumbled
- 1/2 cup chopped fresh cilantro
- 8 corn tortillas, softened
- Garnish: Chopped cilantro, sour cream

Direction

- To make the sauce: Wash the beans carefully in cold water. Drain them. Soak the beans overnight in 4 cups of chicken broth. Transfer to a saucepan, bring to a boil, reduce the heat, and simmer for 1 1/2 hours. Sauté the onion, garlic, and jalapeno chilies in hot oil in a skillet and add to the beans. Continue to simmer,

adding more broth if necessary. When the beans are done, remove them, and drain off some of the liquid. Place the beans, some of the liquid, sherry, lime juice, zest in a blender or food processor and puree until smooth.
- To make the filling: Combine the chili, garlic, cumin and oregano and toss the chicken in the mixture to coat. Sauté the onion in the oil in a skillet. Add the chicken and cook until no longer pink. Add the tomato and cook for two minutes.
- Preheat the oven to 350 degrees.
- To assemble: Place some of the chicken mixture on 2 softened tortillas (one on top of the other) on a plate. Sprinkle the cheese and cilantro over the chicken and roll.
- Pour some of the sauce over the top of each enchilada and heat for 10 minutes to melt the cheese.
- Garnish with additional cilantro and a dollop of sour cream, and serve.

147. Chicken And Spinach Calzones Recipe

Serving: 6 | Prep: | Cook: 17mins | Ready in:

Ingredients

- 2 tsps olive oil
- 1 pound boneless, skinless chicken breasts
- 1 package (10 ounces) frozen chopped spinach, thawed and drained. I used about 3 ounces of spinach..it was a perfect amount.
- 8 ounces of part-skim ricotta cheese
- 1 tbs. minced garlic
- 1tbs chopped parsley
- 4 tsp. parmesan cheese
- 2 egg whites, divided
- 1 frozen whole-wheat bread dough loaf(16 ounces), thawed, not risen

Direction

- Preheat the oven to 350°. Lightly coat a baking sheet with cooking spray. I use my pizza stone covered with parchment paper.
- Cut chicken into small pieces.
- In a large, nonstick frying pan, heat olive oil over medium high heat. Add chicken and sauté, turning occasionally until golden brown, about10 to 12 min.
- In a small bowl, combine the spinach, ricotta cheese, garlic, parsley, parmesan cheese and 1 of the egg whites. Mix until well blended, Set aside.
- In another bowl, using a wire whisk or fork beat the remaining egg white lightly.
- Cut the bread dough into 6 equal-sized pieces.
- On a floured surface, press each piece into a circle.
- Using a rolling pin, roll each dough piece into ovals 8 inches long and 6 inches wide. Brush the edges of the dough ovals with the lightly beaten egg white.
- Place 1/6 of the chicken cubes in the center of each oval.
- Add 1/6 of the spinach mixture to each.
- Fold the dough over the filling, pressing the edges together.
- Crimp with a fork and place on the prepared pan.
- Bake until browned and crispy, about 15 to 20 mins.
- Serve immediately.
- Goes nice with a salad.
- Nutritional Analysis per serving (1 calzone):
- Calories 359
- Cholesterol 60 mg
- Protein 33 g
- Carbohydrate 40 g
- Total fat 9 g
- Saturated fat 2 g
- Monounsaturated fat 2 g
- Sodium 626 mg
- Fiber 4 g
- Potassium 239 mg
- Calcium 118 mg

148. Chicken In Champagne And Mushroom Sauce Recipe

Serving: 4 | Prep: | Cook: 35mins | Ready in:

Ingredients

- 1/4 cup (50 mL) all purpose flour
- 1/2 tsp. (2 mL) salt
- 1/4 tsp. (1 mL) black pepper
- 2 tbsp. (30 mL) olive oil
- 4 skinless, boneless chicken breasts (about 6 oz/170 g each)
- 1 tbsp. (15 mL) butter
- 3 cups (750 mL) sliced mushrooms
- 1 cup (250 mL) champagne (or other sparkling white wine)
- 1 cup (250 mL) whipping cream

Direction

- In a small bowl, combine the flour, salt and pepper. Dredge the chicken breasts in this mixture, one at a time, and arrange them on a plate.
- In a large skillet, heat the olive oil over medium-high heat. Add the chicken breasts and cook quickly until lightly browned on both sides, turning once -- 1 to 2 minutes per side. (You may have to do this in two batches.) The chicken should be browned but not cooked through. Remove to a plate.
- Add the butter to the skillet, then dump in the mushrooms. Cook, stirring frequently, until the mushrooms have released their liquid and it has evaporated. Pour in the champagne, stir around to dissolve any crusty bits from bottom of the pan, then stir in the whipping cream. Bring to a boil, then lower the heat and let the sauce simmer for about 5 minutes. Return the chicken breasts to the skillet, nestling them into the mushroom sauce, lower the heat to medium and cook, uncovered, until the chicken is cooked through and the sauce is thickened -- 6 to 8 minutes.
- Serve immediately with crusty bread or steamed rice to soak up the sauce.

149. Chicken In Creamy Pesto Sauce Recipe

Serving: 3 | Prep: | Cook: 150mins | Ready in:

Ingredients

- 3 chicken breasts (thawed an trimmed)
- one jar of alfredo sauce
- 2 or 3 tablespoons of pesto (homemade or jar) (to taste)
- salt and pepper
- nonstick spray

Direction

- Spray inside of slow cooker
- Sprinkle both sides of chicken with salt and pepper
- Lay side by side in slow cooker
- In a bowl mix Alfredo sauce with pesto
- Pour over chicken
- Cook on high for about 2 hours
- Chicken should temp at 165 degrees
- Serve over pasta

150. Chicken In White Cream Sauce With Garam Masala Recipe

Serving: 4 | Prep: | Cook: 1mins | Ready in:

Ingredients

- 3 med red onions
- 3 garlic cloves (peeled)
- 3 inch piece of fresh ginger (peeled & sliced)
- 1/3 cup canola oil
- 1 inch cinnamon stick

- 12 green cardamon pods (broken open)
- 16 whole cloves
- 1/2 tsp cumin seeds
- 1/4 tsp coriander seeds
- 5 bay leaves
- 1/4 tsp white or black peppercorns
- 3 whole dried red chiles
- 1 tsp salt
- 2 tsp ground coriander
- 1 cup plain yogurt
- 2 lbs boneless chicken breasts cut into pieces
- 3/4 cup hot water
- 1/2 tsp garam masala
- 1/2 cup heavy cream

Direction

- Mince onions, garlic, and ginger (set aside).
- Combine oil, cinnamon, cardamom, cloves, cumin, coriander seeds, bay leaves, peppercorns, and red chiles in a large skillet over a medium heat. Cook, stirring, until the cinnamon unfurls and the other ingredients are lightly brown (about 1-2 mins).
- Add onion mix and salt; continue cooking until onions are lightly brown (about 15 mins). Keep a cup of water nearby until the onion cooks. As the pieces caramelize in the bottom of pan and add 1 tsp. of water at a time. Scrape the bottom of the pan and stir. Do this until the onions are golden.
- Add the ground coriander and cook, stirring for 1 minute. Add 3 tbsps. of yogurt and cook while stirring until the yogurt is blended. Continue adding yogurt in this manner until you've used all the yogurt.
- Add the chicken and cook while stirring (about 5 mins). Add hot water and stir. Bring to a boil then turn the heat down to low. Cover and simmer until the chicken is cooked through (additional 5 mins).
- Stir in the garam masala and cook, stirring (2 mins). Stir in heavy cream and remove from the heat.
- Let the dish rest for about an hour. When ready to serve heat over low heat and drizzle with a little heat cream.

151. Chicken With Creamy Cassis Sauce Recipe

Serving: 0 | Prep: | Cook: | Ready in:

Ingredients

- 4 boneless, skinless chicken breast halves or cutlets (about 1 1/4 pounds)
- 1/3 cup flour
- Salt
- Freshly ground black pepper
- 2 tablespoons extra virgin olive oil
- 1/3 cup dry white wine
- 1/4 cup crème de cassis (or a teaspoon of Dijon)
- 1/4 cup heavy cream
- 2 tablespoons unsalted butter

Direction

- 1 Dredge chicken: Rinse the chicken breasts and pat dry with paper towels. Dredge them in flour, shake off the excess flour and season with salt and pepper.
- 2 Brown chicken on both sides: Heat oil in a large skillet on medium high. Place the chicken breasts in the skillet and cook, turning once, until both sides are golden brown and the chicken is just cooked through, about 10 minutes.
- Transfer the chicken to a platter, cover with foil to keep warm.
- 3 Make sauce: Discard excess fat in the skillet. Add the wine and deglaze, scraping up the browned bits. Boil the wine down for half a minute, add the crème de cassis and the cream.
- Continue to boil down the mixture until it is reduced by a third. Whisk in the butter. Add salt and pepper and spoon over chicken breasts to serve.

152. Chicken Zucchini Alfredo Recipe

Serving: 0 | Prep: | Cook: 30mins | Ready in:

Ingredients

- kosher salt
- 3 tablespoons extra-virgin olive oil
- 2 cloves garlic, minced
- 2 zucchini, thinly sliced into half-moons
- 4 4-ounce thin skinless, boneless chicken breasts
- Freshly ground pepper
- 12 ounces fettuccine (preferably whole wheat)
- 1 tablespoon all-purpose flour
- 1 cup cold low-fat milk (1%)
- 1/2 cup evaporated nonfat milk
- 3/4 cup freshly grated parmesan cheese
- 1/4 cup chopped fresh parsley

Direction

- Bring a large pot of salted water to a boil. Heat 1 tablespoon olive oil in a nonstick skillet over medium heat. Add 1 clove garlic and cook 30 seconds. Add the zucchini, cover and cook until tender, stirring, about 6 minutes. Transfer to a bowl.
- Heat another tablespoon oil in the skillet over medium-high heat. Season the chicken with 1/4 teaspoon each salt and pepper and cook through, 2 to 3 minutes per side. Transfer to a plate.
- Cook the pasta in the boiling water as the label directs. Drain, reserving 1/2 cup cooking water; return the pasta to the pot.
- Meanwhile, whisk the flour and low-fat milk in a bowl. Place the remaining 1 clove garlic and 1 tablespoon oil in the skillet and cook over medium-high heat, 30 seconds. Add the flour-milk mixture and bring to a boil, stirring. Reduce the heat to low and cook, stirring, 2 minutes. Add the evaporated milk, 1/2 teaspoon salt and the cheese; stir to melt, 1 minute.
- Cut the chicken into strips. Toss with the pasta, sauce, zucchini and parsley, adding the reserved pasta water to loosen.

153. Chili Spiced Chicken Recipe

Serving: 4 | Prep: | Cook: 15mins | Ready in:

Ingredients

- 1 medium yellow onion, quartered
- 2 cloves garlic
- 2 tablespons chili powder
- 2 teaspoons ground cumin
- 2 teaspoons fresh lime juice
- 4 skinless, boneless chicken breast halves (about 4 oz each)
- ------------FOR THE SALSA----------
- 2 cups canned black beans, rinsed an drained
- 1/2 cup diced red bell pepper
- 1/4 cup chopped red onion
- 1/4 cup diced cucumber
- 2 tablespoons fresh lime juice
- 2 tablespoons red-wine vinegar
- 1/2 teaspoon ground cumin

Direction

- To prepare salsa, in a medium bowl, combine beans, bell pepper, red onion, cucumber, lime juice, vinegar and cumin. Mix well. Cover with plastic wrap; set aside.
- In a blender or food processor fitted with the metal blade, process yellow onion and garlic until smooth. Add chili powder, cumin, and lime juice; process until a paste forms.
- Spread chili paste over both sides of chicken. Place chicken. Place chicken in a shallow dish. Cover with plastic wrap and marinate for 10 to 20 minutes.
- Preheat broiler. Line broiler pan with foil. Broil chicken, 4 inches from heat, turning once, until cooked though and no longer pink about 12 minutes.

- Cut chicken, on diagonal, into thin slices.
- Spoon salsa evenly onto 4 serving plates. Fan chicken over salsa.
- Serve immediately.

154. Chinese Almond Chicken Recipe

Serving: 4 | Prep: | Cook: 30mins | Ready in:

Ingredients

- • 1 pound boneless, skinless chicken breast or thighs, cut into 1-inch cubes. I use duck now and turkey will work. Delicious.
- • 1 egg white
- • ½ tsp. salt
- • 2 tsp. cornstarch
- • 1 scallion, chopped
- • ½ cup peas, frozen works.
- • 1 1/2 Tbs. soy sauce, I prefer a light soy.
- • 1 Tbs. Chinese rice wine, Sake or dry sherry.
- • ¼ cup roasted slivered or sliced almonds, sliced is best.

Direction

- 1. In a medium bowl, combine the chicken with the egg white, salt, and cornstarch.
- 2. Stir until the cornstarch is fully dissolved. Let sit for 10 minutes.
- 3. In a small pot, bring about 1 quart of water to boil. Add 1 Tbs. of the oil to the water.
- 4. Add the chicken, and blanch for 1 minute, until the chicken is white on the outside but not cooked through. Drain the chicken well and set aside.
- 5. In a wok or large skillet, heat the remaining 1 Tbs. of oil over medium-high heat.
- 6. Add the chopped scallions and stir-fry briefly until aromatic, about 20 seconds.
- 7. Add the chicken and peas and stir-fry for 1 minute.
- 8. Add the soy sauce and sherry and cook for another 1 to 2 minutes.
- 9. Sprinkle in the almonds and stir so they are well-coated with the sauce.
- 10. Transfer to a plate and serve.
- I serve this with steamed or fried rice, pickled veggies and maybe steamed broccoli or cauliflower.

155. Chinese Chicken Balls Recipe

Serving: 6 | Prep: | Cook: 30mins | Ready in:

Ingredients

- 4 boneless chicken breasts cut-up in 1 inch cubes
- 1 1/4 cup all purpose white flour plus 1/4 cup for coating the chicken
- 2 tsp baking powder
- 1 tsp salt
- 1/4 tsp pepper
- 2 eggs
- 3/4 cup milk
- 1 to 2 tbsps cooking oil

Direction

- Cut up chicken breasts in 1 inch cubes and set aside.
- Mix together 1 1/4 cup of white flour with the baking powder, salt, pepper (reserve 1/4 cup for coating chicken pieces before dipping into this mixture). Add the 2 eggs and the milk. Mix all together well.
- Take the chicken pieces and dip them in the 1/4 cup of flour, then dip into this batter to coat the chicken. Fry the chicken pieces in hot cooking oil until browned on all sides and serve with my chicken balls red sauce.

156. Chinese Fire Pot With Fish Balls Recipe

Serving: 12 | Prep: | Cook: 5mins | Ready in:

Ingredients

- 2 pounds flank steak, sliced thinly against the grain
- 2 pounds chicken breast, thinly sliced
- 1 pound large shrimp, U-15's peeled and deveined (15 shrimp per pound)
- 20 fish balls
- 2 pounds bay scallops
- 3 packages soaked mung bean noodles
- 4 Shanghai cabbage, whole leaves
- 4 baby bok choy, whole leaves
- 1 napa cabbage large chopped
- 2 quarts chicken stock
- 1 pound shiitake mushrooms, de-stemmed
- boiling water
- For the table, jars/small bottles of the following to make your own dipping sauce:
- Samba Oelek
- peanut butter
- Chinese sesame paste
- sesame oil
- oyster sauce
- rice wine vinegar
- shaoxing wine
- Thin soy sauce
- 2 cups chopped scallions
- 2 cups chopped cilantro
- eggs (optional)

Direction

- Thread beef, chicken, shrimp, fish balls and scallops on wooden skewers and set aside. Combine water and chicken stock in an electric wok and bring to a boil. Add mung bean noodles, cabbage, bok choy and shiitake mushrooms. Place skewers in pot and cook according to individual taste. Ladle broth into bowls with skewered meats and seafood and serve with condiments.
- FISH BALLS:
- 2 pounds Chilean sea bass or other fatty white fish
- 4 eggs, separated
- 1 teaspoon white pepper
- 1 teaspoon kosher salt
- 1 teaspoon sesame oil
- 1 tablespoon fish sauce
- 3 minced Thai bird chilies
- 1/3 cup sliced scallions
- In a food processor, puree fish with egg yolks until smooth. Add pepper, salt, sesame oil, fish sauce, and chilies; pulse processor a few times. Transfer mousse to a large, chilled bowl and fold in the scallions. Using a mixer, lift the egg whites to a stiff peak. Gently fold in the egg whites with the mousse. Cook a very small portion either in boiling water or in a microwave oven to verify seasonings. Using wet hands, make small balls (1-inch in diameter). Quickly blanch in salted boiling water for only 2 minutes. Drain and set aside to cool.
- Huge appetite,
- The serving will be round 8 to 12 depending the each person serving.

157. Chipotle Chicken And Noodles Recipe

Serving: 0 | Prep: | Cook: 480mins | Ready in:

Ingredients

- 1 Cup water
- 24 Ounces Boneless skinless chicken breasts cut into 1-inch pieces
- 1 Can Hunt's crushed tomatoes 28 oz.
- 2 Tablespoons chipotle peppers in adobo sauce, chopped
- 6 Ounces Dry egg noodles, uncooked

Direction

- Combine chicken, tomatoes, chipotle peppers and water in slow cooker. Cover with lid.

- Cook on LOW 8 hours (or on HIGH 4 hours), stirring in noodles for the last 30 minutes of the cooking time.
- Stir before serving.

158. Coco Ichibanya Cocos Style Chicken Cutlet Curry Recipe

Serving: 4 | Prep: | Cook: 20mins | Ready in:

Ingredients

- 4 servings short grain white rice, cooked and kept warm
- 4 boneless, skinless chicken breasts
- 2 cups fine breadcrumbs(panko, if possible)
- 2 eggs, beaten
- 1 block S&B Golden® curry sauce mix(med/hot)*
- 12oz sliced fresh mushrooms(variety, if possible)
- 2 cups shredded Monterey or pepperJack cheese
- 2 1/2 cups water
- 2 pieces of bacon, chopped or 1T bacon grease
- 2T peanut oil
- salt, pepper and cayenne
- *there are 3 heat variations of S&B...if you're looking for a "level 1 or 2", please try the MILD version of the curry block.

Direction

- In large stir fry pan or wok, cook bacon (or just add the bacon grease) until just crispy.
- Add mushrooms and sauté about 5 minutes.
- Add water and entire brick of curry sauce mix to mushrooms.
- Let simmer on high to thicken, stirring occasionally while preparing chicken.
- Pound chicken breasts out to about 1/2 inch thickness. Season with salt and pepper.
- In pie plate, combine breadcrumbs with salt, pepper and other desired seasonings (i.e. garlic or onion powder, cayenne, parsley, etc.)
- Dredge chicken in egg then in breadcrumbs until evenly coated.
- Cook chicken in large skillet with peanut or vegetable oil.
- Cook about 5 minute each side, until chicken is cooked through.
- To arrange dish, place serving of rice on plate, top with sliced chicken breast, then about 1/2 cup shredded cheese, then top with sauce.
- **CoCo's curry is a messy dish of yummy goodness according to those who've tasted the real thing. You can adjust the heat of this recipe by the use of cayenne or the pepper jack cheese, but I don't suggest using any commercial curry powders...they will change the flavor, noticeably. **

159. Coconut Chicken Phase 1 Recipe

Serving: 2 | Prep: | Cook: 30mins | Ready in:

Ingredients

- 1 tablespoon extra-virgin olive oil
- 1/2 pound chicken breast tenders
- 1/2 tablespoon chicken broth
- 1/2 medium onion, chopped
- 1 clove garlic, minced
- 1/2 teaspoon dried cilantro
- 1/2 teaspoon grated fresh ginger
- 1/2 teaspoon finely grated lemon peel
- pinch of ground cumin
- 1/2 pinch of ground turmeric
- 1/2 cup light coconut milk (no sugar added)
- 1 tablespoon macadamia nuts, finely ground
- 1/2 teaspoon sugar substitute
- 1/8 teaspoon ground red pepper (or to taste)
- 1/2 tablespoon tamarind paste (available in Indian and specialty food markets)
- 1 teaspoon water

- Chopped scallion, for garnish

Direction

- Heat the oil in a large skillet over medium-high heat. Add the chicken and cook for 5 minutes per side, or until browned and no longer pink in the center. Remove the chicken to a plate and set aside.
- Heat the broth in the same skillet. Add the onion, garlic, cilantro, ginger, lemon peel, cumin, and turmeric and cook for 5 minutes, or until the onion is tender but not browned. Stir in the coconut milk, nuts, sugar substitute, and red pepper. Return the chicken to the skillet, cover, and simmer for 10 minutes, or until the chicken is cooked through.
- Remove the chicken to a plate and keep warm. Do not discard the sauce in the pan.
- In a small bowl, combine the tamarind paste and water. Stir into the sauce in the skillet and gently boil until thickened and the mixture measures about 1/2 cup.
- Evenly divide the chicken among 2 serving plates. Top with sauce and garnish with the scallion.
- Nutritional Information:
- 360 calories
- 25 g total fat (14 g sat)
- 66 mg cholesterol
- 10 g carbohydrate
- 28 g protein
- 3 g fiber
- 60 mg sodium

160. Copycat California Pizza Kitchens Chicken Tequila Fettuccine Recipe

Serving: 4 | Prep: | Cook: 30mins | Ready in:

Ingredients

- 1 lb. uncooked spinach fettuccine
- 1 1/4 boneless, skinless chicken breasts, diced
- 1/2 cup fresh cilantro
- 2 Tbsp. minced garlic
- 1 Tbsp. minced jalapeno pepper, seeds and membrane
- removed
- 3 Tbsp. butter, (reserve 1 Tbsp. for saute)
- 1/2 cup chicken stock
- 1 1/2 cups heavy cream
- 2 Tbsp. gold tequila
- 2 Tbsp. freshly squeezed lime juice
- 3 Tbsp. soy sauce
- 1/4 medium red onion, thinly sliced
- 1/2 medium red bell pepper, thinly sliced
- 1/2 medium yellow bell pepper, thinly sliced
- 1/2 medium green bell pepper, thinly sliced

Direction

- Boil salted water to cook pasta; cook until al dente, 8-10 minutes for dry pasta, 3 minutes for fresh. Pasta may be cooked ahead of time, rinsed and oiled and then reheated in boiling water.
- Cook 1/3 cup cilantro, garlic, and jalapeno in 2 Tbsp. butter over medium heat for 4-5 minutes
- Add stock, tequila, and lime juice. Bring the mixture to a boil and cook until reduced to a paste like consistency; set aside.
- Pour soy sauce over chicken; set aside for 5 minutes.
- Meanwhile, cook onion and peppers, stirring occasionally, with remaining butter over medium heat. When the veggies have become limp have become limp, add chicken and soy sauce; toss and add reserved tequila lime paste and cream.
- Bring the sauce to a boil; boil until chicken is cooked through and sauce is thick.
- Toss with drained fettuccine and reserved cilantro.

161. Corn And Bell Pepper Chicken Bake Recipe

Serving: 6 | Prep: | Cook: 30mins | Ready in:

Ingredients

- 1 2/3 cups hot water
- 1 pkg (6 ounces) Stove Top cornbread stuffing mix
- 1 1/2 pounds boneless skinless chicken breast, cut into 6 serving-size pieces
- 16 ounce package fromen stir-fry pepper and onion blend, thawed
- 10.75 ounce can cream of chicken soup
- 10 ounce package frozen corn

Direction

- Preheat oven to 425.
- Mix stuffing mix with hot water and set aside.
- In a 13x9 baking dish, place chicken pieces, then cover with the stir-fry vegetables.
- Mix corn and soup together and spoon over the chicken and vegetables in dish.
- Top with moistened stuffing.
- Bake until chicken is cooked all the way through, about 30 minutes.

162. Country Captain Recipe

Serving: 8 | Prep: | Cook: 120mins | Ready in:

Ingredients

- 1 (5 1/2 - 6 lb) stewing hen, cleaned and dressed OR equivalent amount of chicken breast and thigh pieces
- 2 quarts chicken stock or water
- 2 large yellow onions
- 2 large sweet green peppers, cored, seeded, and coarsely chopped
- 2 cloves garlic, peeled and crushed
- 2 Tbsp olive oil
- 1 cup dried currants or seedless raisins
- 1 Tbsp curry powder
- 1 tsp cayenne pepper
- 1/2 tsp black pepper
- 1 tsp thyme
- 1/4 tsp ground cloves
- 1 tsp salt
- 2 (28 oz) cans diced tomatoes (do not drain)
- 3 cups reserved chicken stock
- 1 cup toasted, blanched almonds (topping)

Direction

- Place chicken in a large kettle with water or stock. Cover and simmer 1 to 1 1/2 hours until tender. Lift chicken from kettle and set aside to cool; strain stock and reserve.
- In the same kettle, cook onions, green peppers, and garlic in oil 8 to 10 minutes over moderate heat until onion is golden. Add all the remaining ingredients except almonds and simmer, uncovered, for 45 minutes, stirring now and then.
- Skin chicken, remove meat from bones, and cut in bite-sized pieces.
- Add chicken to sauce and simmer, uncovered, for 15 minutes.

163. Cranberry Chicken Recipe

Serving: 2 | Prep: | Cook: 60mins | Ready in:

Ingredients

- 1/2 cup cranberry juice
- 2 tablespoons soy sauce
- 2 tablespoons worcestershire sauce
- 2 garlic cloves, minced
- 2 bone-in chicken breast halves
- Hot cooked rice, optional

Direction

- In a resealable plastic bag, combine the first four ingredients.

- Add chicken and turn to coat.
- Seal bag and refrigerate 8 hours or overnight.
- Place chicken and marinade in a small ungreased baking pan.
- Bake, uncovered, at 350 degrees for an hour or until meat juices run clear.
- Place over hot rice if desired.

164. Crazy Coconut Chicken Recipe

Serving: 8 | Prep: | Cook: 15mins | Ready in:

Ingredients

- 2 tbs shredded coconut
- 4 whole chicken breasts (about 4 pounds)
- 1 c canned coconut milk
- 1/2 c chicken broth (see Soups: chicken broth)
- 1/4 c sugar
- 2 tbs lemon juice
- 1 tbs + 1 1/2 teaspoons cornstarch
- 2 tsp ginger root juice
- 2 tsp vegetable oil
- 1 tsp salt
- 1/8 tsp white peppers
- vegetable oil
- 1/4 c all-purpose flour
- 1/4 c water
- 2 tbs cornstarch
- 2 tbs vegetable oil
- 1/4 tsp baking soda
- 1/4 tsp salt
- 1 egg white

Direction

- Heat oven to 300°. Bake coconut, stirring occasionally, 10 minutes or until golden brown. (Watch carefully so coconut does not burn.)
- Remove bones and skin from chicken breast; cut each chicken breast lengthwise into 2-inch strips.
- Heat coconut milk, broth, sugar, lemon juice, 1 tablespoon plus 1 1/2 teaspoons cornstarch, the gingerroot juice, 2 teaspoons vegetable oil, 1 teaspoon salt and the white pepper to boiling.
- Cook, stirring constantly, until thickened. Remove from heat; keep warm.
- Heat vegetable oil (2 inches) in wok to 350°.
- In bowl, mix flour, water, 2 tablespoons cornstarch, 2 tablespoons vegetable oil, the baking soda, 1/4 teaspoon salt and the egg white in medium bowl.
- Dip chicken into batter then fry a few pieces at a time 3 minutes or until very light brown; drain on paper towels.
- Cut each chicken piece crosswise into 1-inch pieces, using a very sharp knife; place in a single layer on heated platter.
- Pour coconut sauce over chicken; garnish with toasted coconut.
- The coconut flavor of this recipe turns everyday chicken into an exotic tropical treat. The white sauce over golden brown chicken makes a very attractive dish. Toasted coconut stores well at room temperature. Keep it in a close jar up to several months.

165. Cream Of Green Chile Chicken Soup Recipe

Serving: 6 | Prep: | Cook: 40mins | Ready in:

Ingredients

- 2 corn tortillas -- * see note
- 3 skinless, boneless chicken breasts, cooked and shredded
- 12 oz tub green chiles -- mild, hot, or x-hot
- 1/2 stick margarine
- 2 cups chopped onion
- 1 garlic clove -- peeled and minced
- 1/2 tsp dried oregano -- crumbled
- 2 bay leaves

- 3 1/2 cups chicken broth -- homemade or canned
- 2 medium baking potatoes -- peeled and cubed
- 1/3 tsp cumin
- 1/2 tsp salt
- 1/4 tsp pepper
- 1/3 cup whipping cream
- 2 cups monterey jack cheese -- grated
- * Preferably 1 of yellow cornmeal and 1 of blue.

Direction

- Cut the tortillas into 1/4 inch wide strips and leave them uncovered at room temperature until they are dry and crisp, about 24 hours (or heat in iron skillet until dry and hot).
- In a 4 quart saucepan over low heat, melt the butter.
- Add the onions, garlic, oregano, and bay leaves and cook, covered, stirring once or twice, for 10 minutes.
- Stir in the chicken broth, potatoes, salt, cumin & black pepper and bring to a boil.
- Lower heat and simmer, partially covered, stirring once or twice, until the potatoes are very tender, about 25 minutes.
- Stir in the cream and chicken, heat through and adjust the seasoning if necessary.
- The soup can be prepared up to 3 days ahead. Cool it completely and refrigerate, covered. Rewarm it over low heat, stirring often, until steaming.
- Ladle the soup into wide bowls, sprinkle the cheese over the soup, and scatter the tortilla strips over the cheese. Serve immediately.

166. Cream Of Mushroom Chicken Recipe

Serving: 4 | Prep: | Cook: 45mins | Ready in:

Ingredients

- 4 - large boneless chicken breasts
- 2 - cans cream of mushroom soup
- 1 1/2 cans milk (measure milk in soup can)

Direction

- Bake chicken at 400 degrees for 30 minutes or until done
- Mix soup and milk in bowl until smooth
- Pour over chicken after it is done.
- Bake until soup mixture bubbles (approx. 15 minutes) at 400 degrees

167. Creamed Smokey Chicken Recipe

Serving: 8 | Prep: | Cook: 60mins | Ready in:

Ingredients

- 8 boneless, skinless chicken breasts
- 2 (2 oz) pkgs chipped beef
- 8 slices bacon, uncooked
- 1 pint sour cream
- 1 (10.75 oz) can cream of mushroom soup
- ½ tsp paprika
- ½ tsp liquid smoke

Direction

- Preheat oven to 350°.
- Line a large baking dish with chipped beef.
- Wrap bacon around each chicken breast; place in baking dish.
- Mix sour cream, soup and liquid smoke; pour over chicken. Sprinkle paprika on top and cover with foil.
- 5 Bake for 1 hour.

168. Creamy Bacon And Mushroom Chicken Recipe

Serving: 8 | Prep: | Cook: 30mins | Ready in:

Ingredients

- 4 large boneless skinless chicken breasts
- 8 slices bacon, uncooked
- 2 cans 10.5 oz cream of mushroom soup
- 8 tbsp cream cheese
- rice, cooked

Direction

- Cut each piece of chicken in half.
- Wrap one slice of bacon around each half of chicken and place in a 9 X 13 inch pan.
- Pour soup over chicken and bake at 350 degrees for 20 minutes. Remove from oven and top each piece of chicken with 1 tbsp. cream cheese.
- Place back into oven for 10 minutes.
- Serve over hot rice.

169. Creamy Chicken Curry Recipe

Serving: 56 | Prep: | Cook: 40mins | Ready in:

Ingredients

- 4 tbsp. lauric oil
- 1 big red onion, thinly sliced
- 2 to 3 gloves garlic, finely chopped
- 1 2-inch piece fresh ginger, finely chopped
- 1/2 tbsp. curry powder
- 1/2 tbsp. luyang dilaw powder (turmeric)
- 3 round potatoes, peeled and quartered
- 1/2 kilo boneless and skinless chicken breast
- 1 cup kakang gata (first pressing of coconut milk)
- 2 cups pangalawang gata (second extract of the coconut milk)
- 1 pc. red bell pepper, thinly sliced
- 1 pc. green bell pepper, thinly sliced
- ground pepper and patis (fish sauce), to taste

Direction

- Heat 2 tbsp. of the oil in a large skillet over medium heat.
- Sauté the onions in skillet and cook until translucent.
- Add garlic, fresh ginger, curry powder and luyang dilaw (turmeric) powder and cook for 3 minutes.
- Add the remaining 2 tablespoons of oil to skillet and raise heat to medium-high.
- Add the chicken and stir-fry until golden, about 8 minutes.
- Add potatoes and stir-fry for 2 minutes more.
- Add the second extract of the coconut milk and simmer for about 8 minutes or until the potatoes are tender.
- When done, add the bell peppers and stir in the kakang gata, reduce heat to medium-low, and simmer gently for 2 minutes.
- Season with ground pepper and patis.
- Remove from heat and serve hot

170. Creamy Pot Pie Recipe

Serving: 0 | Prep: | Cook: 2hours | Ready in:

Ingredients

- 3 medium potatoes, chopped
- 4 carrots, chopped
- 1 small leafy heart from a bunch if celery, chopped
- 1 large onion, diced
- 6 cloves garlic, minced
- 1/4 - 1/2 cup of peas
- 1 chicken breast, cooked and chopped (optional)
- 1/4 cup fresh Italian parsley, chopped
- 1 1/2 tsp. poultry seasoning
- 2 tbs. extra virgin olive oil
- 2 tbs. butter
- 4 cups vegetable broth
- 1 8oz. pack cream cheese
- 1 cup whole milk
- salt and pepper to taste

- 1 recipe for pie crust that makes 2 crusts

Direction

- In a soup pot combine the olive oil and butter and heat on medium heat.
- To the butter and oil add the onion and celery and sauté till tender crisp.
- Next add the garlic and sauté for 1 minute.
- Add the rest of the vegetables and vegetable broth and cook till the vegetables are tender.
- Add the chicken (optional), peas, parsley, poultry seasoning, salt, pepper, milk, and cream cheese to the vegetables.
- Stir really well and set aside,
- Preheat the oven to 375 degrees.
- Divide the pie crust into 8 - 12 balls.
- Roll the crust to fit inside the ramekins and to top the pies.
- Pour the creamy soup inside the crusted ramekins and top with the remaining crusts.
- Press the crusts together around the ramekins to keep the pie filling in.
- Cut an air hole in the top middle of each pie.
- Place in a 375 degree oven.
- Bake for 30 - 45 minutes or until the crust is golden brown.
- Serve after about 15 - 20 minutes out of the oven.
- Enjoy!

171. Creole Chicken Bonne Femme Recipe

Serving: 2 | Prep: | Cook: 1hours | Ready in:

Ingredients

- Creole chicken Bonne Femme
- 1/4 Cup Extra Virgin Olive Oil
- 1 Tbsp Unsalted butter
- 2 Boneless, skinless chicken breasts, pounded lightly for even cooking
- 2 Medium Russet Potatoes, peeled and sliced into 1/8" rounds
- 3/4 Cup Spanish Onion, diced
- 1/8 Cup Green Onions, Sliced
- 2 cloves of Garlic, minced
- 1 Cup Ham, diced
- Kosher Salt & black pepper, to taste
- 1/4 Cup White Wine
- 1 Tbsp Italian Parsley, finely chopped
- 2 Tbsp Unsalted butter
- Sliced Green Onions for Garnish

Direction

- Preheat an oven to 350 degrees F.
- Season the chicken breast liberally with salt and pepper. Add the Olive Oil and 1 Tbsp. of Unsalted Butter to a medium high sauté pan. When hot add the chicken breasts and sauté until golden brown on both sides, set aside.
- Add the potatoes to the hot sauté pan and sauté until tender. Add the onions, ham, and garlic, sauté until the onions are translucent, fold or stir gently as to not break up the potatoes. Deglaze the pan with the white wine, cook for 2 minutes. Season the "sauce" with salt & black pepper to taste. Gently nestle the chicken breasts in the sauce and place in the oven until the chicken is just cooked through.
- Remove from the oven, place the chicken on 2 heated serving plates. Add the parsley, and the remaining 2 Tbsp. Unsalted Butter to the sauce, shake the pan until it is incorporated. Divide the sauce over each chicken breast, garnish with the green onions and serve.
- Serves 2.

172. Creole Chicken Fried Chicken With Creole Ranch Dressing Recipe

Serving: 6 | Prep: | Cook: 20mins | Ready in:

Ingredients

- 1/2 cup paprika
- 1/2 cup granulated garlic

- 1/4 cup granulated onion
- 3 tablespoons ground black pepper
- 2 teaspoons ground white pepper
- 2 teaspoons cayenne pepper
- 1/4 cup dried oregano
- 1/4 cup dried thyme
- 2 tablespoons ground cumin
- 2 tablespoons sugar
- 2-1/4 pounds small boneless skinless chicken breasts
- 1-1/2 cups buttermilk
- 2 cups flour
- 2 tablespoons kosher salt
- vegetable oil for frying
- Dressing:
- 1-1/4 cups mayonnaise
- 1 cup buttermilk
- 1 tablespoon red wine vinegar
- 2 teaspoons minced garlic
- 1/4 cup finely chopped chives
- 1 tablespoon lemon pepper
- 1/4 cup freshly grated parmesan
- 1 teaspoon kosher salt
- 1/2 teaspoon freshly ground black pepper
- 1 teaspoon spice mix used to coat chicken

Direction

- Combine all spice ingredients.
- Pull off chicken tenders from the breasts then sprinkle both sides of tenders with spice mix.
- Line them up in a non-reactive baking pan and pour on the buttermilk.
- Cover and let marinate in the refrigerator for at least 4 hours.
- Mix flour, 1/4 cup spice mix and salt then spread out in a flat pan.
- Remove chicken pieces out of buttermilk and press into the flour mixture coating them well.
- Pour 1/4" of oil in bottom of a heavy skillet then heat over medium high until almost smoking.
- Add chicken pieces without crowding the pan.
- Turn down heat to medium and fry 5 minutes on each side.
- Serve hot until crisp and golden with some ranch dressing ladled on top.
- To make dressing whisk all dressing ingredients together in a bowl.
- Transfer to a container with a lid and store in refrigerator until needed.

173. Crisp And Creamy Baked Chicken Recipe

Serving: 4 | Prep: | Cook: 35mins | Ready in:

Ingredients

- 4 Small Boneless, Skinless, chicken breasts (1lb/500g)
- 6 Tbsp. (1/2 of 1 pouch) Shake'N Bake Extra Crispy Orginal Coating Mix
- 1-1/2 Cups instant white rice, uncooked.
- 2/3 Cup condensed cream of celery soup
- 1/4 Cup milk
- 1 Cup Marble Shredded cheese (or either Mozza or Cheddar)

Direction

- Preheat oven to 400.
- Coat chicken with coating mix as directed on package; place in greased 9X13 baking dish.
- Bake 20 min. or until chicken is cooked through (170'F)
- Meanwhile, cook rice as directed on package.
- Beat Soup and milk with wire whisk until well blended.
- Pour evenly over chicken; sprinkle with Cheese.
- Bake an additional 5 mins, or until cheese is melted and sauce is bubbly.
- Serve with Rice

174. Crock Pot Italian Chicken Stew Recipe

Serving: 6 | Prep: | Cook: 10hours8mins | Ready in:

Ingredients

- 3-4 boneless skinless chicken breast halves, cut into 1-1 1/2-inch pieces
- 1 can cannellini beans, or chickpeas drained, rinsed
- 1 can light or dark kidney beans, drained, rinsed
- 1 can diced tomatoes, un-drained
- 1 cup chopped celery
- 1 cup onion chopped (I used white it's what I had)
- 1 cup (2 medium) sliced carrots
- 2 small garlic cloves, minced or chopped (I just keep a large jar of minced garlic in the fridge we go thru it fairly quickly)
- 1 cup water
- 1/2 cup white wine (or whatever you have available I'm not picky)
- 1 can (6oz) tomato paste
- 1 can un-drained green beans
- 1can drained black olives (optional)
- 3-4 tsp dried Italian seasoning
- 1 tsp salt (or to taste)
- 1 tsp pepper (or to taste)

Direction

- In 4 to 6-quart slow cooker, combine all ingredients mix well.
- Cover; cook on low setting for 8 to 10 hours or on high setting for 5 to 6 hours or until vegetables are tender.
- Makes 4 (2-cup) servings
- Serve over Polenta

175. Crock Pot Italian Chicken And Potatoes Recipe

Serving: 4 | Prep: | Cook: 480mins | Ready in:

Ingredients

- 4 -6 boneless, skinless chicken breast halves, flash-seared in 1T. olive oil
- 1/2-2/3 cup Italian salad dressing (use at least 1/2 cup), divided
- 1 teaspoon italian seasoning (or mix basil, oregano, crushed red pepper, and garlic powder to equal same)
- 1/2 - 2/3 cup grated Parmesan or romano cheese
- 4 to 6 medium potatoes, cut into wedges or thick slices (I prefer peeled)

Direction

- Place chicken in bottom of Crock Pot.
- Sprinkle with half of the Italian dressing, herbs, and the grated cheese.
- Put the potatoes on top of the chicken.
- Sprinkle with the rest of the dressing, herbs, and cheese.
- Cook on low for about 6-8 hours, or until the chicken is done and potatoes are tender.

176. Crockpot Bacon Ranch Chicken Recipe

Serving: 6 | Prep: | Cook: 4hours | Ready in:

Ingredients

- 4 boneless skinless chicken breasts
- 4 tablespoons real bacon bits OR
- 8 slices of bacon, cooked and crumbled
- 1 teaspoon minced garlic
- 1 package ranch dressing mix
- 1 can cream of chicken soup
- 1 cup sour cream
- egg noodles or rice

Direction

- Place chicken in greased 5-6 quart slow cooker.
- Combine bacon, garlic, ranch dressing mix, soup, and sour cream; mix well.
- Pour over chicken in the crock pot.
- Cook on high 3-4 hours.
- Shred the chicken using two forks.

- Serve over cooked egg noodles or rice.

177. Crockpot Chicken And Mushroom Gravy Recipe

Serving: 6 | Prep: | Cook: 480mins | Ready in:

Ingredients

- 3 whole chicken breasts, halved
- 1/4 c. dry white wine or chicken broth – I used Chardonnay wine
- 1 can cream of chicken soup
- 1 (4 oz.) can mushrooms, sliced
- salt & pepper to taste

Direction

- Brown chicken in small amount of oil or butter then place chicken pieces in crock pot. Season with salt and pepper. Mix wine and soup. Pour over chicken. Add mushrooms. Cover and cook on low for 7 to 9 hours or high 3 to 4 hours. Recipe may be doubled in 5-quart crock pot.

178. Crunchy Chicken Chunks With Thai Peanut Sauce Recipe

Serving: 8 | Prep: | Cook: 35mins | Ready in:

Ingredients

- chicken Chunks
- 1 1/2 cups Country® corn flakes cereal, crushed (1/2 cup)
- 1/2 cup Original Bisquick® mix
- 3/4 teaspoon paprika
- 1/4 teaspoon salt
- 1/4 teaspoon pepper
- 1 lb boneless skinless chicken breasts, cut into 1-inch pieces
- cooking spray
- Thai peanut sauce
- 1/2 cup plain low-fat yogurt
- 1/4 cup creamy peanut butter
- 1/2 cup fat-free (skim) milk
- 1 tablespoon soy sauce
- 1/8 teaspoon ground red pepper (cayenne), if desired

Direction

- 1. Heat oven to 400°F. Line 15x10x1-inch pan with foil. In 2-quart resealable food-storage plastic bag, mix cereal, Bisquick mix, paprika, salt and pepper until well blended. Shake about 6 chicken pieces at a time in bag until coated. Shake off any extra crumbs. Place chicken pieces in pan. Spray chicken with cooking spray.
- 2. Bake uncovered 20 to 25 minutes or until coating is crisp and chicken is no longer pink in center.
- 3. In 10-inch non-stick skillet, mix all sauce ingredients. Cook over medium heat 3 to 4 minutes, stirring occasionally, until mixture begins to thicken. Serve chicken chunks with sauce.

179. Crunchy Chicken Fingers Recipe

Serving: 4 | Prep: | Cook: 10mins | Ready in:

Ingredients

- 1/3 cup cornflake crumbs
- ½ cup finely chopped pecans
- 1 tablespoon dried parsley flakes
- 1/8 teaspoon salt
- 1/8 teaspoon garlic powder
- 4 skinless chicken breasts, cut into 1x3 inch strips
- 2 tablespoons skim milk

Direction

- In a shallow dish, combine cornflake crumbs, pecans, parsley, salt, and garlic powder. Dip chicken in milk, then roll in crumb mixture. Place in a 15x10x1 inch baking pan.
- Bake in a 400 degree oven for 7 to 9 minutes or until chicken is tender and no longer pink.

180. Cumin Fried Chicken Recipe

Serving: 4 | Prep: | Cook: 15mins | Ready in:

Ingredients

- 1 cup buttermilk
- 1 tablespoon ground cumin
- 1/4 teaspoon cayenne pepper
- 1 pound boneless skinless chicken breast halves cut into strips
- 1/2 cup all purpose flour
- 1 teaspoon salt
- 1/4 cup vegetable oil
- 2 teaspoons fresh lime juice

Direction

- Combine buttermilk, 1-1/2 teaspoons cumin and 1/8 teaspoon cayenne in plastic bag.
- Shake gently to blend then add chicken and seal and toss well to coat.
- Refrigerate at least 1 hour or up to 6 hours.
- Combine flour, remaining cumin and 1/8 teaspoon cayenne and salt on waxed paper.
- Drain chicken then blot with paper towelling and coat chicken pieces evenly with flour mixture.
- Heat oil in large non-stick skillet over medium high heat.
- Working in batches if necessary to avoid crowding skillet add chicken to hot oil.
- Cook 8 minutes per batch or until golden and crisp turning pieces over halfway through cooking.
- Remove with slotted spoon to paper towelling to drain then arrange on platter.
- Drizzle with lime juice and serve.

181. Deep Fried Monte Cristo Sandwiches Recipe

Serving: 2 | Prep: | Cook: 30mins | Ready in:

Ingredients

- For 2 sandwiches
- 4 slices white or wheat bread, but I think Brioche is best!
- 4 slices cooked, sliced chicken breast
- 4 slices cooked ham
- 2 slices American cheese
- 2 slices Swiss or Gruyere cheese
- Batter:
- 1 large egg
- ½ cup plus 2 tablespoons water
- 1/4 tsp. salt
- 1 tsp. granulated white sugar
- ¾ cup flour
- ½ Tbs. baking powder
- Peanut Oil (for deep frying)…you will need about 1" deep oil in a deep sided skillet.
- Powdereed sugar, for dusting finished sandwiches
- Fruit jam, of your choice, for serving

Direction

- On two pieces of bread, place 2 slices chicken and 1 slice of Swiss or Gruyere cheese, then 2 slices ham and 1 slice American cheese. Place second slice of bread on top of layers, and secure the sandwiches in the corners with long tooth picks.
- For batter, place egg in mixing bowl, add water and beat together. Add salt, sugar, flour, and baking powder. Beat batter until smooth. Dip sandwiches in batter, making sure to cover all sides and surfaces.
- Carefully place dipped sandwiches in about 1" of hot oil (about 350 degrees), in a heavy, deep skillet, frying until golden. Carefully flip and

brown other side of sandwich. When sandwiches have fried to a golden brown, remove from pan with a slotted spatula, and place on paper towel to soak up any excess oil. Let cool for a few minutes before removing the tooth picks. Before serving slice into fourths and sprinkle with powder sugar. Serve with any fruit jam, such as strawberry, raspberry or blueberry!

182. Dotties Chicken And Broccoli Alfredo Recipe

Serving: 6 | Prep: | Cook: 30mins | Ready in:

Ingredients

- 9 ounces uncooked fettuccine
- 1 1/2 cup fresh or thawed and drained broccoli
- 3 tablespoons butter
- 1 1/2 pound skinless, boneless chicken breasts, cubed
- 1 1/2 (10-3/4 oz) can condensed cream of mushroom soup
- 3/4 cup milk
- 3/4 cup shredded parmesan cheese
- 1 cup sour cream
- 3/8 teaspoon ground white pepper
- 3/4 teaspoon salt, or to taste

Direction

- Cook fettuccine noodles to desired doneness.
- Add broccoli the last 4 minutes.
- Drain well.
- In a non-stick skillet over medium-high heat, heat butter.
- Add chicken and cook until brown and juices run clear.
- Stirring often.
- Add soup, milk, cheese, sour cream, pepper and fettuccine mixture.
- Cook through until smooth and hot.
- Stir constantly.

- Serve and enjoy with crusty bread to soak up all the sauce.

183. EASY Crunchy Honey Chicken Nuggets Recipe

Serving: 4 | Prep: | Cook: 17mins | Ready in:

Ingredients

- 1 pound skinless, boneless chicken breasts, cut into 1 or 1 1/2 inch bite-size pieces
- 1/4 cup honey (slightly warmed)
- 1/4 cup water
- 1 cup crushed corn flakes
- Additional honey for dipping.

Direction

- Preheat the oven to 425F.
- In small bowl combine honey and water.
- Place corn flakes in a shallow bowl.
- Dip chicken strips into honey mixture, then coat with corn flake crumbs.
- Put on a lightly greased baking sheet. Bake for 15-17 minutes, or until cooked at center, turning chicken over at halfway point.
- Serve with additional honey for a dipping sauce if desired

184. Easy Chicken Scampi Recipe

Serving: 6 | Prep: | Cook: 30mins | Ready in:

Ingredients

- 2 cloves garlic, finely chopped
- 1 tsp. dry mustard
- 1 tsp. salt
- 1/2 tsp. pepper
- 4 tbls. parsley, chopped

- 1/4 tsp. oregano, dried
- 1/4 tsp. basil, dried
- 1/4 cup lemon juice
- 1/2 cup olive oil
- 1 1/2 lb. boneless, skinless chicken breast, cut into 1 inch chunks
- 1/2 cup seasoned bread crumbs
- Box of linguine

Direction

- Preheat oven to 350
- In 9 inch baking dish, add first 9 ingredients
- Add chicken and coat with marinade
- Cover and put in fridge for 2 hours
- Sprinkle with bread crumbs
- Bake 30 minutes
- Cook Linguine according to box directions
- Serve chicken Scampi over linguine

185. Easy Chicken Stir Fry Recipe

Serving: 0 | Prep: | Cook: | Ready in:

Ingredients

- 1 bag of frozen stir fry, your choice
- 6 servings of brown or white rice
- 4 tbl soy sauce
- 4 tbl sugar
- 2 - 3 chicken breast, cubed

Direction

- In a pan, cook rice as directed.
- In a fry pan, cook stir fry as directed.
- In a pan or fry pan, boil cubed chicken in water till done.
- On medium heat, in fry pan, mix rice, stir fry, and chicken.
- Add soy sauce and sugar, stir until blended, remove from heat.
- I have tried it wrapped in a soft tortilla and it was good that way as well.

186. Easy Chicken And Noodles Recipe

Serving: 8 | Prep: | Cook: 20mins | Ready in:

Ingredients

- 4 cups (Small bag of coleslaw)
- 1/2lb-1lb chicken breast (cut into strips)
- 1 small red bell pepper
- 1 small green bell pepper
- 1 small onion
- 2 packages of chicken flavored ramen noodles (broken apart)
- soy sauce
- 2 tbsp. vegetable oil
- black pepper(optional)

Direction

- Cut bell peppers and onions into preferred size of slices. Set aside.
- In skillet add 1 tbsp. veg. Oil. Heat on medium temperature.
- Add chicken. Cook chicken until most of it is white on the outside. Add bell peppers and onions. Cook until chicken is done and peppers and onions are heated, yet still crispy.
- While that is cooking, you can prepare the noodles in a separate pan, saving the noodle seasoning.
- After the chicken and peppers are done, set aside and cover in a bowl.
- Add the remaining 1 tbsp. Of veg. Oil to skillet.
- Add 4 cups of coleslaw and stir fry until heated completely. Remove from heat.
- Drain noodles.
- Add noodles, chicken and peppers, and coleslaw into a large bowl or pan. Stir until mixed.
- Add chicken flavored ramen noodle seasoning.
- Stir.

- Add desired amount of soy sauce. Approx. 1/8-1/4 of a cup. It depends on your taste.
- Add pepper (opt.)

187. Easy Elegant Cheesy Chicken Recipe

Serving: 4 | Prep: | Cook: 30mins | Ready in:

Ingredients

- 4 bonless chicken breasts
- 1C cheddar cheese
- 8 fresh asparagus spears (i iike to use 2 or 3 in each chicken breast but it depends on the size of the asparagus,,, if it is big i only use 1)
- lemon pepper
- toothpicks or butcher string to hold/tie chicken together

Direction

- Cut pockets into your chicken breast as you do for stuffing them (in the thick side) being careful not to cut through.
- Stuff with two pieces of asparagus and with a generous portion of shredded cheese.
- Roll the chicken and tie with two pieces of butcher string one on the top and on the bottom of the chicken breast, or hold together with two or three toothpicks.
- Sprinkle generously with lemon pepper (or your other favorite seasonings) and bake with open side up for 30-40 mins at 350 until juices run clear.

188. Easy Sunday Afternoon Chicken Recipe

Serving: 6 | Prep: | Cook: 60mins | Ready in:

Ingredients

- 4 boneless, skinless chicken breasts
- 1 can cream of chicken soup
- 1/2 can water
- 1 1/2 tsp curry powder
- 2 T lemon juice
- 1 cup cheddar, grated
- 1 cup chicken broth
- 1 8 oz package stuffing mix

Direction

- Preheat oven to 350°
- Lay chicken breasts in a 9x13" casserole dish
- Combine soup and water in a small bowl
- Pour the soup mixture over the chicken
- Mix the remaining ingredients into the stuffing mix
- Spread the stuffing mix over the chicken.
- Bake 1 hour
- If the stuffing gets too brown, cover loosely with aluminum foil.

189. Electric Skillet Chicken Recipe

Serving: 4 | Prep: | Cook: 55mins | Ready in:

Ingredients

- 6 chicken breasts, skinned & deboned
- 1/4 cup oil
- 1 bell pepper
- 1 large onion
- 1 can tomatoes with green chilies
- 1 can cream of chicken soup
- 1 small can tomatoes
- salt & pepper
- angel hair pasta or rice

Direction

- Brown chicken in electric skillet in oil. Slice peppers and onions in rings. Add to skillet, cover and steam about 10 minutes. Stir in other ingredients, except pasta. Simmer on low heat until chicken is tender. Serve over pasta or rice.

190. Elegant Chicken Recipe

Serving: 8 | Prep: | Cook: 60mins | Ready in:

Ingredients

- 6 boneless, skinless chicken breasts, cut into bite-sized pieces
- 1 sm. can sliced water chestnuts, drained
- 6 slices Swiss or cheddar cheese
- 2 cans cream of chicken soup
- 1 box chicken-flavor Stove Top stuffing
- 1 stick butter or margarine, melted

Direction

- Preheat oven to 350°F. Grease 13" x 9" glass dish and layer chicken (uncooked) on bottom. Sprinkle water chestnuts over chicken. Cover with cheese slices. Top with soup and sprinkle dry stuffing mix over soup. Drizzle melted butter or margarine over all. Lay foil over top, but don't seal. Bake approximately one hour or until chicken is cooked through.
- Serve with steamed green beans or a lightly dressed green salad.

191. Farmhouse Chicken And Dumplings Recipe

Serving: 4 | Prep: | Cook: 1hours31mins | Ready in:

Ingredients

- 2 bone-in split chicken breasts
- 2 quarts water
- 2 stalks celery, cut in half (to be removed later, or sliced thinly if you plan on leaving it in. I remove it.)
- 2 medium carrots, cut in large pieces (to be removed later, or sliced thinly if you plan on leaving it in. I remove it.)
- 1/2 cup coarse chopped onion
- 1 tsp salt, or more to taste
- 1/2 tsp. dried parsley (or 2 tsp. fresh chopped)
- 1/2 tsp pepper, or more to taste
- DUMPLINGS
- 2 cups self-rising flour
- 1/4 tsp. ground pepper
- 1/2 tsp. dried parsley
- 1/4 cup butter or margarine
- 3/4 cup broth, cooled (taken from that used to cook chicken)
- 1/2 cup extra flour for dusting cut dumplings
- OR
- 2 cups all purpose flour
- 2 tsp. baking powder
- 1/2 tsp. salt
- 1/4 tsp. ground pepper
- 1/2 tsp. dried parsley
- 1/4 cup butter or margarine
- 3/4 cup broth, cooled (taken from that used to cook chicken)
- 1/2 cup extra flour for dusting cut dumplings

Direction

- Place chicken in large stew pot or Dutch oven
- Add celery, carrots, salt, pepper and water
- Bring to a boil, then reduce to low simmer and cover
- Cook until chicken is done, about 30 mins, depending on size of breasts
- Remove chicken when done and allow to cool until comfortable to handle
- Remove 3/4 cup of broth and allow to cool while you bone and cut/shred chicken and start the dumplings
- Remove bone and skin from chicken and cut or shred into bite-sized pieces and set aside
- Remove and discard carrots/celery. (Skip this step if you want more of a vegetable chicken stew. personally, I don't care for them in chicken and dumplings) the onions will mostly be in tiny bits and really add to the final dish

- *******
- Dumplings
- Add pepper and dried parsley to flour, mixing well (or flour, baking powder, salt if not using self-rising flour)
- Add 3/4 cup reserved and cooled broth, stirring until moistened and workable.
- Turn onto floured surface, handling the dough gently, and pat into a little over a 1/4 inch thick rectangle.
- Dust with some of the remaining flour
- Cut into roughly 1 1/2 x 1 1/2 inch squares. (I use a pizza cutter)
- Turn up heat and let broth come to a boil while you're dredging the dumplings.
- *Adding the dumplings is a quick process, not a difficult one, so make sure you have all of them dusted in flour and ready to drop into the broth*
- Dredge each dumpling in the remaining flour to coat each cut side and replace on floured surface, or add them one at a time to a small bowl with the flour in it, until all are in the bowl. The main thing is to get them all ready quickly. Coating them helps to thicken the broth as the dumplings cook
- When broth is boiling, drop each dumpling, one at a time, stirring gently while you are quickly adding the dumplings.
- When all are in, lower heat to simmer, cover tightly and allow dumplings to cook about 6-8 mins, until they have risen and float. DO NOT OVERCOOK if you want them light and fluffy inside. Size and thickness will affect cooking time.
- Add boned, cut up chicken, stir in remaining parsley and serve immediately.
- * PLEASE!!!!!! Don't be scared off by the instructions for the dumplings. I just want to stress the fact that having them all ready to go into the boiling broth is essential to get them all done at the same time. It's not hard, it's just a matter of having all of them ready before you add the first one. Pick whatever works best for you... either laying them back onto the floured surface or keeping them all in a bowl with the flour so you can stir them around before you start to drop them into the broth. If there is anything unclear, please let me know. I hope you enjoy this as much as we do!
- You can save some time by cooking the chicken ahead of time, even the day before and just throw the dumplings together when you're ready to eat. If I do this, I heat the chicken in a tiny bit of the broth before stirring it in after the dumplings are done.

192. Focaccia Chicken Sandwich Recipe

Serving: 6 | Prep: | Cook: | Ready in:

Ingredients

- 3 skinless and boneless chicken breast halves
- 2 tablespoons prepared brown mustard
- 2 cups broccoli florets
- 2 cups shredded mozzarella cheese
- 1 loaf focaccia bread (cut in half horizontally)

Direction

- Preheat your oven to 350F (175C). Spread the mustard onto the breasts, and put them in a baking dish. Bake them for approximately 30 minutes or until the juices run clear.
- While that is baking, boil 1/2 inch of water in a small saucepan with a lid. Add in your broccoli florets and cook for approximately 7 minutes (tender and bright green when ready). Drain this and set it aside.
- Shred (or cube) your chicken, and put in the bottom half of the focaccia bread. Spread out the broccoli on the chicken and top it off with your mozzarella.
- Bake this part of the sandwich (bottom part NOT the top) for approximately 10 minutes (the cheese should be melted when good). Place top of bread over the filling and pop back into the oven to bake for an extra 5 minutes to heat. Cut into smallish squares and serve.

193. Foil Baked Garden Chicken Recipe

Serving: 2 | Prep: | Cook: 60mins | Ready in:

Ingredients

- 2 Boneless skinless indivdual chicken breasts (I used organic chicken)
- One weighed 1/2 lb and the other was 1/4 lb
- I Small sliced onion enough to cover the top of the chicken
- (I used a red onion and not all of it)
- 4 or 5 mushrooms or more sliced (optional)
- A few slices of zucchini small or medium sized (optional)
- A couple of slices of swiss cheese, mozzarella or cheese you enjoy. Low fat cheese will work too!
- 1 sliced and chopped tomato or a few cherry tomatoes sliced
- 1 sliced and chopped red bell pepper or any other colour is fine.
- 1 1/4 teaspoon parsley chopped or dried
- 1/4 teaspoon garlic powder
- 1 1/4 teaspoon oregano chopped or dried. basil works well also
- A drizzle of light olive oil or flavoured oil of you choice or balsamic vinegar would do very nicely instead of the oil too.
- Pam or whatever non stick spray brand you use.
- salt and pepper to taste
- You could also use sliced peppers as a suggestion but I omitted them this time.

Direction

- Preheat oven to 350F
- Cover an oven proof pan like a 9"x9" cake pan with foil fitting it flat to the bottom and to the edges one way and then another sheet on top of that the other way. Spray the foil evenly with Pam and place the cleaned patted dry chicken breasts on top of the foil in the center of the pan. Sprinkle the chicken with a bit of garlic powder, parsley, oregano and salt and pepper.
- Now from here on is just a guideline. I have done this several ways such as leaving the cheese off it until the last 10 minutes so it melts nicely that works well too.
- Top the chicken with zucchini slices evenly, then onion, mushrooms, peppers, cheese and top with sliced tomatoes. Sprinkle with a bit of garlic powder, parsley, oregano, salt and pepper again. Drizzle the top with a bit of oil or balsamic vinegar. Wrap up the foil sealing it like a little package. If the amount of foil doesn't cover it totally cover with an additional piece of foil. Bake for approximately 35 to 45 minutes and remove from the oven. Carefully open the foil to expose the chicken and place back in the oven for approximately 10 more minutes until done.
- Serve immediately. Clean up is a breeze just toss the foil in the garbage when it has cooled down but be careful there will be lots of juice from the veggies on the bottom of the foil.

194. Foil Pack Chicken Fajita Dinner Recipe

Serving: 4 | Prep: | Cook: 35mins | Ready in:

Ingredients

- 1-1/2 cups instant white rice, uncooked
- 1-1/2 cups hot water
- 1 Tbsp. TACO BELL® HOME ORIGINALS® taco seasoning Mix
- 4 small boneless skinless chicken breast halves (1 lb.)
- 1 each green and red pepper, cut into strips
- 1 jalepeno pepper, seeded and sliced thinnly
- 1/2 cup TACO BELL® HOME ORIGINALS® Thick 'N chunky salsa 1/2 cup KRAFT Mexican Style Finely Shredded taco cheese

- sour cream, garnish

Direction

- Heat oven to 400°F.
- Fold up all sides of each of 4 large sheets of heavy-duty foil to form 1-inch rim; spray with cooking spray. Combine rice, water and taco seasoning; spoon onto foil. Top with remaining ingredients.
- Bring up foil sides. Double fold top and ends to seal each packet, leaving room for heat circulation inside. Place in 15x10x1-inch pan.
- Bake 30 to 35 min. or until chicken is done (165°F). Let stand 5 min. Cut slits in foil to release steam before opening packets.
- Garnish with sour cream, if desired.
- Nutrition Information
- Calories 350
- Total fat 8g
- Saturated fat
- 3.5 g Cholesterol
- 80 mg Sodium
- 510 mg Carbohydrate
- 37 g Dietary fibre
- 2 g Sugars
- 3 g Protein
- 31 g Vitamin A
- 25 %DV Vitamin C
- 70 %DV Calcium
- 15 %DV Iron

195. French Country Chicken Dinner Recipe

Serving: 4 | Prep: | Cook: 60mins | Ready in:

Ingredients

- For the chicken
- 4 boneless, skinless chicken breast halves
- 1/2 cup white flour
- salt and pepper
- 1 Tbl butter
- 1 Tbl olive oil
- For the vegetables and sauce
- 1 Tbl butter
- 1 Tbl olive oil
- 1 Tbl fresh thyme leaves removed from the stems
- 4 regular sized carrots cut on the diagonal into 1" slices
- 2 cups frozen tiny onions (right from the freezer bag)
- 1 cup white wine (dry is preferable)
- 1/2 cup chicken broth
- One pound small potatoes cut into halves or quarters; depending on how large the potatoes are
- 3/4 cup of creme fraiche *
- 1 cup frozen baby peas (the ones without the butter sauce)
- 1 cup grated gruyere cheese (large grate is fine)

Direction

- Preheat oven to 350 degrees F.
- To coat chicken I put the flour in a zip lock bag.
- Add a few shakes of salt and pepper and then put in each piece of chicken, one at a time
- Shake it around until it's coated and remove it and set it aside.
- When you have all of your chicken coated, get out a large sauté pan and add the butter and olive oil.
- Heat so the butter melts and add the chicken, smooth breast side down. Sauté on medium high until the first side of the chicken is a nice, crisp, golden brown. This should take about 5 minutes.
- Then turn the chicken over and slightly brown the underside. You are not trying to cook the chicken all the way through. You are just browning it. When this is done place the chicken breasts in an oven proof 9 X 13 pan and put it in your 350-degree oven. The chicken will finish now by baking for 30 minutes. This process gives the chicken a nice

crunch on the outside and your chicken will remain moist on the inside.
- For the veggies and sauce
- In a medium sized soup pot put in the butter and olive oil. Heat on medium till the butter melts.
- Add the thyme, carrots, and onions. Sauté and stir just until the mixture starts to loosen.
- Now add the wine and chicken broth and potatoes.
- Turn to medium high to get this mixture bubbling and then turn to medium and let it simmer. Cover the pot to keep the moisture inside.
- Open periodically to stir but otherwise let this mixture cook the potatoes and veggies.
- It will also begin to reduce so you have a rich sauce. If you get too close to running out of liquid you can add more wine and broth, but this should not be necessary unless your burner is running too hot.
- You'll know when this mixture is done by poking the potatoes and carrots. If they are soft, it's ready.
- While this mixture is cooking, boil your peas in a separate pan in water. Follow package directions. When they are finished just hold them aside until the meal is ready.
- Add the crème fraiche to the veggies and stir. Turn off. You now have a savory, rich sauce coating your vegetables.
- Pull the chicken out of the oven. Check one of the pieces of chicken to make sure you have no pink in the middle and then you are ready to serve. Put veggies and sauce on the plate. Add the chicken on top. Drain the peas and sprinkle on top of the chicken, and let them roll off. Cooking the peas separately leaves them a nice, vibrant green; instead of being coated in sauce. Sprinkle on the Gruyére and serve.
- * If you cannot find Crème Fraiche, you can make your own. Add a small amount of cultured buttermilk or sour cream to normal heavy cream, and allowing to stand for several hours at room temperature until the bacterial cultures act on the cream. For this recipe, I would add about a teaspoon of buttermilk or sour cream to a 3/4 cup minus 1 teaspoon heavy cream. I prefer to use the buttermilk, as crème fraiche is not as sour as sour cream.

196. Fried Lumpia Recipe

Serving: 0 | Prep: | Cook: 2hours | Ready in:

Ingredients

- - lean ground pork
- - chicken breast fillet, shredded
- - shrimp, diced OR crab meat, shredded OR both
- - singkamas (jicama) OR water chestnut, thinly sliced
- - tomato sauce or paste
- - lumpia wrapper
- - garlic, minced
- - onion, minced
- - cooking oil
- - salt
- - pepper

Direction

- In a large wok, heat oil and sauté onion and garlic until fragrant. Add ground pork and cook until no longer pinkish. Add shredded chicken and shrimp (and/or crab meat) and cook until shrimp turns pink. Add singkamas or water chestnut. Then add tomato sauce or paste. Mix well. Add salt and pepper to taste. Make sure you are constantly stirring the mixture all this time to avoid the ingredients from getting stuck together or from getting clunky. Once done, set aside to let the mixture cool down. Also, try to drain excess sauce. Then scoop a little portion and wrap in lumpia wrapper. Fry until golden brown.

197. Garlic Chicken Breasts Recipe

Serving: 1 | Prep: | Cook: 50mins | Ready in:

Ingredients

- 1/2 cup grated Parmesan cheese
- 1 envelope garlic and herb or Italian salad dressing mix
- 2 boneless skinless chicken breast halves (6 ounces each)

Direction

- In a large resealable plastic bag, combine cheese and dressing mix; add chicken. Seal bag and shake to coat.
- Place chicken in a greased 8-in. square baking dish. Bake, uncovered, at 400° for 20-25 minutes or until a thermometer reads 170°.
- Nutrition Facts
- 1 chicken breast half: 289 calories, 10g fat (5g saturated fat), 112mg cholesterol, 1668mg sodium, 5g carbohydrate (4g sugars, 0 fiber), 42g protein.

198. Garlic Garlic Chicken Recipe

Serving: 4 | Prep: | Cook: 30mins | Ready in:

Ingredients

- 2 tablespoons minced garlic
- 1/4 cup olive oil
- 1/4 cup dry bread crumbs
- 1/4 cup grated parmesan cheese
- 4 skinless, boneless chicken breast halves

Direction

- Preheat oven to 425 degrees F (220 degrees C).
- Warm the garlic and olive oil to blend the flavors in a small pan on low heat while the oven is preheating.
- In a separate dish, combine the bread crumbs and Parmesan cheese. Dip the chicken breasts in the olive oil and garlic mixture, then into the bread crumb mixture.
- Place in a shallow baking dish.
- Bake in the preheated oven for 30 to 35 minutes, until no longer pink and juices run clear.

199. Garlic Pecan Fried Chicken Recipe

Serving: 2 | Prep: | Cook: 20mins | Ready in:

Ingredients

- 1 lb boneless chicken breast
- 2 oz pecans
- 1 tsp salt
- 2 tsp spices (any of your choice)
- 4 cloves garlic
- 1/2 tsp grnd pepper
- 1 tsp sugar
- 1 cup buttermilk
- 3 cups flour
- 1/2 tsp garlic powder
- 1/2 tsp oregano
- 1/2 tsp grnd pepper
- 1 tsp salt
- vegetable shortening for frying

Direction

- Place the pecans, 1 tsp. salt, the spices, and the garlic
- Cloves, half the pepper, the sugar and the buttermilk in a blender. Pulse and blend until the garlic and pecans are chopped up very finely.
- Place the chicken in a nonreactive bowl and pour the buttermilk mix over it.

- Mix everything so that all the chicken is evenly coated.
- Place the bowl in the fridge and marinate for at least two hours and up to eight hours or more.
- Stir every once in a while.
- Get the flour coating ready.
- In a strong plastic food storage bag, or a doubled weak bag, place the flour and the remaining spices.
- Shake it up a bit to get things evenly mixed.
- Get your fry pan ready by heating enough shortening to reach halfway up your chicken pieces to a good fry temperature.
- It will be hot enough when a pinch of flour will sizzle a bit when dropped in.
- When you're ready, take a piece of chicken, making sure to coat it with buttermilk as much as you can, and place it in the bag of flour. Shake the bag to get the piece totally caked in flour. Doing this too much is better than not doing it enough.
- When it's good and caked, take the piece out and put it into the hot oil.
- Fry one side completely and then fry the other. Don't flip things back and forth.
- Don't crowd the pieces at all. Give them plenty of room. As each piece is done, drain it on paper towels.
- Cut open the first piece to make sure you're timing things right. Rinse, repeat.

200. Garlic Smothered Chicken Recipe

Serving: 4 | Prep: | Cook: 45mins | Ready in:

Ingredients

- 4 chicken breast
- olive oil
- 1 stick butter
- 1/4 cup thinly sliced garlic (about 8 to 10 cloves)
- 1 large white onion, chopped fine
- 4 oz. sliced or chopped fresh mushrooms
- 1 teaspoon fresh chopped basil
- dash creole seasoning
- dash cracked black pepper
- garlic salt
- salt

Direction

- Preheat oven to 375
- Generously season breast with garlic salt, salt and pepper.
- Drizzle olive oil in the bottom of a roasting pan.
- Place chicken in pan and bake for 30 minutes or until chicken is completely cooked.
- In skillet, heat butter over medium heat.
- Add garlic slices and sauté' 2 to 3 minutes.
- Stir in mushrooms and onions and cook until onions are transparent (about 3 to 4 minutes)
- Add fresh basil and a dash of creole seasoning and cracked black pepper.
- Remove chicken from oven.
- Pour garlic sauce over chicken and return chicken to oven.
- Lower heat to 350 and continue to cook for 5 minutes.
- Remove from oven.
- Serve over cooked rice or pasta.

201. Garlicky Chicken Pasta With Veggies Recipe

Serving: 6 | Prep: | Cook: 15mins | Ready in:

Ingredients

- 1 box bow tie pasta
- 1 T butter
- 1 T olive oil
- 3 pinches kosher salt
- 3 T olive oil
- 2 T butter

- 1 package skinlesss, boneless chicken breast tenderloins
- 1 med white onion, rough chopped
- 1/2 red bell pepper, chopped
- 3-4 heaping forksful chopped garlic
- 3/4 tub chopped fresh mushrooms
- 1 small tub grape tomatoes
- 3 handsful frozen chopped spinach (I buy it in the bag, and just reach in a get what I need. Probably half of a 10 oz box).
- italian seasoning
- Seasoned salt
- garlic pepper
- red pepper flakes
- 1/2 c Parmesan
- chicken stock or wine
- Add'l parmesan, olive oil, butter as needed
- ** About 1/4 c sour cream, and 6-8 oz of cream cheese are great additions for creamier sauce. You could also add a bechamel sauce, or cream of mushroom soup (or cream of celery, cream of chicken, etc.).

Direction

- Bring pot of water to boil, add olive oil, butter and kosher salt.
- When boiling add pasta
- Cook until al dente
- While pasta is cooking, cut chicken into bite sized pieces; chop onion, and pepper
- Add olive oil and butter to large skillet
- Add chicken, onion and red pepper to skillet
- Season with Italian Seasoning, Garlic Pepper and Seasoned Salt
- When chicken has cooked through, add spinach and mushrooms
- Add chicken broth to deglaze. (White wine could also be used)
- Stir in pasta, cheese, red pepper flakes and grape tomatoes

202. George Foreman Awesome Chicken Sandwich Recipe

Serving: 4 | Prep: | Cook: 15mins | Ready in:

Ingredients

- 4 boneless chicken breast
- olive oil
- coarse salt
- fresh ground pepper
- avo classic spicy guacamole
- swiss cheese
- lettuce
- tomato
- 4 sandwich bun

Direction

- Pre-heat George Foreman Grill.
- Wash & dry chicken breasts.
- Dip in olive both sides.
- Salt & Pepper.
- Place chicken on grill and grill for 5 minute on one side then flip and grill another 5 minute.
- Take chicken off then slice each chicken in half lengthwise and place on bun.
- Top with Swiss cheese.
- Then guacamole.
- Then tomato & lettuce.
- Enjoy!

203. Ginger Black Sesame Chicken Recipe

Serving: 2 | Prep: | Cook: 25mins | Ready in:

Ingredients

- 1 tsp ginger juice
- 1/2 tsp wasbi powder
- 3 cloves garlic, minced
- 2 tbsps lime juice

- 1 tbsp black sesame seeds
- salt
- 2 chicken breasts

Direction

- Combine first 6 ingredients. Put chicken into a Ziploc bag and pour in the marinade.
- Seal the bag and squish to get the marinade to coat the chicken.
- Let it sit in the refrigerator for one hour or up to overnight.
- Grill until cooked through.

204. Glazed Chicken Recipe

Serving: 46 | Prep: | Cook: 42mins | Ready in:

Ingredients

- 4-6 chicken breast -boneless, skinless
- 1 can campbell's golden mushroom soup
- 1-2 TBS. crushed sage
- 1 cup shredded cheddar cheese
- 2-3 green onions-chopped
- black pepper to taste

Direction

- Spray 9x13 baking dish with Crisco or pam.
- Arrange chicken breast in baking dish
- In mixing bowl combine soup, crushed sage, and 1/2 green onions, black pepper.
- Pour ingredients over chicken breast
- Sprinkle cheddar cheese over sauce, top with remaining green onions.
- Bake uncovered 30 minutes at 400 degree oven.
- If using bone in chicken then bake for 55 min.
- Serve with white rice or mash potatoes.

205. Grandma's No Peek Chicken Casserole Recipe

Serving: 6 | Prep: | Cook: 1hours | Ready in:

Ingredients

- 4 boneless skinless chicken breasts
- 1 cup long grain rice
- 1 can golden mushroom soup
- 1 packet of Lipton Onion Soup Mix
- 1 can of water (use empty soup can)
- salt and pepper to taste

Direction

- Whisk together soup, soup mix, salt and pepper and water together.
- Stir in rice.
- Lay chicken breast over rice mixture and bake at 350 degrees for 1 hour or until chicken done.

206. Greek Chicken Breasts Recipe

Serving: 4 | Prep: | Cook: 10mins | Ready in:

Ingredients

- 4 skinless, boneless chicken breasts, pounded to uniform thickness
- 1 tablespoon Greek seasoning
- 1 or 2 tomatoes, sliced
- ¼ cup crumbled feta cheese
- 1 tablespoon pine nuts, toasted (see note)

Direction

- Preheat oven to 350 F.
- Sprinkle chicken with Greek seasoning. In a large, lightly oiled skillet over medium-high heat, add chicken and brown on both sides, 3 to 5 minutes per side. Transfer to a baking pan or rimmed baking sheet. Top each breast with tomato slices and sprinkle with feta and pine

nuts. Bake 10 minutes or until heated through. Makes 4 servings.
- Note: To toast pine nuts, place in a small skillet over medium-high heat. Shake skillet occasionally. When lightly browned and fragrant, pine nuts are done.
- PER SERVING: Calories 228 (27% fat) Fat 7 g (2 g sat) Cholesterol 98 mg Sodium 558 mg Fiber 1 g Carbohydrates 3 g Protein 36 g

207. Greek Chicken Recipe

Serving: 4 | Prep: | Cook: 480mins | Ready in:

Ingredients

- 4 chicken breasts/skinless,boneless
- 1 medium head of cabbage,quartered
- 1 lb. carrots cut into `1 inch pieces
- water to cover all.
- 4 cubes chicken boullion
- 1 tsp. poultry seasoning.
- 1/4 tsp. Greek style seasoning
- 2 tbsp. cornstarch
- 1/4 cup water

Direction

- Rinse chicken and place in crockpot.
- Rinse the cabbage place on top of the chicken, then add the carrots.
- Cover all this with the water.
- Add bouillon cubes and sprinkle liberally with poultry seasoning.
- Add Greek seasoning to taste.
- Cook on low for 8 hours or on high for 4 hours.
- TO MAKE GRAVY:
- When ready to eat, pour off some of the juice and place into a saucepan.
- Bring it to a boil.
- Dissolve corn starch in about 1/4 cup of water and add to the saucepan.
- SIMMER all together until thick.
- Serve the gravy over chicken and vegetables.

- Make some mashed potatoes or rice to combine with others.

208. Greek Chicken In The Crockpot Recipe

Serving: 5 | Prep: | Cook: 68mins | Ready in:

Ingredients

- 4 + chicken breasts (depending on how many you're cooking for)
- 1/4 cup olive oil
- 1 cup lemon juice
- 4 cloves garlic, minced
- 1 tsp oregano
- 1 tsp seasoned salt (or regular)
- 1/2 tsp salt
- 1/2 tsp pepper

Direction

- Place chicken in crock pot
- Whisk all other ingredients in bowl and pour over chicken.
- Cook for 6-8 hours on low.

209. Greek Gods Pasta Salad With Marinated Chicken Breast Recipe

Serving: 6 | Prep: | Cook: 40mins | Ready in:

Ingredients

- 4 cups drained and cooled rotini
- 2 chicken breasts, grilled or sauted
- (Marinated overnight in 2 Tbsp olive oil, 2 cloves crushed garlic, 2 Tbsp lemon juice, 2 tsp oregano flakes, and ½ tsp dry mint)
- ½ cup finely chopped sweet red bell pepper
- ½ fine chopped sweet green bell pepper

- ½ cup finely chopped green onion
- 2 tsp dry basil
- 1 tsp fresh ground black pepper
- salt to taste
- 2 cloves crushed garlic
- ½ cup pitted sliced kalamata olives
- 1/3 cup good mayonnaise
- 3 Tbsp extra virgin olive oil
- 1 Tbsp fresh lemon juice
- feta cheese

Direction

- Marinate chicken breasts overnight in olive oil, garlic, lemon, oregano and mint in a covered container.
- Grill or sauté over medium heat until tender and juices run clear. Remove from heat and cool in refrigerator.
- In a large bowl, combine cooked rotini, chopped peppers, chopped green onion, and chopped olives.
- Add garlic, oregano, basil and black pepper.
- Add salt.
- Add mayonnaise, olive oil and lemon juice.
- Toss gently.
- Arrange rotini salad in a decorative shallow salad dish and decorate the top with cooked chicken breasts, which have been cut into strips.
- Crumble feta cheese over chicken
- Serve with Grecian bread and pepperoncini

210. Green Curry Recipe

Serving: 4 | Prep: | Cook: 15mins | Ready in:

Ingredients

- 4 chicken breasts (boneless- skinless)
- 1cup coconut cream
- 1/4 cup green curry paste
- 3 cups coconut milk
- 1-1/2 cups yam or sweet potato, diced
- 2 Tbsp. fish sauce
- 1 Tbsp. brown sugar
- salt to taste
- 1/2 Tbsp. cilantro leaves
- 3 red chiles
- 1/2 cup basil leaves
- plain yogurt

Direction

- Cut the meat into large bite-sized pieces; reserve.
- In a medium saucepan, warm the coconut cream over medium heat until it boils gently. Adjust heat to maintain a gentle boil and cook for 6-8 minutes, stirring occasionally. The coconut cream should become fragrant as it cooks. When tiny pools of oil glisten on the surface, add the curry paste and stir to dissolve. Continue cooking for 1-2 minutes.
- Add the chicken pieces; stir to coat evenly. Continue cooking for about 2 more minutes. Increase heat and add the coconut milk, yams, fish sauce, sugar, and salt; stir well.
- Stir in the cilantro and chilies. Adjust heat to maintain an active gentle boil; cook for 8-10 minutes, stirring occasionally. Taste and adjust the seasoning with more fish sauce, sugar, or curry paste. When the chicken is done and the yams are tender, remove from the heat - - if it's too hot, you can use yogurt to cut the heat a bit.
- At this point, transfer to a serving bowl. Serve with white rice
- Garnish with additional basil and cilantro leaves.

211. Grilled Almond Chicken With Savory Plum Sauce Recipe

Serving: 2 | Prep: | Cook: 20mins | Ready in:

Ingredients

- 1 egg
- 1/4 cup cornstarch

- 2 tablespoons soy sauce
- 1 large garlic clove minced
- 2 whole boneless skinless chicken breasts cut into strips
- 2-1/2 cups finely chopped almonds lightly toasted
- 2 tablespoons minced dried or fresh parsley
- 4 fresh plums halved and pitted
- 1 teaspoon chopped fresh tarragon
- savory Plum Sauce:
- 1 cup plum preserves
- 1/2 cup prepared chutney chopped
- 2 cloves garlic minced
- 2 tablespoons brown sugar
- 2 tablespoons lemon juice
- 2 teaspoons soy sauce
- 2 teaspoons minced fresh ginger

Direction

- Combine egg, cornstarch, soy sauce and garlic in plastic bag.
- Add chicken pieces and marinate 15 minutes then drain well.
- Place almonds and parsley in plastic bag.
- Place chicken pieces a few at a time in almond mixture.
- Shake thoroughly.
- Grill over medium direct heat for 8 minutes.
- Spoon plum sauce over chicken.
- To make sauce combine all ingredients in saucepan.
- Cook and stir over medium until preserves melt.

212. Grilled Bacon Wrapped Chicken Breast Recipe

Serving: 4 | Prep: | Cook: 40mins | Ready in:

Ingredients

- 3 lbs. of chicken breasts cut to about 1/2 pound per serving. (I just cut the side of a full breast in half)
- 1 lbs. sliced hickory bacon
- black pepper to taste.
- For the sauce.
- 5 cups of your favorite BBQ sauce.
- 3/4 cup of Italian dressing
- 1 cup of brown sugar.
- 1 medium onion diced
- water as needed

Direction

- To make the sauce combine all the sauce ingredients and simmer for 30 minutes on low/medium heat. The object is to get the sauce to about the consistency of tomato sauce from a can. Use a little water to achieve this.
- While the sauce is on the grill. Take each slice of bacon and run it through your thumb and for-finger, pinching it as you go along. This will make it longer.
- Wrap each breast half with the 1 slice of bacon.
- Lay them out on a cookie sheet and sprinkle with black pepper.
- Grill on a medium flame, turning occasionally as to not burn.
- When the chicken appears to be almost done, reduce flame to low and with a set of tongs dip each breast into the basting sauce and place on the top shelf of the grill and cover. If you don't have a top shelf then make sure you place them off the flame to finish off.
- Redip each breast in the sauce every 10 minutes, rotating the cooking side and place on the grill. Let them finish off for 30 minutes total time off direct flame.

213. Grilled Chicken Roller Recipe

Serving: 1 | Prep: | Cook: 20mins | Ready in:

Ingredients

- 1 small boneless, skinless chicken breast half (1/4 lb.)
- 1 American cheese slice or whatever kind of cheese you want
- 1 slice center cut bacon
- 1 Tbs balsamic vinaigrette dressing

Direction

- Heat grill to medium heat. Pound chicken to 1/4" thickness
- Top with cheese; roll up tightly. Wrap bacon around long sides of roll covering exposed cheese, stretching bacon as necessary to fit; secure with toothpicks.
- Grill 15 to 20 mins or till chicken is done (165) turning frequently and brushing with dressing the last 5 mins. Discard toothpicks before serving.
- Note: Can use 2 Tbs shredded cheese instead of slices.

214. Grilled Chicken With Curry Lime Sauce Recipe

Serving: 0 | Prep: | Cook: 5mins | Ready in:

Ingredients

- 4 grilled boneless, skinless chicken breasts
- 1/2 C reduced-fat sour cream
- 1 1/2 tbsp fresh lime juice
- 1 1/4 tsp curry powder
- 1/4 tsp garlic powder
- 1/4 tsp onion powder

Direction

- 1. In small bowl, whisk together the sour cream and lime juice. Add in the curry powder, garlic powder, and onion powder. Whisk until well-combined.
- 2. Spoon sauce over chicken. Enjoy!

215. Grilled Chicken With Portobello Mushroom Sauce Recipe

Serving: 4 | Prep: | Cook: 25mins | Ready in:

Ingredients

- 4 chicken breasts, boneless, skinless
- 2 Tablespoons butter
- 3/4 cup Portobello mushrooms, chopped
- 1/4 cup onions, diced
- 2 Tablespoons flour
- 2 cups milk
- salt and pepper to taste

Direction

- Melt the butter in a saucepan. Add the mushrooms and onion. Cook until just soft. Add the flour and cook for 3 minutes. Whisk in the milk and simmer for 20 minutes, stirring frequently. Check seasonings. Grill the chicken. Top with the warm sauce.

216. Grilled Chicken And Red Pepper Taco Recipe

Serving: 2 | Prep: | Cook: 8mins | Ready in:

Ingredients

- 1 1/2 lb boneless, skinless chicken breasts
- 2 red bell peppers roasted & peeled
- 2 stalks celery, washed and sliced
- 1 med red onion, peeled and chopped
- 1/2 c black beans (about 2, Cooked
- 1/4 c cilantro leaves, Chopped
- 1/4 c balsamic vinegar
- 1/4 c oil
- 1/4 c orange juice
- 1/4 c lime juice
- 2 cloves garlic, peeled and minced

- 1 t coriander seed, Ground
- 1/2 t pepper
- 1/2 t salt
- 1/4 c sour cream (or non-fat -yogurt)
- 6 (8-in) flour tortillas

Direction

- Preheat your grill. Pound the chicken breasts to an even thickness, and grill or broil on both sides until cooked through, but not dried out, about 4 minutes on a side.
- It makes sense to grill the peppers at the same time. Slice, and set aside.
- Combine the bell peppers, celery, onion, black beans and cilantro in a mixing bowl.
- Combine the vinegar, oil, orange juice, lime juice, garlic, coriander, pepper.
- Combine with salt and sour cream or yogurt in a jar with a tight-fitting lid. Shake well, and pour the dressing over the vegetables. Marinate the vegetables for 1 hour at room temperature. Do not marinate the vegetables for more than 1 hour.
- Place a large skillet over medium heat, and grill the tortillas for 30 seconds on a side to soften.
- To serve, divide the chicken among the tortillas, placing it at the center of the tortilla. Divide the vegetables and their dressing on top of the chicken, and roll the tortilla into a cylinder.

217. Grilled Cumin Chicken With Fresh Tomatillo Sauce Recipe

Serving: 4 | Prep: | Cook: 20mins | Ready in:

Ingredients

- 2tsp olive oil
- 1/2tsp ground cumin
- 1/8 tsp pepper
- 2 garlic cloves, minced
- 4 skinless, boneless chicken breast halves
- 1/2lb tomatillos
- 1/2c chicken broth
- 1/4c cilantro leaves
- 1/4c chopped green onion
- 2 tbs fresh lime juice
- 1/2tsp sugar
- 1/4tsp salt
- 1 garlic clove, chopped
- 1 jalapeno pepper, seeded and chopped
- 1/4 tsp salt
- cooking spray

Direction

- Combine first 4 ingredients in large bag. Add chicken, seal and let stand 15 mins.
- Discard husks and stems from tomatillos. Combine tomatillos and broth in small saucepan over med-high heat; cover and cook 8 mins. Drain; cool slightly. Combine tomatillos, cilantro and next 6 ingredients (through jalapenos) in food processor. Process till smooth.
- Remove chicken from bag; discard marinade. Sprinkle chicken evenly with 1/4tsp salt. Place on grill rack coated with spray; grill 6 mins. each side or till chicken is done. Serve with tomatillo sauce.

218. Grilled Lemon Thyme Chicken Breasts Recipe

Serving: 4 | Prep: | Cook: 35mins | Ready in:

Ingredients

- 4 teaspoons chopped fresh thyme leaves
- 1 tablespoon freshly grated lemon peel
- 2 teaspoons garlic salt
- 1/2 teaspoon pepper
- 4 boneless skinless chicken breasts (about 1 1/4 pounds)

Direction

- If using charcoal grill, place drip pan directly under grilling area, and arrange coals around edge of firebox. Spray grill rack with cooking spray. Heat coals or gas grill for indirect heat.
- In small bowl, mix all ingredients except chicken. Sprinkle mixture over chicken.
- Cover and grill chicken over drip pan or over unheated side of gas grill and 4 to 6 inches from medium-high heat 15 to 20 minutes, turning once, until juice of chicken is clear when center of thickest part is cut (170°F).
- Garnish with additional fresh thyme if desired.

219. HAWAIIAN CHILI Recipe

Serving: 8 | Prep: | Cook: 300mins | Ready in:

Ingredients

- 1 whole clove of garlic chopped
- 1 bottle of beer
- 1 can of tomatoes (large can)
- 2 large sweet vidalia onions (chopped fine)
- 3 bell peppers chopped fine
- 1 pineapple chopped finely
- 3 skinless chicken breasts (I also substitute pork loin)
- 1 can white kidney beans
- 2 large carrots chopped fine
- 3 stalks of celery chopped fine
- 2 jalapeno peppers chopped
- 2 tablespoons of cumin
- chili powder to taste
- 1/2 cup of soy sauce
- 1/4 cup of finely grated ginger root (fresh only)
- Lots of chopped basil
- 1 cup of honey
- water don't use stock ...I found that it doesn't add nor take away from the flavor so just use old fashioned water (just enough to cover)

Direction

- Put in a large pot in no particular order and simmer all day. Serve with Colby cheese or sour cream. This chili freezes great and becomes more mild the second day.

220. Harissa Grilled Chicken And Vegetables Recipe

Serving: 4 | Prep: | Cook: 30mins | Ready in:

Ingredients

- 2 large chicken breasts
- 1 tbsp olive oil
- 1 tbsp harissa
- 1/2 tsp dried thyme
- pepper
- 2 cups broccoli florets
- 1 large bell pepper, any color, cut into 1" strips
- 1 medium red onion, cut into small wedges
- About 2 cups summer squash, cut into 1/2" rounds
- 1 tbsp olive oil
- salt & pepper
- 1 tsp za'atar
- lemon juice
- olive oil

Direction

- Preheat lightly greased grill pan (or grill) over medium-high heat.
- Pound chicken breasts to about 1/2" thickness
- Mix harissa, 1 tbsp. oil, thyme and pepper and brush onto chicken pieces
- Grill chicken for about 4 minutes each side (reduce heat slightly). Remove chicken and set aside.
- Meanwhile, toss vegetables with olive oil, salt & pepper. Add to grill pan, in batches if necessary (you want them in a single layer to cook evenly) and grill about 5 minutes, turning occasionally, for about 5 minutes.

- Cut chicken into 3/4" slices and add to veggies in pan. Add zaatar and cook, stirring or shaking, to incorporate some of the harissa flavor onto the veggies.
- Garnish with a squeeze of lemon juice and drizzle of olive oil and serve.
- NOTES:
- Harissa is a spicy North African condiment - the one I used was prepared and contained hot peppers, smoked paprika, roasted red peppers, preserved lemon and spices such as coriander and cumin. There are many variations. Zaatar is a Middle Eastern spice blend - mine was thyme, sesame seeds and salt, but often other herbs are represented, such as sumac.

221. Hawaiian Chicken Parmigiana Recipe

Serving: 2 | Prep: | Cook: 20mins | Ready in:

Ingredients

- 2 chicken breast fillets
- 1 Lightly Beaten egg
- 2 Cups bread Crumbs
- 1 Cup Plain flour
- 4 tbp tomato ketchup
- Shaved English ham
- pineapple, cut into rings
- vegetable oil
- Grated cheese

Direction

- Lightly coat each chicken fillet in flour then dip into egg.
- Cover with breadcrumbs.
- Pan fry in hot oil.
- When golden brown, remove and place on baking dish.
- Spread each fillet with Ketchup, then layer with ham and pineapple.
- Sprinkle with cheese.
- Place under grill (broiler) until cheese is melted.
- Serve with corn and mash potatoes.

222. Hawaiian Chicken Recipe

Serving: 68 | Prep: | Cook: 45mins | Ready in:

Ingredients

- 3 to 4 boneless chicken breasts
- 1 tsp salt
- 1 1/2 instant rice, uncooked
- 3 1/2 oz of coconut
- 20 oz can pineapple chunks, drained (reserve liquid)
- 3/4 cup water
- 2 tsp lemon juice
- 4 Tbsp orange marmalade
- 4 Tbsp butter, melted
- 4Tbsp soy sauce
- 2 1/2 tsp ground ginger

Direction

- Cut chicken into 1" cubes and place half of the chicken into a large shallow baking dish.
- Sprinkle with 1/2 tsp salt.
- Sprinkle uncooked rice over chicken.
- Place the rest of the chicken over the rice layer.
- Sprinkle with remaining 1/2 tsp salt.
- Sprinkle with coconut and then layer pineapple chunks over coconut.
- Dot with marmalade.
- Mix water, lemon juice, and pineapple juice and pour over all.
- Pour melted butter and soy sauce all over baking dish.
- Sprinkle with ginger.
- Bake, covered, in a 350 degree oven for 40 minutes or until chicken and rice are done.
- Remove cover and brown in oven for 5 minutes.

223. Home Made Enchiladas Recipe

Serving: 6 | Prep: | Cook: 5mins | Ready in:

Ingredients

- Round corn tortillas
- chicken breast, Shredded meet, or cheese (whatever you want the inside to be)
- 10 Green tomatillos
- 5 Paste tomatoes make sure the color is truly red (not the big tomatoes)
- 3 Chiles Pasilla (if you want to only)
- 1 Jalapeño (add more if you like spicy)
- 2 cayenne Chiles (not powder)
- 1/2 of an onion
- 1 cup of cilantro
- 3 Cups of shredded Monterrey Jack cheese
- 1 avocado thinly sliced
- Thinly sliced lettuce
- oil (as needed)
- sour cream
- Knorr Mexican chicken powder stock or cubes

Direction

- First: You will cook in a sauce pan the: green tomatillos, tomatoes, chili pasilla, jalapeño, cayenne chilies, and onion. Once it's cooked remove the skin from the tomatoes and remove the insides (seeds and vain) from the pasilla chilies.
- Second: You will blend all ingredients together and add Knorr chicken power stock to taste and some of the water where you cooked the items.
- Third: You will add the cilantro and blend until it's finely chopped. Make sure that the sauce is not watery.
- Forth: In a frying pan add about 2 table spoons of oil & let it get warm/hot, put in the tortilla and turn don't let the tortilla get hard you only want to sauté/bathe it in the hot oil. Set it aside and add the shredded chicken (or whatever) and role. Continue this until you make as many as you need. (You will continue to add oil as you go and depending on how many enchiladas you are making)
- Fifth: Warm up another sauce pan and add 1 tbsp. of oil and let it get warm/hot then add the sauce to it and let it cook for about 2 to 3 minutes on medium high and turn off.
- Now you will put the enchiladas that you are eating on a plate and you will add the sauce on top (as many as you want) then add the shredded cheese and put in the micro or conventional oven for about 3 minutes or until the cheese is melted. (I usually add ½ of the sauce and put in the micro and when I take it out I add some more so that my enchiladas will be juicy and not dried up).
- Lastly: I add the avocado, lettuce and the sour cream on top of my enchiladas and they are ready to be eaten. You can add some buttered white rice as a side if you like.
- ENJOY ;D)…

224. Honey Orange Chicken Recipe

Serving: 2 | Prep: | Cook: 30mins | Ready in:

Ingredients

- for the chicken :
- 2 chicken breast cut into 1 inch pieces
- 1 cup of flour
- garlic salt, pepper
- for the sauce:
- 1/2 cup of honey
- 2 Tbs orange juice
- 2 Tbs sesame oil
- 2 Tbs rice vinegar
- red pepper flakes to taste
- 1 Tbs corn starch
- 1 Tbs water

Direction

- In a saucepan over medium heat, add the honey, sesame oil, red pepper flakes and rice vinegar. Whisk and bring to a boil.
- In a separate bowl stir together the cornstarch and water. Once the mixture is boiling, while continuing to whisk, slowly add the cornstarch mixture. Bring back to a boil and then turn down to simmer for 10 minutes.
- Remove from the heat and allow to finish thickening.
- Cut chicken into 1 inch pieces, put flour into a gallon zip bag, add garlic salt and pepper and shake.
- Meanwhile, heat just enough oil to cover the bottom of a heavy skillet over medium heat. Once the oil is hot cook the chicken, turning occasionally until golden and cooked through, about 3-5 minutes.
- Drain on a paper towel and then toss in the sauce and serve over sticky rice.

225. Idiot Chicken Recipe

Serving: 4 | Prep: | Cook: 35mins | Ready in:

Ingredients

- 4 boneless skinless chicken breasts
- Sauce:
- 1 (8 ounce) package Philadelphia cream cheese
- 1 (2 7/8 ounce) package Italian salad dressing mix
- 1 (10 ounce) can cream of chicken soup or cream of mushroom

Direction

- Beat all ingredients (other than chicken) together.
- Place chicken in sprayed pan. I use a 9x13 cake pan.
- Pour sauce mixture over chicken cover with foil. Cook at 375 degrees 35-40 minutes. I usually take the foil off for the last 5 minutes.
- Serve over rice or noodles.

226. Improved Chicken Divan Recipe

Serving: 4 | Prep: | Cook: 20mins | Ready in:

Ingredients

- 2 bunches brocolli
- 2 tbsp olive oil
- 1 chicken breast
- 1 can cream of mushroom soup
- 1/2 cup sour cream (fat free option works great too!)
- 1/2 cup mayo (fat free also!)
- juice of 1/2 lemon
- 3 tsp curry powder
- 1/2 cup cheddar cheese
- 1/4 cup bread crumbs
- 4 cups brown rice ((cooked)

Direction

- Preheat oven to 400 F. Put a chicken breast in a small baking dish, season with salt and pepper and bake for about 20 minutes. Let it cool
- Meanwhile in a bowl mix together cream of mushroom soup, sour cream, mayo, lemon juice and curry powder.
- Fill up a pan with 2 cups of water. Put cut up broccoli in it. Cover and let it cook for 10 minutes. After its cooked strain it.
- After the chicken is cooked and cooled, shred it.
- Mix chicken, chicken mushroom soup mixture and broccoli together. Put in in an 8x8 baking dish (or bigger!)
- Sprinkle cheese and bread crumbs on top and let it bake for 20 minutes at 400 F or until the mixture is bubbly and heated through.
- Don't forget to eat it over yummy brown rice!

227. Indian Curry Chicken Recipe

Serving: 2 | Prep: | Cook: 30mins | Ready in:

Ingredients

- 2 Tblsp of vegetable, sunflower or canola oil
- 2-3 Tblsp of curry powder (your own blend if possible) store bought is fine
- 1 Tblsp of white or brown sugar (more or less to taste)
- 1 (16oz.) can of coconut milk
- 1-2 garlic cloves (minced or paste)
- 1 inch piece of fresh ginger (minced or paste)
- 1 small onion (thinly sliced)
- 2 green chilies (seeded and chopped) OR 1 (4oz.) can of chopped chilies
- 1-2 medium potatoes (peeled and diced)
- 1 small tomato (seeded and chopped) if using canned drain and rinse them
- (1 1/2 lbs.) of boneless skinless chicken breast (cut into bite size pieces)
- salt & black pepper to taste

Direction

- Mix the oil, curry powder, garlic-ginger paste and onion in a glass mixing bowl and create some sort of a paste.
- Over medium heat put a 5 quart pan or just a large sauté pan and heat the condiment paste just until fragrant 3-4 minutes.
- (Your nose will lead the way, trust me on that)
- Add the chopped green chilies, the coconut milk, the sugar and stir to mix and dissolve the paste stirring in a slow rolling boil.
- (Taste the sauce to adjust flavors according to your personal taste).
- Bring in the tomatoes, chicken pieces and potatoes, stir to coat well all the ingredients with the curry sauce.
- Cover and simmer for 25-30 minutes stirring occasionally.
- Serve with plain white basmati or brown rice, yellow cardamom rice is another good option too.

228. Italian Baked Chicken And Rice Recipe

Serving: 4 | Prep: | Cook: 25509mins | Ready in:

Ingredients

- 1 - 1 1/2 lbs skinless/boneless chicken breast
- salt and pepper
- 1 cup white rice
- 1 can (14 oz) tomatoes
- 1 small onion, diced
- 1/2 cup shredded mozzarella cheese
- 2 tsp. oregano
- 1 clove garlic, minced
- 1/2 cup grated parmesan cheese

Direction

- Dice the chicken, season the pieces with salt and pepper. Set aside.
- In a shallow baking dish sprayed with cooking spray, put the rice, tomatoes, onions, mozzarella, oregano, garlic and 1 cup water.
- Stir in the chicken pieces and sprinkle with Parmesan cheese.
- Bake in a 325 degree oven, covered loosely with foil, for 45 minutes.
- Uncover and bake 10 to 15 minutes longer, until rice and chicken are cooked.

229. Italian Chicken Flat Bread Recipe

Serving: 2 | Prep: | Cook: 10mins | Ready in:

Ingredients

- 1 package garlic Naan bread(2 pieces)
- 1/2 small boneless and skinless chicken breast (sliced thin
- 1/2 zucchini, sliced thinly or julienne sliced
- 1/2 yellow squash, sliced thinly or julienne slice1/2 cup sliced mushroon
- 1 small Roma tomato, sliced
- Tsp Italian seasoning
- Tsp Garluc and herb spice(zatarains)
- Dash garlic salt
- Tsp sliced fresh basil
- Cup fresh spinach
- Dash whipping cream
- 1/4 cup shaved Parmesan
- Cup shredded mozzarella
- Oilive oul, few drizzles
- 1 tablespoon butter, optional

Direction

- Heat olive oil in skillet
- Stir in chicken and sautéed 2-3 minutes
- Stir in zucchini, mushrooms and squash and sauté 2. -3 minutes
- Stir in tomatoes, seasoning, spice, and cook 1 minute
- Add Parmesan and heavy whipping cream
- Divide mixture and spread over Naan bread
- Top with fresh spinach and mozzarella and sprinkle with basil
- Place on baking sheet and place under broiler
- Broil until lightly brown
- Enjoy

230. Italian Margarita Chicken Recipe

Serving: 4 | Prep: | Cook: 20mins | Ready in:

Ingredients

- 4 chicken breasts
- 1 container Italian salad dressing (pick your favorite - even cheap dressings work well for this marinade)
- 2 limes
- margarita mix
- tequila
- garlic powder

Direction

- Arrange chicken breasts together in a pan, puncture with a fork so the marinade sinks in fully
- Splash Italian dressing over the chicken until the breasts are half-submerged
- Cut the limes in half and squeeze juices over the chicken
- Apply a liberal amount of garlic powder
- Add in two parts margarita mix and one part tequila (for a nice, subtle flavor, not much tequila, one shot or so, is needed)
- Work all the ingredients into the chicken with a loving rub
- Let the chicken sit in its lovely little marinade for a half hour to an hour
- Toss the chicken onto the grill and cook, using indirect heating (works best to turn the outer burners on full, keep the middle burners off, and place chicken in the center of the grill), for 8-10 minutes per side
- Let cool, and serve chicken with whatever your heart desires

231. Italian Marinade Chicken Recipe

Serving: 5 | Prep: | Cook: 3hours2mins | Ready in:

Ingredients

- 6-8 Boneless, Skinless chicken breast tenders
- 1 Cup Italian dressing
- 1/2 Cup of water
- 1 Tsp dried rosemary

- 1 Tsp salt (I like to use the Himalayan Pink salt on this dish)
- 1/2 Tsp ground clove
- 1 Tsp dried sage
- 1 Tsp pepper
- 2 cloves of Fresh Chopped garlic
- 1 Tbsp Fresh Chopped ginger
- 1-2 Tbsp extra virgin olive oil
- 1/2 Cup Chopped onion

Direction

- Marinade:
- Whisk all items together and add chicken to the mixture. Wrap in plastic wrap and marinade in the fridge for 2-3 hours.
- Coat pan with Olive Oil add chicken and about a cup of the marinade.
- Cook in a deep pan with a lid on a medium heat and flip after about halfway through.
- This is also really nice grilled on a low temp.

232. Jamaican Jerk Chicken Recipe

Serving: 4 | Prep: | Cook: 15mins | Ready in:

Ingredients

- 1 tbs. allspice, jamaican if you can get it
- 1 tbs. thyme
- 1 1/2 tsp. cayenne pepper
- 1 1/2 tsp. sage
- 3/4 tsp. nutmeg
- 3/4 tsp. cinnamon
- 2 tbs. salt
- 2 tbs. garlic powder
- 1 tbs. sugar
- 1/4 cup olive oil
- 1/4 cup soy sauce
- 3/4 cup white vinegar
- 1/2 cup orange juice
- 1 lime, juiced
- 1 seeded and chopped habanero pepper
- 3 green onions chopped
- 4 skinless boneless chicken breasts

Direction

- Combine dry ingredients in bowl
- Whisk in wet ingredients, pepper, and onion
- Marinate chicken 1 hour or more, I marinate overnight if I can
- Grill chicken until done
- Boil leftover marinade and serve over chicken

233. Jamaican Jerked Chicken Recipe

Serving: 6 | Prep: | Cook: 10mins | Ready in:

Ingredients

- 6 boneless chicken breasts
- for the marinade:
- 1-3 habanero chiles (scotch bonnet peppers), seeded and chopped – Use fewer if a more mild sause is desired –this is HOT
- 10 green onions, chopped
- 1/2 cup chopped onion
- 4 cloves garlic, chopped
- 1 3-inch piece ginger, peeled and chopped
- 1/4 cup whole allspice
- 4 bay leaves, crushed
- 1/3 cup fresh thyme
- 1 teaspoon freshly-ground nutmeg
- 1 teaspoon freshly-ground cinnamon
- 1 teaspoon sea salt (to taste)
- 1 tablespoon freshly-ground black pepper
- 1/4 cup olive oil
- 1/4 cup soy sauce
- 1/4 cup white vinegar
- 1/4 cup lime juice.
- 1/2 cup orange juice

Direction

- Seed and finely chop habanero peppers (wear gloves).

- Trim chicken of fat.
- In a large bowl, combine the garlic, ginger, allspice, bay leaves, cinnamon, nutmeg, thyme, pepper, and salt. With a wire whisk, slowly add the olive oil, soy sauce, vinegar, orange juice, and lime juice.
- Add the Scotch Bonnet pepper, onion, green onions, and mix well.
- Add the chicken breasts, cover and marinate for at least 1 hour, longer if possible, but NOT overnight.
- Cook the breasts on the grill until thoroughly cooked. The marinade can be made into a sauce by reducing it on the stove top and adding about 2 teaspoons of cornstarch mixed in a quarter cup of water. Warning: this sauce sneaks up on you... don't eat too quickly!
- I like this served on coconut rice with black beans.

234. Japanese Chicken Katsu Recipe

Serving: 2 | Prep: | Cook: 10mins | Ready in:

Ingredients

- 2 skinless, boneless chicken breast halves - pounded to 1/2 inch thickness
- 1/2 cup all-purpose flour
- 1/2 cup panko bread crumbs
- salt and pepper to taste
- 1 egg, beaten
- 1 cup canola oil for frying, or as needed
- -SAUCE-
- 1/2 cup worcestershire sauce
- 1/4 cup ketchup
- 2 tablespoons soy sauce
- pepper to taste

Direction

- For the sauce, stir together the Worcestershire sauce, ketchup, and soy sauce, and a pinch of pepper to taste. Set aside.
- Heat 1/4 inch of oil in a large skillet over medium-high heat
- Season flattened chicken with salt & pepper.
- Dip flattened chicken pieces first into flour, then egg, and lastly bread crumbs.
- Fry breaded chicken breasts in preheated oil until golden brown and no longer pink in center, about 3-4 minutes per side.
- Transfer to a paper towel-lined plate to absorb excess oil. Slice chicken into thin strips and top with a drizzle of sauce.
- Serve remaining sauce on the side for dipping.

235. Junes Chicken Florentine Recipe

Serving: 4 | Prep: | Cook: 60mins | Ready in:

Ingredients

- Chicken: 3 boned chicken breasts, skinned
- or 4-6 chicken breasts
- 1/2 cup flour
- 1/2 tsp salt
- 1/4 tsp pepper
- 1/4 tsp oregano
- Spinach: 2 ten ounce pkgs of frozen spinach - well drained or 3-4 sixteen ounce bagged spinach
- Creamed Sauce:
- 6 Tbsp butter
- 1 cube chicken bouillon cubes or granules
- 1/4 cup and 2 Tbsp flour
- 1 & 1/2 cups milk
- 1/4 tsp salt and 1/8 tsp pepper

Direction

- Mix flour and seasonings.
- Coat chicken and brown both sides in pan
- Sauce:
- Melt butter over low heat, dissolve chicken bouillon cube in butter
- Remove from heat, blend in flour till smooth

- Gradually add milk stirring constantly
- Add salt and pepper
- Cook over low-med heat, stirring constantly until sauce thickens and boils
- Reduce heat and cook 2 more minutes
- Stir spinach into sauce, pour into casserole dish, and place chicken breasts on top of spinach and top with generous amount of shredded mozzarella
- Bake at 325 degrees for 50-60 minutes

236. Junes Chicken Parmigiana Recipe

Serving: 4 | Prep: | Cook: 15mins | Ready in:

Ingredients

- 4 chicken breasts
- 1 egg beaten w/ a little water
- 3/4 cup italian seasoned bread crumbs -mix
- 1/2 cup grated parmesean - mix
- 1 (15 ounce) jar of spaghetti sauce or homemade sauce
- 1 cup shredded mozzerella
- favorite pasta: angel hair, mostaccioli, linguini

Direction

- Preheat oven to 400 degrees
- Slightly pound chicken breasts w/mallet to tenderize
- Dip chicken into egg/water mix
- Coat with bread crumbs/parmesan cheese mix
- Cook chicken in headed olive oil until well browned on each side
- Pour sauce into 11x7 dish
- Place chicken on sauce and top with mozzarella cheese
- Bake for 15 minutes in 400 degrees
- Add pasta to side

237. Kai Sarap Crispy Chicken And Pork Adobo Flakes Recipe

Serving: 6 | Prep: | Cook: 30mins | Ready in:

Ingredients

- 1/2 kilo pork, cut into strips
- 1/2 kilo chicken breast fillet, cut into strips
- 4 pcs bay leaf
- 1 cup soy sauce
- 1/2 cup vinegar
- freshly ground black pepper
- 4 cloves garlic crushed, more if you're using native Ilocos garlic
- 1 teaspoon sugar
- vegetable or canola oil for frying

Direction

- Mix all the ingredients together in a bowl, except for the oil. Marinate for 2-4 hours.
- Remove the pork and chicken flakes from the marinade and fry until desired texture.
- Put the marinade in low heat and add the fried meat strips.
- Let simmer for half an hour or slow cook for 1 hr.
- Serve with rice.

238. Kane's Favorite Chicken Enchiladas Recipe

Serving: 0 | Prep: | Cook: 1hours30mins | Ready in:

Ingredients

- 3 to 4 large boneless, skinless chicken breasts
- 1 Tablespoon margarine or butter
- 1 package beef taco seasoning mix (not chicken).
- 2-3 Tablespoons sour cream
- 3-4 Cups shredded colby-Jack cheese (or mild cheddar cheese)

- 1 Large and 1 small can mild or hot beef enchilada sauce
- 1 dozen 6"-7" soft flour tortillas
- 1 Box cheesy Mexican rice mix
- Dash salt
- Dash pepper

Direction

- Pre-heat oven to 350 degrees.
- In large skillet melt tablespoon of butter. Place chicken breasts in skillet, salt and pepper chicken, cover skillet and cook over medium high heat until done. (Try not to brown the chicken it gets tough on the outside). While chicken is cooking prepare the cheesy Mexican rice mix as directed on box. Drain chicken and cut into 1" cubes, discard all fatty pieces.
- Place cubed chicken back in skillet and pour 1/2 of large can of enchilada sauce over chicken. Mix in beef taco seasoning, sour cream, and 2 – 2 ½ cups shredded cheese. Heat until cheese is melted and mixture is hot through and through (taste and make sure you do not need to add anything – more sour cream, more sauce, or cheese – make it the way you like)!
- Spray 11" x 7" baking pan with non-stick cooking spray. Place about 1-1/2 to 2 tablespoons of chicken mixture in center of enchilada and top with about 1-1/2 tablespoons of cheesy Mexican rice. Roll enchiladas up "burrito style" with ends tucked inside. Use a little of the chicken mixture to seal enchiladas closed - you can also lace a tooth pick through the tortillas to secure them closed. Place enchiladas in baking pan, seam side up. Pour remaining enchilada sauce over the enchiladas making sure they are well covered and then sprinkle a generous amount of shredded cheese over the enchilada sauce. Bake uncovered in 350 degree oven for approximately 20-30 minutes, checking to make sure the cheese is not drying out. Remove from oven when cheese is melted and enchilada sauce is bubbling! Top enchiladas with additional sour cream if desired. Serve with remainder of cheesy Mexican rice as a side dish.

239. Kennedys Pub Chicken Vienne Recipe

Serving: 2 | Prep: | Cook: 15mins | Ready in:

Ingredients

- 1c all pupose flour
- 2(6oz.each)boneless chicken breasts,pounded to 1/4" thickness
- 3Tbs. olive oil
- 1/2c. white wine
- 1c chicken broth
- 1/4c julienned sun-dried tomatoes
- 1 1/2tsp chopped fresh garlic
- salt and pepper to taste
- 3/4c chopped fresh spinach

Direction

- Dredge the chicken in the flour until coated on all sides. Heat the oil in a sauté pan. Sauté the chicken until brown on both sides. Leaving the chicken in the pan, add the white wine and let simmer until the liquid is reduced by half.
- Add the chicken broth, sun-dried tomatoes, garlic, salt and pepper. Simmer on medium heat till sauce thickens. Add the spinach and cook for 2 mins. Serve over linguine or rice.

240. Key West Chicken Recipe

Serving: 4 | Prep: | Cook: 30mins | Ready in:

Ingredients

- 3 TB soy sauce
- 1 TB honey
- 1 TB vegetable oil
- 1 tsp lime juice

- 1 tsp chopped garlic
- 4 skinless, boneless chicken breast halves

Direction

- In shallow container, blend soy sauce, honey vegetable oil, lime juice, garlic. Place chicken breast halves into mixture and turn to coat. Cover and marinate in refrigerator at least 30 mins
- Preheat outdoor grill for high heat.
- Lightly oil gas grate. Discard marinade and grill chicken 6 to 8 mins a side, until juices run clear.

241. Kickin Kitchen Sink Stir Fry Recipe

Serving: 6 | Prep: | Cook: 10mins | Ready in:

Ingredients

- 2 large boneless skinless chicken breasts - cut into thin strips, then bite size pieces
- garlic pepper
- seasoned salt
- Durkee's Citrus Grill seasoning **** I have had a hard time finding this lately, just google, and it's now called Tone's Citrus Grill seasoning. Same manufacturer, recipe, etc.
- EVOO
- 1 red pepper, cut into thin strips, then cut in half
- 1 white onion, cut into strips
- 2 handsful baby carrots
- 2 handsful brocoli florets
- 1/2 tub fresh mushrooms, sliced
- 1 small can water chestnuts, drained
- 1 yellow squash, sliced
- 1 zuchini, sliced
- 1/2 tub grape tomatoes
- 3 T Kikoman's Stir Fry Sauce
- 1 T worcestershire
- 3 T chopped garlic
- 1/2 t dry mustard

- zest and juice from half a lemon
- parmesan cheese
- brown rice

Direction

- Cut chicken and season pieces with seasoned salt, garlic pepper, and citrus grill.
- Drizzle nonstick skillet or wok with EVOO.
- Sauté chicken until pink color disappears.
- Mix together stir-fry sauce and following ingredients up to parmesan.
- Add veggies to large mixing bowl and toss with sauce mixture.
- Using a large slotted spoon, add veggies to pan. (I don't pour in, as the veggies produce water as cooked, and I don't want the extra liquid in there).
- Sauté until veggies are cooked but still firm.
- Serve over brown rice and garnish with parmesan cheese.

242. Kickin Pasta Recipe

Serving: 8 | Prep: | Cook: 5mins | Ready in:

Ingredients

- tomatoe sauce
- lasagna pasta
- chicken breasts
- provolone cheese
- ginger
- onion salt
- mushrooms
- jalapenos
- tomatoes
- garlic
- salt
- paprika
- pepper
- pot of water
- season all

Direction

- Begin boiling your pasta
- Trim the excess fat from your chicken breasts / cut the breasts into small strips - about a cm apart / cut each strip in half or thirds / add seasoning, paprika, and jalapenos as you fry your chicken.
- Start your sauce in a small pot / pour tomato sauce in and add onion salt- ginger- fresh, or pre-diced tomatoes -minced garlic- salt and pepper.
- By now your pasta should be soft / drain the pasta and set it on your clean cutting board horizontally. Cut vertically each cut about a half inch away from the next.
- Add your pasta, chicken, sauce, provolone cheese, and mushrooms together and blend the wonderful tastes together as the cheese melts.
- For a little more kick add more jalapenos as you mix everything together.
- When you serve it just slice a piece of provolone cheese in one direction and place it on top of the serving in a stripe formation to decorate.

243. Kung Pao Chicken Recipe

Serving: 4 | Prep: | Cook: 10mins | Ready in:

Ingredients

- 1 1/2 boneless and skinless chicken breasts
- 3 Tbsp of roasted peanuts
- 8-12 dried red chilies (but I used only 4 pcs) (remove the seeds and cut into halves)
- 3 Tbsp of cooking oil
- 5 slices of fresh ginger (peeled)
- 2 garlic cloves (sliced diagonally)
- 1 stalk scallion or onion leaves (chopped)
- For the marinade:
- 1 Tbsp of cornstarch
- 2 Tsp soy sauce
- 1 Tsp sesame seed oil
- 1 Tbsp shaoxing wine (but I did not even used this!) (check my breaded pork recipe.I used the seasoning mixture there as a substitute)
- For the sauce:
- 1 1/2 Tbsp of light soy sauce
- 1 Tsp of dark soy sauce
- 1 Tsp sugar
- 1/4 Tsp of black vinegar
- 2 Tbsp of water
- 1 Tsp cornstarch

Direction

- Cut the chicken meat into small cubes and marinate for at least 30 mins.
- Mix the sauce ingredients in a small bowl and set aside.
- Heat up a wok with 1 Tbsp. of cooking oil and stir-fry the marinated chicken until they are about 70% cooked. Remove from the wok and set aside.
- In a frying pan, add in the remaining 2 Tbsp. of cooking oil.
- When the pan starts to smoke, Add the garlic and ginger and so a quick stir then add the dried red chilies.
- Stir fry until the chilies smell spicy, then add the chicken.
- Add the roasted peanuts then stir evenly.
- Pour the sauce and stir continuously until all the chicken are well coated.
- Add in the scallions and sir evenly.
- If you think the sauce is not enough. Turn off the heat then make another sauce mixture. Turn on the heat again then pour the additional sauce mixture. If the taste is too salty for you, add some more sugar and water to expel the saltiness. (But for me, this mixture is perfect)
- Dish out and serve with hot rice. This goes best with garlic rice.

244. Kung Pow! Chicken Recipe

Serving: 2 | Prep: | Cook: 1hours30mins | Ready in:

Ingredients

- 1 ½ lbs. of chicken breast meat
- 3 tbls. of aged soy sauce
- ¼ cup of rice wine vinegar
- 3 tbls. of vegetable oil
- 3 tbls. of cornflour
- ¾ cup of peanuts
- 1 ½ cup of flour
- --- DARK chicken SAUCE---
- 1 quart of dark chicken stock
- 2 cups of demi-glaze
- 2 carrots
- ¼ bunch of celery
- 1 med onion
- 1 cup of mushroom pieces
- bell pepper trimmings
- Half an oz. of fresh ginger
- 2 tbls. of honey
- Pale roux
- ---STIR FRY---
- Half a bunch of celery
- 1 bunch of scallions
- 1 cup of fresh tender snow peas
- 2 red bell peppers
- Dried schezwan red peppers
- More toasted peanuts (very crisp)
- More chopped fresh ginger if you like it that much
- Fresh minced garlic
- Peanut oil and a wokish type sauté pan

Direction

- FOR CHICKEN: Cut the chicken into 1 ½ inch long and half an inch thick strips. Mix the soy sauce, vinegar, oil and corn flour together and set the chicken to soak for an hour.
- Put the peanuts and the flour into a food processor and chop them till the peanuts are evenly reduced to the texture of a coarse grained sand. Completely coat the chicken with this mixture and deep-fry it in oil, but do not let the nuts burn…and they will if you are not on the ball!!!
- FOR THE SAUCE: Cut up the carrot, celery, onion and combine them to the stock in a large sauce pan, along with the pepper and mushroom scraps and set it over a moderate flame to cook for about 30 minutes. Add the ginger, demi-glaze and the honey and cook a further 30 minutes at a gentle pace. Thicken slightly with the roux and strain well.
- FOR THE STIR FRY: Cut the celery into thin diagonals, cut the scallions into long thin slivers, cut the bell peppers into small triangles and leave the peas be.
- Heat the pan until it is extremely hot, add the celery and the peppers and cook them dry for 1 minute. Add enough oil to make things sizzle and then put in the garlic, ginger, and a few of the dried peppers. Cook a minute more then fling in the snow peas and fry away for another 1-2 minutes, tossing it often.
- Add the sauce, scallions and the chicken. Cook it only so long as to nicely tighten it and keep the chicken still somewhat crisp.
- TO SERVE: Serve it with the toasted peanuts sprinkled on top and to further complicate things, I serve it with a cold "salad" made from firm long grained rice, bean sprouts and mushrooms tossed in a sesame oil/plumb vinegar dressing.

245. Lazy Roast Chicken Recipe

Serving: 4 | Prep: | Cook: 120mins | Ready in:

Ingredients

- salt
- Marjoran
- basil
- oregano
- Peper

- 1 onion
- 5 garlic cloves
- 1 table spoon of mustard
- 1 lemon
- 1 chicken breast and 4 drums with skin and bones
- (aby other chicken parts will do too)
- 1 can of beer

Direction

- Wash the chicken.
- Rub it with salt and freshly grinded pepper under the skin, taking care not to rip it.
- On a mortar smash the garlic, herbs, mustard and lemon juice
- Rub the paste around the chicken also under the skin
- Place the chicken parts in a bowl and pour the beer over it
- Cover it and take to the fridge to marinate for at least 6 hours (will taste better if left overnight)
- Cover the bottom of a roast pan with olive oil
- Pour also some olive oil over the chicken still in the bowl and stir it
- Place the chicken in the roast pan, pour the liquid left in the bowl,
- Cover the pan with tinfoil closing it very well on the sides so the steam won't scape
- Take it to the oven on maximal temperature and after 15 mins set it to 115C (low temperature) leave it for 1 hour and a half
- Remove the tin foil and set the oven to medium temperature (180C) roast it until it is golden brown

246. Lean Portola Valley Chicken Recipe

Serving: 6 | Prep: | Cook: 60mins | Ready in:

Ingredients

- 1 tblsp corn-oil margarine
- 3 tblsp flour
- 3/4 cup fat-free chicken stock
- 1/2 cup nonfat milk
- 1/4 tsp salt
- Dash of garlic powder
- Dash of pepper
- 1/2 tsp curry powder
- 1/2 cup cold water
- 1/2 cup nonfat mayonnaise dressing
- 1/2 cup raw white rice
- 1 pkg (10 ounces) frozen chopped spinach, thawed and squeezed dry
- 4 boneless, skinless chicken breast halves (1 pound) You can use the breasts as is, or cut them up into bite-size pieces.
- 1/2 cup grated parmesan cheese

Direction

- Preheat the oven to 350 degrees. Spray an 11-by 7-inch baking dish with non-stick vegetable coating.
- SAUCE
- In a saucepan over medium heat, melt the margarine.
- Add the flour and stir for 1 minute; do not brown.
- Add stock and milk and stir, using a wire whisk, until mixture comes to a boil.
- Add salt, garlic powder, pepper and curry powder and continue to cook for 1 minute. Remove from heat, stir in water and mayonnaise and set aside.
- ASSEMBLY
- Sprinkle the rice over the bottom of the baking dish.
- Layer the spinach evenly over the top.
- Cover the spinach with half of the sauce mixture, then the chicken, then the remaining sauce.
- Sprinkle the cheese over the top and bake, uncovered, for 1 hour.
- Nutritional Value per Serving: 336 calories

247. Lemon Cumin Grilled Chicken Breast Recipe

Serving: 4 | Prep: | Cook: 8mins | Ready in:

Ingredients

- 4 skinless, boneless chicken breast halves (about 1-1/4 lbs
- 1 tsp ground cumin
- 1/2 tsp salt
- 1/4 tsp fresh ground black pepper
- 2 tsp olive oil
- nonstick cooking spray
- 2 Tbs lemon juice

Direction

- Put chicken between 2 pieces of plastic wrap and pound slightly with a mallet or rolling pin so it is an even thickness of about 1/2".
- In a small bowl, combine cumin, salt and pepper. Rub chicken breasts on both sides with olive oil, then rub the spice mixture on both sides.
- Spray a grill or non-stick grill pan with cooking spray and heat over medium-high heat. Cook chicken till grill marks form and chicken is no longer pink, about 3-4 mins a side. Remove from heat, let rest 5 mins. Drizzle with lemon juice
- The chicken will keep for up to 3 days in airtight container in refrigerator.

248. Lemon Apricot Chicken Recipe

Serving: 4 | Prep: | Cook: 30mins | Ready in:

Ingredients

- 1 egg
- 1/4 cup margarine or buter melted
- 2 tablespoons water
- 1 cup Bisquick mix
- 1 tablespoon grated lemon peel
- 1/4 teaspoon garlic powder
- 4 small boneless skinless chicken breasts (1 1/4 lb)
- 2/3 cup apricot preserves
- Lemon-apricot Sauce:
- 2 tablespoons lemon juice
- 1/2 teaspoon soy sauce
- 1/4 teaspoon ground ginger
- lemon slices, if desired

Direction

- 1. Heat oven to 425°F. Spread 1 tbsp. of melted butter in pan.
- In shallow bowl, beat egg and water slightly.
- In another shallow bowl, mix Bisquick mix, lemon peel and garlic powder.
- 2. Between pieces of plastic wrap or waxed paper, place each chicken breast smooth side down; gently pound with flat side of meat mallet or rolling pin until about 1/2 inch thick.
- Dip chicken into egg mixture, then coat with Bisquick mixture. Place in pan. Drizzle remaining butter over chicken.
- 3. Bake uncovered 20 minutes. Turn; bake 10 minutes longer or until juice is no longer pink when centers of thickest pieces are cut. Cut chicken crosswise into 1/2-inch slices.
- 4. In 1-quart saucepan, mix all remaining ingredients except lemon slices. Cook over medium-low heat until hot, stirring frequently. Cut chicken crosswise into 1/2-inch slices; pour sauce over chicken. Garnish with lemon slices.
- Serve with white or fried rice.

249. Light Sesame Chicken Recipe

Serving: 4 | Prep: | Cook: 45mins | Ready in:

Ingredients

- ■3 T. honey

- ▪2 T. sesame seeds
- ▪2 T. soy sauce
- ▪1-2 tsp. rice wine vinegar (optional -this wasn't in the original recipe)
- ▪3 cloves garlic, finely chopped
- ▪2 egg whites
- ▪1/4 c. cornstarch
- ▪1 1/2 lb. chicken breast; boneless, skinless, and halved
- ▪salt and pepper to taste
- ▪2 T. vegetable oil
- ▪1 1/2 lb. broccoli florets; steamed until tender

Direction

- 1. In a small bowl; combine honey, sesame seeds, soy sauce, rice wine vinegar and garlic. Set aside.
- 2. In a large bowl; whisk together egg whites and cornstarch. Add chicken, seasoning with salt and pepper. Toss to coat.
- 3. In a large skillet; heat 1 tablespoon (15 ml) oil over medium-high heat. Add half the chicken. Cook, turning occasionally, until golden and cooked through, for 6 to 8 minutes.
- 4. Transfer chicken to plate; repeat with remaining oil and chicken.
- 5. Return all chicken to skillet. Add cooked broccoli, honey mixture and gently toss.
- 6. Serve with rice.

250. Lime Tequila Chicken Recipe

Serving: 4 | Prep: | Cook: 20mins | Ready in:

Ingredients

- 1 cup water
- 1/3 cup teriyaki sauce
- 2 tablespoons lime juice
- 2 teaspoons minced garlic
- 1 teaspoon mesquite liquid smoke flavoring
- 1/2 teaspoon salt
- 1/4 teaspoon ground ginger
- 1/4 teaspoon tequila
- 4 chicken breast fillets
- Dressing:
- 1/4 cup mayonnaise
- 1/4 cup sour cream
- 1 tablespoon milk
- 2 teaspoons minced tomato
- 1-1/2 teaspoons white vinegar
- 1 teaspoon minced canned jalapeno slices
- 1 teaspoon minced onion
- 1/4 teaspoon dried parsley
- 1/4 teaspoon Tabasco pepper sauce
- 1/8 teaspoon salt
- 1/8 teaspoon dried dill weed
- 1/8 teaspoon paprika
- 1/8 teaspoon cayenne pepper
- 1/8 teaspoon cumin
- 1/8 teaspoon chili powder
- 1/8 teaspoon garlic powder
- 1 teaspoon freshly ground black pepper
- 1 cup shredded pepper jack cheese
- 2 cups crumbled corn chips

Direction

- Prepare marinade by combining marinade ingredients in medium bowl.
- Add chicken to bowl then cover and chill 3 hours.
- Make dressing by combining all ingredients in a medium bowl and mix until smooth.
- Cover and chill until needed.
- Preheat oven to high broil or grill to high heat then cook chicken 5 minutes per side.
- Arrange cooked chicken in a baking pan and spread with a layer of dressing.
- Sprinkle with 1/4 cup cheese then broil chicken 3 minutes to allow cheese to melt.
- Spread a bed of crumbled corn chips on four plates then top with a chicken breast.

251. MY Butter Chicken Recipe

Serving: 4 | Prep: | Cook: 45mins | Ready in:

Ingredients

- 1 lb chicken thighs, chopped into bite size pieces (half may be substituted with chicken breast, however, it will be dryer and less flavourful)
- 8 oz tomato paste
- 1 white onion, diced
- 1/2 cup plain yogurt (or 1/2 cup heavy cream; i like to use both)
- 1/4 cup heavy cream, half and half (or homo milk),
- 4 tbsp butter, divided
- 1 1/2 tbsp garam masala (or more, if you like it a little more spicy)
- 1/2 tsp turmeric (optional)
- 1/4 tsp ground coriander (optional)
- up to 1/2 tbsp chili powder (depending on heat)
- 1/2 tbsp cumin (i like the extra cumin, just cause)
- 3 cups rice of choice - jasmine is the usual rice, however, i like brown or black (forbidden) rice.

Direction

- In a large frying pan (at least twice as much room than the chicken will need), place about 1 1/2 tbsp. butter, and chicken, and cook on medium heat until sealed (white on the outside, still pink inside)
- Start making your rice now so it's done at about the same time
- Add diced onion, garam masala, turmeric, coriander, chili powder and cumin, stir and cook until onions are transparent but not limp (about 3 minutes)
- Add tomato paste and the rest of the butter, stir and cook about 2 minutes.
- Mound chicken in the middle of the frying pan, and while stirring, pour in heavy cream and plain yogurt.
- Cover and cook about 15 minutes on medium-low heat, sauce will thicken and possibly separate a little - it may look like red oil top
- Serve hot over or beside rice.
- This recipe can also be made in a slow cooker for potlucks and office parties - just double the recipe, keeping the fully cooked chicken separate from the sauce, and combine in crockpot on high heat for 4 hours before the start of the party/function.

252. Mango Lime Chicken Recipe

Serving: 4 | Prep: | Cook: 1hours | Ready in:

Ingredients

- 4 chicken breasts or thighs
- 1 ripe mango
- 2 limes
- 2 T. oil
- 2 T. brown sugar
- 2 cloves garlic, minced
- salt and pepper to taste

Direction

- Get the fruit from one mango and add to a blender. Add the juice of the two limes. I zested both of them as well. Add the oil, brown sugar, garlic, salt and pepper as well. Blend until smooth.
- Place the chicken and 3/4 of the marinade in a baggie together and let the chicken marinade for 1-6 hours. Cook on a grill. Use the reserve marinade to baste the chicken as it grills.

253. Mediterranean Chicken And Village Salad Recipe

Serving: 4 | Prep: | Cook: 30mins | Ready in:

Ingredients

- chicken
- 4 boneless skinless chicken breast fillets
- 1/4 cup lemon juice, freshly squeezed
- 1 tbsp olive oil
- 3 cloves garlic, minced
- 2 tbsp fresh oregano leaves, roughly chopped
- pinch red pepper flakes
- 1/4 tsp sea salt
- 1/4 tsp black pepper, freshly ground
- Village Salad
- 2 roma tomatoes, diced (I de-seed)
- 1 medium seedless cucumber, diced
- 1/4 cup fresh parsley, roughly chopped
- 1/4 cup kalamata olives, chopped
- 2 green onions, chopped
- 4 oz. feta cheese, cut into small cubes
- 2 tbsp olive oil
- 1 tbsp white wine vinegar
- S&P – to taste

Direction

- Chicken
- Combine all ingredients except for chicken in a non-reactive bowl. Whisk together to incorporate. Add chicken and marinate for 30 minutes.
- Heat skillet over medium-high. Add a drizzle of olive oil and place chicken into skillet. Cook for 4 minutes on each side, or until cooked through and juices run clear. The chicken may also be done on a grill, under the broiler, or baked in the oven.
- Village Salad
- Combine all ingredients and toss well to incorporate.

254. Mediterranean Chicken Breasts With Avocado Tapenade Recipe

Serving: 4 | Prep: | Cook: 15mins | Ready in:

Ingredients

- 4 boneless skinless chicken breast halves
- 1 tablespoon grated lemon peel
- 5 tablespoons fresh lemon juice, divided
- 2 tablespoons olive oil, divided
- 1 teaspoon olive oil, divided
- 1 garlic clove, finely chopped
- 1/2 teaspoon salt
- 1/4 teaspoon ground black pepper
- 2 garlic cloves, roasted and mashed
- 1/2 teaspoon sea salt
- 1/4 teaspoon fresh ground pepper
- 1 medium tomato, seeded and finely chopped
- 1/4 cup small green pimento stuffed olives, thinly sliced
- 3 tablespoons capers, rinsed
- 2 tablespoons fresh basil leaves, finely sliced
- 1 large avocado, halved, pitted, peeled and finely chopped

Direction

- In a sealable plastic bag, combine chicken and marinade of lemon peel, 2 tablespoons lemon juice, 2 tablespoons olive oil, garlic, salt and pepper. Seal bag and refrigerate for 30 minutes.
- In bowl, whisk together remaining 3 tablespoons lemon juice, roasted garlic, remaining 1/2 teaspoons olive oil, sea salt and fresh ground pepper. Mix in tomato, green olives, capers, basil and avocado; set aside.
- Remove chicken from bag and discard marinade. Grill over medium-hot coals for 4 to 5 minutes per side or to desired degree of doneness.
- Serve with Avocado Tapenade.

255. Mexican Chicken Corn Chowder Recipe

Serving: 8 | Prep: | Cook: 20mins | Ready in:

Ingredients

- 1 1/2 boneless chicken breast
- 1/2 cup chopped onion
- 1-2 cloves minced garlic
- 3 tbsp butter
- 2 chicken bouillon cubes
- 1 cup hot water
- 1/2-1 tsp cumin
- 2 cups half and half cream
- 2 cups shredded monterey jack cheese
- 1 can cream corn
- 1 can green chilies, undrained and chopped
- 1 teas hot pepper sauce
- 1 can rotel tomatoes; drained

Direction

- Cut chicken into bite-size pieces.
- Brown chicken, onion and garlic in butter.
- Dissolve bouillon in hot water.
- Add to pan along with cumin; bring to boil.
- Cover and simmer for 5 minutes.
- Add cream, cheese, corn, chilies and hot sauce.
- Cook and stir over low heat until cheese is melted.
- Stir in tomatoes.
- Serve immediately.

256. Moms Easy Chicken Piccata Recipe

Serving: 4 | Prep: | Cook: 20mins | Ready in:

Ingredients

- 1.5 Pounds boneless, skinless chicken breast pieces
- 1/4 cup grated parmesan cheese
- 1/2 cup flour
- sea salt
- Freshly ground pepper
- 4 Tablespoons olive oil
- 4 Tablespoons butter (divided)
- 3/4 cup dry white wine
- 3 Tablespoons lemon juice
- 1/3 cup capers in brine (drained)

Direction

- Butterfly your chicken breasts and flatten to 1/4 inch thick with the flat side of a meat mallet (if you don't have a mallet, a rolling pin works as well.) I suggest placing the chicken between layers of plastic wrap to flatten, it keeps the mess in check.
- Rinse the chicken well in water.
- Mix together the flour, Parmesan, sea salt and pepper in a large, flat bowl.
- Dredge the chicken in the flour and cheese mix until well covered. Set aside.
- In a large, heavy bottomed skillet, heat the olive oil and half the butter over medium high temperature. Add chicken pieces and brown well on each side. About 5 minutes per side, but make sure you check that they are cooked thoroughly.
- Transfer chicken to a plate and cover with foil to keep it warm while you prepare the sauce.
- To the skillet, add white wine, lemon juice and capers. Make sure to get all those yummy browned bits off the bottom of the pan, they add wonderful flavor to the sauce! Simmer until it is reduce by about half. To finish the sauce, whisk in the remainder of the butter. Serve the sauce over the chicken.

257. Monterey Chicken Recipe

Serving: 8 | Prep: | Cook: 35mins | Ready in:

Ingredients

- 8 boneless, skinless, chicken breasts
- 1 (7 oz.) can chopped mild green chilies*

- ½ lb. monterey jack cheese, cut into 8 strips
- ½ cup fine dry bread crumbs
- ¼ cup freshly grated parmesan cheese
- 1 to 3 teaspoons chili powder
- ½ teaspoon salt
- ¼ teaspoon ground cumin
- ¼ teaspoon freshly ground black pepper
- 6 tablespoons butter, melted
- tomato sauce (recipe follows)
- ****
- Tomato Sauce:
- 1 (15-oz.) can plain tomato sauce or 1 can rotel
- or mix the two together. Some of the sauce can be spooned
- on top of each breast before cooking.
- ½ teaspoon ground cumin
- 1/3 cup sliced green onion
- salt and freshly ground black pepper to taste
- Garnish:
- sour cream
- Fresh limes
- cilantro

Direction

- Pound the chicken breasts between 2 sheets of waxed paper until thin.
- Spread each breast with 1 tablespoon of the green chilies.
- Place 1 cheese strip on top of each portion of chilies.
- Roll up each chicken breast and tuck ends under.
- Combine the bread crumbs, Parmesan cheese, chili powder, salt, cumin and pepper in a shallow dish.
- Dip each stuffed breast into the melted
- Butter and roll in the bread crumb mixture.
- Place the breasts in a baking dish, seam side down.
- Drizzle with remaining butter.
- Cover and chill for at least 4 hours or overnight.
- Preheat the oven to 400 degrees F.
- Bake for 25 to 40 minutes, or until done.
- Serve with Tomato Sauce and garnish with sour cream and fresh limes.
- Sprinkle with finely chopped cilantro. (Optional)
- *I use whole green chilies and wrap 1 cheese strip in 1 whole chili and then put it into the breast; it's less messy and I like the flavor of more chili.
- Serve with rice or how about couscous??

258. More Kunfunky Chicken Really Fried This Time Recipe

Serving: 3 | Prep: | Cook: 20mins | Ready in:

Ingredients

- 2 large boneless, skinless chicken Breasts, or ready made thin cutlets to make life easy.
- 1 cup all-purpose flour
- 1 Packet Hidden Valley Ranch seasoning
- 1 1/2 cups whole milk, Half n Half or heavy cream
- 2 1/2 cups plain breadcrumbs, or more if needed
- 1 egg
- 3 cloves garlic, diced, or garlic powder
- 1/4 bunch Fresh tarragon, chopped
- Regular or Smoked sea salt, pepper, crushed rosemary
- 1 cup (2 sticks) margarine for the pan
- For dipping sauce: (equal parts)
- Frank's red hot sauce
- honey

Direction

- If the chicken isn't already sliced thin, go ahead and slice the breasts into thin strips the long way. If you want, you can pound them to make them thinner, but it's not necessary.
- Mix flour with ranch packet contents.
- Coat the chicken cutlets in the flour mixture.
- Dip them in the Milk, but not too long or the flour will wash off.

- Plunge them into the dry breadcrumbs, coating them evenly. If a corner doesn't coat, stick that corner back in the milk for a second.
- Melt a Tbsp. of margarine in a large frying pan over medium heat. Fry up the breaded cutlets, sprinkling the fresh tarragon, salt, pepper and garlic powder over them as they cook on both sides.
- If you're using fresh garlic, sauté it in the pan for a minute or so before adding the chicken.
- Cook chicken, making sure to keep a good layer of margarine at the bottom of the pan or the breading will stick and rip. Remember, a general rule of frying is that bread loves to swim. Yeah, it's unhealthy, but it tastes good! If you want, you can use oil instead, but I've got ulcers and need to avoid it.
- ***As to not waste, we mixed the remaining breadcrumbs, seasoned flour, milk, 1 egg, and some of each of the spices, formed them into patties and sautéed them in the last of the margarine. These came out fantastic and you must try them.
- We tried several dipping sauces for these: Balsamic vinegar, which was alright. Ranch, which was good, but it didn't seem like enough somehow. Mayonnaise, which was a lot better later when eating it cold on a sandwich, but the winner had to be a mix between Frank's Red Hot and honey. OMG. Seriously, just give it a try. It's pretty much a necessity on the wish meat patties, makes them so much better. Try it, you won't be disappointed!!

259. Moroccan Chicken And Lentils Recipe

Serving: 12 | Prep: | Cook: 35mins | Ready in:

Ingredients

- 8 cups water
- 3 teaspoons salt, divided
- 1 pound dried brown lentils, rinsed, drained
- 1 cup plus 2 tablespoons olive oil
- 1/2 cup red wine vinegar
- 3 tablespoons ground cumin, divided
- 2 tablespoons plus 2 teaspoons chili powder
- 2 garlic cloves, minced
- 1 large onion, chopped
- 1 1/2 pounds skinless boneless chicken breast halves, thinly sliced
- 1/4 teaspoon ground cinnamon
- 1 cup chopped fresh parsley

Direction

- Combine 8 cups water and 1 teaspoon salt in heavy large saucepan over high heat. Add lentils; bring to boil. Cover, reduce heat to medium, and simmer until lentils are tender, about 20 minutes. Drain well; rinse with cold water and drain again. Place in large bowl.
- Whisk 1 cup olive oil, vinegar, 2 tablespoons cumin, 2 tablespoons chili powder, garlic, and 1 teaspoon salt in large measuring cup. Pour 1 cup dressing over warm lentils and toss. Cool.
- Heat 2 tablespoons olive oil in large skillet over high heat. Add onion; sauté until dark brown and soft, about 5 minutes. Add chicken; sauté 2 minutes. Add 1 teaspoon salt, 1 tablespoon cumin, 2 teaspoons chili powder, and cinnamon. Sauté until chicken is cooked through, about 3 minutes longer.
- Arrange lentils on large platter. Place sliced chicken atop lentils. Drizzle with remaining dressing and sprinkle with parsley. (Can be made 2 hours ahead. Let stand at room temperature.)

260. Moroccan Chicken Pie Recipe

Serving: 8 | Prep: | Cook: 60mins | Ready in:

Ingredients

- 1 pkg filo or puff pastry - I prefer puff pastry

- 2-3 whole chicken breasts, 3 for a 10 inch pie
- Just enough water or chicken broth (I used broth) to cover chicken in a pot
- 3 large eggs, 4 for 10 inch recipe
- 2-3 Tbs fresh chopped parsley
- 2 tsp cinnamon or more
- 4 tsp sugar- or more
- salt and pepper to taste
- 1/4 cup butter melted
- powdered sugar for the topping
- Other options for filling: chopped almonds, fine chopped dates, golden raisins- saffron strands for the broth

Direction

- Poach chicken breasts in broth, gently till done about 8-10 minutes
- Remove and cool, reserve 1/2 cup broth
- Then cube into bite size pieces
- In a small bowl whisk eggs with 1/2 cup warm chicken broth and the parsley and set aside
- Optional: dissolve some saffron threads in the liquid, really kicks it up a notch
- Roll out one sheet of pastry very thinly to cover you 9 or 10 inch pie plate, metal is better than glass (In Morocco they have a metal tin for this)
- Spread half of diced chicken on pastry
- Pour on half the egg mixture over the chicken
- Sprinkle with granulated sugar and cinnamon
- Place on another layer of chicken, egg mixture, sugar and cinnamon
- Cover with 2nd sheet of rolled out pastry
- Fold edges of bottom pastry over top pastry, sealing to enclose
- Brush with the melted butter
- Sprinkle again with some sugar and cinnamon
- Bake 375-400F until pastry is golden, about 30 minutes
- When removed for the oven, let cool briefly
- Dust heavily with powdered sugar.
- Directions using filo: Using Filo instead of Puff pastry:
- 7- 9 sheets of Filo
- Butter each sheet (use 5) and place each sheet in a pan with an overhang
- After the buttered 5th sheet:
- Spread entire chicken mixture (mixed with egg mixture) evenly in pan
- Sprinkle with sugar and cinnamon
- Lay on remaining sheets over the chicken
- Brush each sheet again with butter
- Fold Filo overhangs over top sheet to seal
- Sprinkle top sheet with sugar, cinnamon etc.
- Bake 375F until puffed, crisp and golden - approx. 30 minutes)
- Sprinkle with powdered sugar before serving
- Note: one wants the top as well as bottom of the pie to be golden.
- Often the pie is flipped onto another oven safe plate to finish browning the bottom crust
- I did not do this step and consider it optional

261. Mos Chicken Salad Recipe

Serving: 6 | Prep: | Cook: |Ready in:

Ingredients

- 2 BBQ chicken breasts(leftover from a rotisserie or El Pollo Loco)
- 1 stem of celery(chopped into little itty bitty cubes, leave as well thankyou)
- 1/2 cup of chopped red roasted bell peppers
- 5 purple grapes or green (whichever you have) or sub for raisins
- 1/4 cup of olive oil Mayo(KRAFT brand)
- salt
- cracked black pepper
- 1 tsp of herbs de provance

Direction

- Dice the chicken (skin and all) into small 1cm by 1cm cubes
- Add diced celery and roasted bell peppers
- Slice grapes thin and add

- Add the Mayo, and herbs, salt to taste and about 1/2 TBSP of cracked black pepper
- Mix everything together well and serve
- If it's too dry add more mayo as needed and for an extra kick, you can add 1 TSP of BBQ sauce (I prefer Bull's Eye) and 1/2 TSP red pepper flakes
- Chill well and serve with crackers or toasted sourdough bread

262. Mourgh Recipe

Serving: 2 | Prep: | Cook: 10mins | Ready in:

Ingredients

- • 2 lg cloves garlic
- • 1/2 ts salt
- • 2 c Plain, whole-milk yogurt
- • juice and pulp of 1 large lemon, 3 to 4 tablespoons
- • 1/2 ts cracked black pepper
- • 2 lg whole chicken breasts, about 2 pounds

Direction

- Long, slow marinating in garlicky yogurt tenderizes, moistens and adds deep flavor, so you end up with skinless grilled chicken that's as delicious as it is nutritionally correct. Serve with soft pita or Arab flatbread and fresh yogurt.
- Put the salt in a wide, shallow non-reactive bowl with the garlic and mash them together until you have paste. Add yogurt, lemon and pepper.
- Skin the chicken breasts, remove all visible fat and separate the halves. Bend each backward to break the bones so the pieces win lie flat.
- Add to the yogurt and turn so all surfaces are well-coated. Cover the bowl tightly and refrigerate. Allow to marinate at least overnight, up to a day and a half. Turn when you think of it.
- To cook, remove breasts from marinade and wipe off all but a thin film. Broil or grill about 6 inches from the heat for 6 to 8 minutes a side, or until thoroughly cooked. Meat will brown somewhat but should not char. Serve at once.

263. MozzaMustard Chicken Recipe

Serving: 2 | Prep: | Cook: 46mins | Ready in:

Ingredients

- 2-4 (depending) Boneless, skinless chicken breasts
- 1 Bottle spicy brown mustard
- 2-4 slices Thick Cut mozzarella cheese
- 1 fresh tomato
- olive oil

Direction

- MAKE SURE THE MUSTARD IS COLD
- Put some olive oil in the bottom of a glass casserole or baking dish.
- Put the chicken in said dish and cover with some aluminum foil.
- Bake it in the oven at 350 degrees for about 45 minutes (until it's done depending on thickness of chicken breast)
- Put the COLD mustard on top of the chicken with a nice thick slice of tomato.
- Put the cheese on top of the mustard and tomato.
- Put it back in the oven on BROIL for about 1 minute just to melt the cheese.
- Serve and enjoy.

264. MrsLynams Cheater Pot Pie Chicken Recipe

Serving: 8 | Prep: | Cook: 30mins | Ready in:

Ingredients

- 2-3 bonless / skinless chicken breasts
- 1/2 bag frozen peas & carrots
- 1 can cream of chicken soup
- 2 frozen pie crusts
- 1 box (of 2) "rolled" pie crusts
- 1 or 2 tbs. oil
- 1/4 cup or 1/2 cup milk (depending)
- salt
- pepper

Direction

- Cut chicken into cubes. Place oil in skillet and add chicken (salt, pepper, garlic, etc.)
- Remove crusts from freezer, allowing them defrost a bit, while preparing chicken. (I place rolled crusts in the fridge the night / morning before)
- Cook chicken until it turns white (done). Place in a medium size mixing bowl. Add the Peas & carrots to the chicken. Pour can of soup in the bowl, adding approx. 1/4 to 1/2 cup of milk. Mix well with spoon, checking desired consistency. (Too thick? Add more milk)
- Spoon mixture into pie crusts.
- Unroll the "rolled" pie crusts ON to the tops of filled pies. Pinch crust edges together or use a crust roller to remove the excess edges of "rolled" crusts.
- Place in oven & bake @350 deg. for approx. 30 minutes or so.
- WATCH edges! May become too dark before pot pie is finished baking. You can cover the edges of the pot pie with foil till about the last 15-20 minutes of baking.

265. Munster Chicken Recipe

Serving: 6 | Prep: | Cook: 30mins | Ready in:

Ingredients

- 6 boneless chicken breast (or 8-12 boneless chicken thighs)
- 2 eggs
- 1 cup Italian or Parmesan bread crumbs
- butter or olive oil to brown chicken
- 1/2 can chicken broth
- Munster cheese sliced
- 1 lemon

Direction

- Whisk eggs.
- Place chicken in eggs and let soak for 5 to 10 minutes
- Dip chicken in bread crumbs
- Heat oil in large skillet
- Brown chicken
- Transfer to 9x13 baking dish
- Pour chicken broth to 1/4 to 1/2 inch up chicken
- Place 1/2 to 1/3 slice of Munster cheese on each piece of chicken (a piece large enough to cover the piece of chicken)
- Bake at 350 degrees until chicken is done and lightly browned
- Squeeze juice of lemon over chicken and serve

266. Mushroom Chicken Bake Recipe

Serving: 6 | Prep: | Cook: 50mins | Ready in:

Ingredients

- 6 boneless skinless chicken breasts
- 2 cans condensed mushroom soup
- 1 can of water
- handful of spinach
- 1/2 large onion chopped
- 1 tbsp garlic chopped
- 1 tbsp butter

Direction

- Preheat oven to 375°F. In a large frying pan, over medium heat, add butter, onion and garlic. Sauté until onions are just tender, about 10 minutes. In a large mixing bowl add mushroom soup, and only 1 can of water. Use whisk to mix together. Add sautéed onions, garlic and butter to soup mixture. In warm frying pan, add spinach and cook until wilted. Once cooked add spinach to soup mixture. Set aside.
- Place chicken in a casserole dish and cook for 20 minutes. Remove from oven and cover chicken with soup mixture. Place back in oven for an additional 30 minutes or until bubbling hot.
- Place chicken breasts on plate and smother with sauce from the casserole dish.
- Serve with rice or pasta, ENJOY!

267. Naked Chicken With Broccolini Recipe

Serving: 24 | Prep: | Cook: 15mins | Ready in:

Ingredients

- 6 each 8 ounce chicken breasts Skin on
- 3 pounds broccolini, rinsed and trimmed
- 6 tablespoons olive oil
- 6 cloves garlic, minced
- 1 1/2 teaspoon kosher salt
- 1 cup panko bread crumbs

Direction

- Spread the panko into on a 1/2 sheet pan and place into the oven for 2 minutes at 425 degrees, or until lightly toasted.
- Trim the broccolini stems to a 4 inch length. Place the broccoli into a mixing bowl and toss with the olive oil, garlic, and kosher salt.
- Add the panko to the bowl with the broccolini mixture.
- Toss to combine.
- Return the mixture to the pan, place in the oven and roast just until the broccoli is tender, 8 to 10 more minutes.
- While broccolini is roasting, cook chicken breast on a flat top grill, or in a large skillet on the stove top, with olive oil and no seasoning (remember, it's naked).
- Slice Chicken breasts lengthwise.
- Plate 2 ounces Broccolini and place 2 ounces of Chicken on top.

268. New Delhi Spiced Chicken Recipe

Serving: 4 | Prep: | Cook: 15mins | Ready in:

Ingredients

- 1 teaspoon ground turmeric
- 1 teaspoon curry powder
- 1 teaspoon coriander
- 1/2 teaspoon ground ginger
- 1/8 teaspoon chili powder
- 1 teaspoon black pepper
- 3 tablespoons butter
- 4 boneless skinless chicken breast halves cubed
- 2 white onions chopped fine
- 2 tomatoes chopped
- 2 green bell peppers chopped fine
- 1 celery stalk chopped fine
- 3 parsley sprigs minced
- 2 garlic cloves minced
- 1/3 cup seedless raisins
- 1 tablespoon dry sherry
- 1-1/2 teaspoon lemon juice

Direction

- Heat two tablespoons butter in a large skillet.
- Place first six ingredients in skillet and brown for 1 minute over high heat.
- Place chicken in skillet with browned spices and stir to coat well then brown 1 minute

- longer or until chicken has turned white on the inside.
- Remove from pan and set aside.
- Add remaining butter to pan and sauté onions over high heat until limp.
- Add remaining ingredients including browned chicken and cook over medium heat until celery is tender but still slightly crisp.
- Serve over brown rice.

269. One Skillet Spicy Chicken Italiano Recipe

Serving: 4 | Prep: | Cook: 15mins | Ready in:

Ingredients

- 1 tablespoon minced fresh garlic.
- 1-1/4 pounds boneless, skinless chicken breast, cut into 1 inch cubes
- 2 cups fresh bite size broccoli florets
- 1 cup oil packed sun dried tomatoes, drained, julienne, reserve 1 tablespoon of the oil.
- 1 cup chopped fresh roma tomatoes
- 1 tablespoon crushed red pepper flakes (optional, I like it hot)
- 1 cup freshly grated mozzarella cheese (buy good cheese and grate it yourself, there IS a difference)
- ¼ cup freshly grated parmesan cheese (not the stuff in the green can, grate some fresh off of a block yourself, you will be pleasantly rewarded for your effort)

Direction

- Preheat broiler while cooking per the following directions
- Heat the tablespoon of oil reserved from the sun dried tomatoes over medium heat
- Add garlic and sauté for 1 minute
- Add the chicken and cook about 5 minutes until lightly browned on all sides
- Add fresh and sun dried tomatoes, broccoli, and crushed red pepper flakes, partially cover skillet and cook about 5 minutes until the fresh tomatoes start to break down and chicken is cooked through.
- Remove from heat, top with the cheeses, place under preheated broiler until the cheese just starts to brown and is bubbly, about 2-3 minutes
- Serve immediately

270. One Step Creamy Chicken Breasts Recipe

Serving: 4 | Prep: | Cook: 50mins | Ready in:

Ingredients

- 4 whole chicken breasts, split and skinned
- 8 thick slices swiss cheese
- 1-10 3/4 ounce can condensed cream of chicken soup
- 1/4 cup dry white wine, DO NOT use cooking wine, please!
- 2 cups stuffing mix
- 1/3 cup butter, melted

Direction

- If desired, debone chicken breasts.
- Arrange in a shallow 7x11 or 9x13-inch baking dish.
- Top with Swiss cheese.
- In a small bowl, stir together soup and wine.
- Spoon evenly over chicken.
- Coarsely crush the stuffing mix and sprinkle over chicken.
- Drizzle evenly with melted butter.
- Bake, uncovered, at 350° for 50-60 minutes, until thickest part of meat is no longer pink when slashed.

271. Orange Amaretto Chicken Recipe

Serving: 6 | Prep: | Cook: 30mins | Ready in:

Ingredients

- 3 Tablespoons all-purpose flour
- 2 teaspoons Hungarian sweet paprika
- 1/2 teaspoon onion powder
- 1/2 teaspoon garlic powder
- 1/2 teaspoon rubbed sage
- 1-1/2 teaspoons kosher salt
- 1/2 teaspoon freshly ground black pepper
- 6 boneless chicken breast halves
- 1 Tablespoon olive oil
- 1 Tablespoon butter
- 1 can (6-1/4 ounces) frozen orange juice concentrate mixed with 3
- ounces water (half of the emptied orange juice can)
- 1 cup amaretto liqueur
- 1-1/2 Tablespoons Dijon mustard
- Chopped parsley for garnish, optional

Direction

- Whisk together flour, paprika, onion powder, garlic powder, sage, salt, and pepper. Sprinkle mixture evenly over both sides of chicken breasts.
- Heat a large, heavy skillet over medium-high heat. Add olive oil and butter, swirling to combine and coat the bottom of the pan. Sear the chicken breasts on both sides until golden, turning only once. (Do this in 2 batches if need be.) Transfer to prepared baking pan.
- Preparation:
- Preheat oven to 350 degrees F.
- Line a 9- x 13-inch baking pan with oiled foil.
- Whisk together flour, paprika, onion powder, garlic powder, sage, salt, and pepper.
- Sprinkle mixture evenly over both sides of chicken breasts.
- Heat a large, heavy skillet over medium-high heat.
- Add olive oil and butter, swirling to combine and coat the bottom of the pan.
- Sear the chicken breasts on both sides until golden, turning only once. (Do this in 2 batches if need be.)
- Transfer to prepared baking pan.
- Add orange juice mixture, amaretto liqueur, and Dijon mustard to the skillet drippings.
- Stir, scraping up any browned bits into the sauce, and boil until reduced by half and thickened, about 5 minutes.
- Pour orange amaretto sauce over chicken breasts.
- Cover with foil and bake for 30 minutes in preheated oven.
- Let chicken rest for 10 minutes before serving.
- Serve chicken breasts drizzled with pan sauce, and garnish with parsley.

272. Orange Chicken Recipe

Serving: 5 | Prep: | Cook: 5mins | Ready in:

Ingredients

- 2 lbs boneless chicken breasts (chopped into cubes)
- 1 cup brown sugar
- 2 cups all purpose flour
- 1 raw egg (beaten)
- 1/4 Tsp salt
- 1/4 Tsp ground black pepper
- 1-1/2 cup water
- 5 Tbsp orange juice
- 2 Tbsp cornstarch (diluted in 2 Tbsp water)
- 1/4 cup vinegar
- 2 Tbsp soy sauce
- 1 Tsp garlic, minced
- 1/2 cup green onions (chopped into small pieces)

Direction

- Pat dry the chicken cubes and season with little salt and pepper.

- Place the flour in a resealable container, add the measured salt and ground black pepper. Cover the container then shake well.
- Dip the chicken cubes on the beaten egg and place inside the container. Close it then shake well until the chicken cubes are nicely coated. (You may place 4 chicken cubes at a time).
- Deep fry the chicken cubes until the color turns golden brown. Drain on paper towels and set aside.
- In a pan, pour the water, soy sauce, vinegar and orange juice. Bring to boil.
- Add the minced garlic and simmer for about 5 mins.
- Add the sugar and simmer for 3 minutes or just until the sugar is fully dissolved. (Adjust the amount of sugar if you used sweetened orange juice).
- Add the chopped green onions and cornstarch mixture. Mix well.
- Add the deep-fried chicken cubes on the pan and cook until the chicken are fully coated with sauce.
- Serve hot.

273. Orange Flavored Bourbon Grilled Chicken Recipe

Serving: 4 | Prep: | Cook: 20mins | Ready in:

Ingredients

- 2 pounds boneless skinless chicken breasts
- 1/2 cup chopped white onion
- 2 cloves garlic minced
- 1 tablespoon olive oil
- 2 teaspoons orange zest
- 1/3 cup orange juice
- 1 tablespoon balsamic wine vinegar
- 1/3 cup bourbon whiskey
- 1/2 cup molasses
- 1/2 cup catsup
- 1 tablespoon steak sauce
- 1/4 teaspoon dry mustard
- 1/2 teaspoon salt
- 1 teaspoon freshly ground black pepper
- 1/4 teaspoon hot pepper sauce
- 1 teaspoon chili powder
- 1/8 teaspoon cloves

Direction

- Mix all ingredients except chicken and stir until well combined.
- Marinate chicken 4 hours then remove from marinade and grill using indirect heat method.
- Baste with marinade frequently then cook to an internal temperature of 160.

274. Orange Glazed Ginger Chicken Recipe

Serving: 4 | Prep: | Cook: 20mins | Ready in:

Ingredients

- 2 tablespoons mustard (your choice, I use cranberry, but dijon works really well, too)
- 1 tablespoon brown sugar
- 1 tablespoon honey
- 1 teaspoon minced fresh ginger (to taste, I use two teaspoons)
- 1/2 cup orange juice
- cooking spray
- 4 halved chicken breasts

Direction

- Preheat oven to 375 degrees F. Mix first five ingredients in bowl for glazing chicken. Cut chicken breasts in half. Spray 11 X 7 pan (or equivalent baking pan) with cooking spray and lay chicken out. Brush glaze mixture over chicken. Cover and bake 15 to 20 minutes or until chicken is done. Uncover and broil chicken 4 inches from heat source for a couple of minutes.

275. Outstanding Grilled Basil Chicken Burgers Recipe

Serving: 4 | Prep: | Cook: 12mins | Ready in:

Ingredients

- 1 package of lean ground chicken breast
- 1/2 medium onion chopped
- 1 large clove of garlic minced
- 1/4c. romano cheese
- 1/4c. Italian style bread crumbs (or more if needed)
- 1/2 tsp. dried oregano
- 1/2 tsp. dried basil
- 15 fresh basil leaves chopped
- fresh cracked pepper to taste
- 2 tsp. olive oil

Direction

- In a small pan, sauté onion and garlic in the olive oil until tender about 5-7 minutes.
- Set aside and let cool.
- Meanwhile, in a large bowl combine the lean ground chicken, Romano cheese, bread crumbs, dried oregano and basil, chopped fresh basil leaves and pepper to taste.
- Add cooled onions and garlic.
- Combine well.
- To avoid this mixture from sticking to your hands, I suggest that you wet both of your hands first, then form into 4 burger patties.
- Spray a heated grill with non-stick cooking spray and place patties on the grill.
- Cook on each side for about 5-6 minutes or until meat is no longer pink.
- Serve with cheese, or top with grilled veggies.
- Enjoy!

276. Oven Fried Chicken Recipe

Serving: 46 | Prep: | Cook: 1mins | Ready in:

Ingredients

- 4 to 6 chicken breast halves
- 1 cup buttermilk
- 2 crumbled corn flakes or dry breadcrumbs(I like the corn flakes the best, it gives it a great crunch)
- 1/2 cup grated parmesan cheese
- 1 tbs. rosemary flakes, thyme, and parsley flakes
- 1 tbs garlic salt
- red pepper to taste
- salt and pepper to taste

Direction

- Remove skin from chicken.
- Mix together corn flake crumbs, parmesan cheese, rosemary, thyme, parsley, garlic salt, red pepper, salt and pepper.
- Dip chicken into buttermilk, then herb mixture.
- Place chicken on a foil-lined pan that has been sprayed with a non-stick vegetable cooking spray.
- Bake 1 hour at 350 degrees

277. Oven Fried Chicken Tenders Recipe

Serving: 4 | Prep: | Cook: 20mins | Ready in:

Ingredients

- 1 pkg (about 1-1/4 lbs) chicken breast tenders
- 1/4 c flour
- 1 egg
- 1 Tbs water
- 1 c plain or Italian panko bread crumbs
- 1/2 c parmesan cheese

- 2 Tbs butter, melted

Direction

- Heat oven to 425 degrees. Line baking sheet with foil; spray with cooking spray.
- In a shallow dish, place flour. Coat chicken with flour. In another shallow dish, mix egg and water. Dip chicken in egg mixture. In another shallow bowl, mix bread crumbs and parmesan cheese. Dip chicken in bread crumb mixture.
- Place on baking sheet. Drizzle with melted butter.
- Bake 15 to 20 mins, turning once, until chicken is no longer pink and coating is golden brown. Serve with favourite dipping sauce, if desired.

278. Overnight Chicken Light Recipe

Serving: 4 | Prep: | Cook: 90mins | Ready in:

Ingredients

- 4 hard-cooked eggs
- 2 cups dry elbow macaroni
- 1-1/2 cups light cheese, such as light Velveeta®, cubed
- 2 cans low fat cream of chicken soup
- 2 cups diced, cooked chicken breast
- 2 cups low-fat milk
- 3/4 cup diced onion

Direction

- Remove and discard two of the egg yolks from the hard-cooked eggs.
- Chop the remaining egg whites and yolks.
- In a large bowl, combine all the remaining ingredients and mix well.
- Cover with plastic wrap and refrigerate overnight.
- The next day, preheat the oven to 350°.
- Coat a 2-1/2-quart casserole dish with non-stick cooking spray.
- Remove bowl from the refrigerator.
- Stir ingredients and pour into prepared dish.
- Bake, uncovered, for 1-1/2 hours.

279. Parmesan Crusted Chicken Breasts Recipe

Serving: 4 | Prep: | Cook: | Ready in:

Ingredients

- 2 cups parmesan cheese, shredded
- 4 boneless, skinless chicken breasts
- black pepper, to taste

Direction

- Roll out a 2 ft. piece of waxed paper or foil near the stove top. Heat a large nonstick skillet over medium high heat -- pan needs to be hot when the chicken is added. Plie the shredded cheese on the work surface created with the wax paper. Season your chicken on both sides with pepper. Then press the chicken firmly into the cheese coating both sides with as much of the cheese as possible. Add 1 TBS olive oil to the skillet. Set breasts into the skillet and cook 7 minutes on each side, until cheese forms an even golden casing on the chicken breasts.
- Drain off any excess oil from the chicken before serving.

280. Parmesan Stuffed Chicken Breasts Recipe

Serving: 4 | Prep: | Cook: 55mins | Ready in:

Ingredients

- 1 cup fresh flat-leaf parsley leaves, chopped

- 1/4 cup plain dried breadcrumbs
- 1/4 cup grated parmesan cheese
- Grated zest of 1 lemon (about 1 tablespoon)
- coarse salt and ground pepper
- 4 bone-in chicken breast halves (about 3 pounds)

Direction

- Preheat oven to 450 degrees. In a small bowl, mix parsley, breadcrumbs, Parmesan, and zest. Season with 1/4 teaspoon each salt and pepper.
- Divide parsley mixture into four mounds. Carefully loosen chicken skin with fingers; tuck parsley mixture under skin (left). Season chicken with salt and pepper. Place in a 9-by-13-inch roasting pan.
- Bake until skin is crispy, chicken is cooked through, and an instant-read thermometer inserted in the thickest part of the meat registers 165 degrees, about 30 minutes.

281. Party Chicken Recipe

Serving: 8 | Prep: | Cook: 180mins | Ready in:

Ingredients

- 8 good size chicken breasts, skinned and deboned
- 8 slices bacon
- 1 4 oz package chipped beef
- 1 can undiluted cream of mushroom soup
- 1/2 pint sour cream

Direction

- Wrap each chicken breast with a strip of bacon. Cover bottom of flat, greased 8 x 12 x 2 inch baking dish with chipped beef. Mix soup and sour cream; pour over chicken. Refrigerate; when ready bake at 275 degrees for 3 hours uncovered. (This may also be cooked in a crock pot on low for 8-10 hours.)

282. Peach Glazed Chicken Breasts Recipe

Serving: 4 | Prep: | Cook: | Ready in:

Ingredients

- 1/3 cup orange juice
- 1 teaspoon cornstarch
- 4 skinless boneless chicken, breast halves
- 1/4 teaspoon salt
- 1/8 teaspoon pepper
- 1 teaspoon olive oil
- 1 clove garlic, minced
- 1/4 cup peach preserves
- 2 cups frozen peach slices
- 1 teaspoon sugar

Direction

- In small bowl, combine orange juice and cornstarch; blend well. Set aside.
- Spray large nonstick skillet with nonstick cooking spray. Heat over med-high heat until hot. Sprinkle both sides of chicken breast halves with salt and pepper; lace in hot skillet. Cook 2 - 3 min on each side or until lightly browned. Remove chicken from skillet; cover to keep warm.
- Reduce heat to med. Add oil and garlic to same skillet; heat 15 seconds. DO NOT BURN. Remove skillet from heat; add cornstarch mixture and spreadable fruit. Return to skillet to heat; blend well.
- Return chicken to skillet; add peaches and sugar. Reduce heat; cover and simmer 14 - 18 min or until chicken is fork-tender and juices run clear. Serve sauce over chicken.

283. Pecan Crusted Chicken In Honey Mustard Sauce Recipe

Serving: 6 | Prep: | Cook: 35mins | Ready in:

Ingredients

- 2 eggs
- 2 Tbsp. water
- 1 pouch SHAKE'N BAKE Extra Crispy Original Coating Mix
- 1 cup finely chopped pecans, toasted
- 6 small boneless skinless chicken breasts (1-1/2 lb./675 g)
- 1/3 cup Miracle Whip Dressing
- 1/3 cup honey mustard

Direction

- HEAT oven to 400°F.
- Beat eggs and water in shallow dish.
- Mix coating mix and nuts in separate shallow dish.
- Dip chicken in eggs, then in coating mixture, turning to evenly coat both sides of each breast.
- Place on foil-covered baking sheet.
- BAKE 18 to 20 min. or until chicken is done (170°F).
- MIX dressing and mustard; spoon over chicken.

284. Pecan Crusted Chicken And Shrimp Recipe

Serving: 12 | Prep: | Cook: 20mins | Ready in:

Ingredients

- 4 (8 ounce) chicken breasts
- 1 pound shrimp, 16/20 count, tails on
- 1 cup buttermilk
- 3 large eggs
- BREADING:
- 3/4 cup all-purpose flour
- 3/4 cup cornmeal
- 2 teaspoons salt
- 2 teaspoons white pepper
- 1 tablespoon paprika, hot or mild
- 1 teaspoon dry mustard
- 1 3/4 cups pecans, ground
- 5 tablespoons butter for sauteing
- SAUCE:
- 1/2 cup Dijon mustard
- 1/2 cup honey

Direction

- Beat eggs and buttermilk with a fork until pale yellow.
- Grind the pecans and place in a bowl OR pie plate.
- Add the flour, cornmeal, salt, pepper, paprika and dry mustard to the nuts.
- Using your finger, dip the chicken into the egg mixture and then press both sides into the pecan mixture.
- Dip the shrimp into the egg/milk mixture and press both sides in the nuts.
- Melt the butter in a skillet over medium high heat.
- Cook the chicken breasts on both sides until cooked through.
- Sauté the shrimp to a nice brown on both sides, about 3 minutes.
- To make the sauce, combine the Dijon and honey well.
- Serve as a condiment on the side.

285. Pegs Chicken Enchiladas Recipe

Serving: 4 | Prep: | Cook: 30mins | Ready in:

Ingredients

- Filling:
- 4 boneless, skinless chicken breasts
- 1 chipotle pepper, seeds and ribs removed, finely chopped
- ¼ red pepper, finely chopped
- ½ medium onion, finely chopped
- ½ tsp. ground cumin
- ½ tsp. chili powder
- ½ tsp. garlic powder

- ¼ cup mexican cheese blend
- 2 T. salsa, I used pineapple salsa
- 2 T. cream of chicken soup
- 6-8 large flour tortillas
- Sauce:
- Remainder of can of soup
- ½ tsp. chili powder
- ½ tsp. garlic powder
- ½ tsp. cumin
- ¼ red pepper, finely chopped
- ½ medium onion, finely chopped
- 2 T. medium salsa
- ½ cup chicken broth (from the breasts you boiled
- ½ cup milk
- ½ C. mexican cheese blend
- lettuce, sour cream and tomatoes.

Direction

- Filling:
- Boil chicken breasts until tender and remove to plate to cool. Save ½ to ¾ cup of the chicken broth for later. Shred the chicken between your fingers and add to large bowl. Add next 9 ingredients and mix to blend.
- Preheat oven to 350.
- Spray a 9x12 pan with cooking spray and sprinkle a little of the chopped onion and pepper into the bottom of the pan to keep the tortillas from sticking.
- Place about 2 T. of the chicken mixture into tortillas and roll up, leaving ends open and place in pan seam side down.
- Repeat until chicken mixture is gone, should make 6-8.
- (You of course could use smaller tortillas and make more enchiladas)
- Sauce:
- Mix soup and next 8 ingredients until well blended and pour over tortillas, moving them around a bit to get sauce in between the tortillas. Sprinkle cheese over the top and bake for 30 minutes.
- Serve with lettuce, tomatoes and sour cream on the side.

286. Poached Italian Chicken With Rice Tabbouleh Recipe

Serving: 0 | Prep: | Cook: | Ready in:

Ingredients

- POACHED chicken
- 4 chicken breasts
- 4-6 bay leaves
- 2 tbsp of Italian herb seasoning mix
- enough water to cover
- i cup of sour cream
- rice TABBOULEH
- 4 cups of cooked brown rice
- 4 ripe tomatoes, finely chopped
- 2 cups of chopped parsley
- 1 tbsp Italian herb seasoning mix
- 1/4 cup of cider vinegar

Direction

- POACHED CHICKEN
- To the saucepan add
- Bay leaves, Italian herbs, chicken breasts
- Add just enough water to cover
- Simmer on very low for 30 mins
- OR until chicken breasts are cooked
- Place saucepan in fridge overnight
- Next day -
- Remove chicken breasts and slice thickly
- Reduce stock by half by boiling off
- Add the sour cream
- Add the sliced chicken breast
- Continue until chicken is warmed thru
- Serve on a bed of rice tabbouleh
- RICE TABBOULEH
- Combine all ingredients
- Cover and leave out for a while for flavours to mingle

287. Pollo Asado And Yellow Vegetable Rice Recipe

Serving: 6 | Prep: | Cook: 60mins | Ready in:

Ingredients

- Pollo Asado
- * 3 whole chicken breasts
- * 1/2 large sliced red or spanish onion
- * 4 smashed garlic cloves
- * 1/2 cup mojo criollo *
- * 1tbsp oregano
- * 2 tsp cumin
- * 2 tsp salt
- * 1/4 lemon wedge
- * 3/4 cup vegetable oil
- Yellow vegetable rice
- * 2.5 cups white rice
- * 3 cups water
- * 1 lb. frozen mixed vegetables
- * * if you prefer fresh vegetables: 1 ear of corn for kernels, 1/4 cup peas, 8 oz. small carrots, 8 oz. small cut green beans
- * 1 packet of Sazon seasoning with achiote (this yellows the rice)(see note below)
- * 3 tbsp vegetable or olive oil
- * 2.5 tbsp salt
- Yellow rice Sofrito
- * 1/2 diced green pepper
- * 2 diced green onion stems
- * 1/2 diced large onion
- * 1 whole tomato
- * 4 minced garlic cloves

Direction

- Pollo Asado
- In large pot, season chicken with garlic and onion, salt, oregano, cumin.
- Pinch chicken with fork to allow seasoning to sit well.
- Add 1/4 cup of mojo to chicken, stir and let marinate for one hour to 90 minutes.
- In same pot, lightly fry chicken breast in vegetable oil until both sides have browned, for 6-7 minutes.
- Add remainder of mojo and squeeze lemon wedge.
- Bring heat down to medium-low, cover and let cook for another 30 minutes.
- If you find your chicken too dry, you can add 1/2 cup of dry white cooking wine. Steam from pot will create the excess mojo sauce.
- Serves 3
- Rice
- In rice cooker, add rice and water to pot.
- Add sofrito, mixed vegetables (frozen or fresh), packet of Sazon seasoning, salt, and oil.
- Stir and click on cook! Should be done in about 20 minutes.
- When cooker chimes, let sit for 5 minutes.
- Fork and comb through rice, lifting the grain.
- Allow to sit for another 5 minutes. Yields enough for 7.
- Sofrito
- In light oil, sauté onion, garlic, green onion (scallion) green pepper and tomato on medium heat, allowing onions to cook down.

288. Pollo Con Crema Ala Donna Recipe

Serving: 4 | Prep: | Cook: 25mins | Ready in:

Ingredients

- 4 boneless skinless chicken breasts
- 1/2 red bell pepper (or green if you like)
- 1/2 sweet onion
- 1 7 oz. can fire roasted green chiles (I like the Hot ones)
- 1 cup chicken broth
- 1 8 oz. cream cheese (I use light)
- 1/2 tsp. cumin (or more)
- 1/2 tsp Mexican oregano
- 1 tsp. ground chipotle pepper (or any kind of spicy pepper, e.g., pasilla, ancho, etc.)
- garlic to taste
- salt to taste

- 3 cups cooked long grain white rice (or whatever kind you like)
- fresh chopped cilantro

Direction

- Make rice according to directions (Or use leftover rice from Chinese takeout- great way to use)
- Chop red bell pepper and onion in size that you prefer (I like mine about 1")
- Sauté in large non-stick pan in a little olive oil (my preference, you can use butter or eliminate) till onion is slightly clear and pepper is still a little firm
- Remove peppers and onion and set aside
- Slice and chop the chicken into bite size pieces
- Heat pan with a little olive oil and add chicken letting it brown slightly (careful not to overcook)
- Add chicken broth and green chilies bring to simmer
- Turn off heat and add cream cheese stirring slowly till incorporated (I use back side of large spoon and press on block of cheese in a circle till it slowly melts in)
- Add spices (I'm not too stringent on this, I just add to taste depending how "hot" we want it)
- (You can serve with dried red pepper flakes for those who like it really hot)
- Add back the peppers and onions
- When it has the consistency you like - to make it thicker, add more cream cheese - thinner, add more chicken broth or milk - serve over cooked rice.
- Top with cilantro

289. Polynesian Chicken Recipe

Serving: 4 | Prep: | Cook: 35mins | Ready in:

Ingredients

- 4 boneless skinless chicken breasts or 8 chicken tenderloins
- 1/2 cup low sodium soy sauce (regular soy sauce would make it way too salty!)
- 1/3 cup honey
- 1 tablespoon hoisin sauce
- 2 star anise (i have used extract when i could not find the spice)
- 2 tablespoon grated ginger

Direction

- Combine all ingredient except chicken.
- I like to put the mixture in a big ziplock bag and then add the chicken and let it marinate for a few minutes.
- Place in baking dish, bake for 35 minutes @ 375 degrees or till chicken is done.

290. Popeye Recipe

Serving: 4 | Prep: | Cook: 5mins | Ready in:

Ingredients

- 4 cooked boneless skinless chicken breasts seasoned with salt & pepper (I grilled mine but you can use any method you like)
- 8 oz. button mushrooms, sliced
- 1 tbsp butter
- black pepper & sea salt, freshly ground to taste
- 1 batch Creamed Spinach
- 1 cup shredded cheese (I used Monterrey Jack/Cheddar/Mozzarella blend)

Direction

- Preheat oven to 350F. Prepare a baking dish with cooking spray.
- Melt butter over medium heat in a skillet. Add mushrooms and season with salt & pepper. Cook, stirring, until they begin to release their own juice. Remove from heat.
- Place chicken breasts in prepared baking dish. Spoon mushrooms over top. Top with

creamed spinach and finally with shredded cheese. Bake for 15 minutes or until heated through and cheese is melted.

291. Pretty In Pink Chicken Salad Recipe

Serving: 4 | Prep: | Cook: 15mins | Ready in:

Ingredients

- 4 boneless, skinless chicken breast halves
- salt, ground black pepper and garlic powder to taste
- leaf lettuce, baby salad greens or greens of choice
- 2 to 3 large ripe tomatoes, sliced
- 2 ounces feta or blue cheese, crumbled
- 1 egg yolk
- 1/2 cup plus 1 tablespoons red wine vinegar
- 6 tablespoons granulated sugar
- 2 1/2 cups vegetable oil
- 3 tablespoons ketchup

Direction

- Pound chicken breasts to a 1/2 inch thickness.
- Season to taste with salt, pepper and garlic powder.
- Grill or broil chicken breasts until cooked through.
- Meanwhile, generously line 4 plates with salad greens.
- Divide tomato slices around rim of plates.
- Thin slices of red onion and cucumber slices may be added as well.
- Crumble cheese over tomato slices.
- In blender or food processor, combine egg yolk, vinegar and sugar. Stream in oil with motor running.
- Arrange chicken in center of plates.
- Drizzle with prepared dressing.

292. Quick Chicken Cacciatore Recipe

Serving: 0 | Prep: | Cook: 22mins | Ready in:

Ingredients

- 4 boneless skinless chicken breast cut into 1-inch strips
- 1 large green pepper chopped
- 1 teaspoon parsley
- 1/2 cup chopped celery
- 1/4 teaspoon salt
- 1 chopped medium onion
- 1/4 teaspoon pepper
- 1 cup sliced mushrooms
- 1 16-ounce can peeled tomatoes
- 2 teaspoon oregano
- 1 8-ounce can tomato sauce
- 1 teaspoon dried basil

Direction

- Spray skillet with non-stick spray
- Preheat pan over heat
- Add chicken, and cook, stirring, for 3-5 minutes, or until no longer pink
- Reduce heat
- Add tomatoes and their juice, tomato sauce, green pepper, celery, onion, mushrooms, oregano, basil, parsley and salt
- Bring to boil; reduce heat and simmer, covered for 10 minutes
- Serve over rice, pasta or potato.

293. Ranch Chicken Recipe

Serving: 4 | Prep: | Cook: 10mins | Ready in:

Ingredients

- 4 boneless skinless chicken breasts
- 1 egg
- 1 teaspoon milk
- 1 package dry ranch dressing

- 2 tablespoons flour

Direction

- Pound out chicken breasts until thin.
- Mix egg and milk then put in a soup bowl.
- Combine dry Ranch dressing with flour then put in soup bowl.
- Dip each breast in the egg mixture then in then ranch mixture.
- Fry 5 minutes on each side.

294. Ranch Chicken Wrap Recipe

Serving: 5 | Prep: | Cook: 30mins | Ready in:

Ingredients

- 3/4 c ranch
- 1/4 cup chopped fresh cilantro
- 1.5 lbs boneless, skinless chicken breast
- 16-25 spinach leaves
- 1 avocado, sliced
- 5 large tortillas

Direction

- Combine ranch, cilantro and set aside 1/4 cup
- Marinate chicken in remaining dressing for hour or more
- Grill and slice
- Place spinach, chicken and avocado on soft tortilla
- Drizzle with reserved dressing
- Roll and slice diagonal

295. Ranch Style Chicken Recipe

Serving: 6 | Prep: | Cook: 15mins | Ready in:

Ingredients

- ½ cups Dijon mustard
- ½ cups honey
- ½ whole (juice Of) lemon
- ½ teaspoons paprika
- ½ teaspoons salt
- Crushed red pepper (optional To Taste)
- 6 whole Boneless, skinless chicken Breasts
- 1 pound Thick Cut bacon
- bacon grease
- sharp cheddar cheese, to taste
- canola oil

Direction

- To begin, make the marinade. In a large bowl mix together ½ cup Dijon or country/grainy mustard with ½ cup honey, juice of ½ lemon, ½ teaspoon paprika, and ½ teaspoon salt and whisk until smooth. Sprinkle in some crushed red pepper flakes or cayenne if you like things a little spicy. Set aside.
- Next, rinse the chicken breasts, place between two sheets of waxed paper and pound to around ½ to ¾ inch thick with a mallet. Next, add the chicken to the bowl with the marinade, cover with plastic wrap and place in the refrigerator for 1 to 3 hours.
- While the chicken marinates, fry up some bacon. When finished cooking, reserve ¼ cup of the bacon grease and clean out the skillet.
- When the chicken is done marinating, preheat the oven to 400 degrees. Remove the chicken from the fridge and pour off excess marinade. Heat half of the reserved bacon grease with an equal quantity of Canola Oil in the clean skillet over medium-high heat. When the grease is nice and hot add two or three pieces of chicken to it. Cook until brownish/blackish, about 1 to 1 ½ minutes per side. Remove chicken to a large baking sheet. If cooking many pieces of chicken, repeat skillet process and remove finished chicken to baking sheet. Place chicken in preheated oven and cook for about 10 minutes. Remove from over.

- Lay a few pieces of bacon over each chicken breast. Sprinkle shredded sharp cheddar cheese over the top of the chicken as generously as you like. Return pan to oven for an additional five minutes until cheese is melted and bacon is sizzling. Serve immediately.

296. Ricotta Baked Chicken Recipe

Serving: 4 | Prep: | Cook: 60mins | Ready in:

Ingredients

- 1 lb boneless skinless chicken breast, flattened to ¼" thick
- 15 oz. container, part skim ricotta cheese
- 4 leaves fresh basil, chiffonned (rolled and cut into small pieces)
- 2 cloves roasted garlic (in a paste-like consistency)
- 2 tbsp. finely chopped banana peppers
- salt and pepper to taste
- ½ c. fine seasoned bread crumbs plus 2 tbsp.
- ½ c. flour
- 1 egg, beaten
- 1 egg beaten with 1 tbsp. water
- 3 tbsp. canola oil
- 2-3 oz. thinly sliced jack or other mild cheese

Direction

- Preheat oven to 325 degrees.
- In a medium sized bowl, mix the ricotta with the beaten egg, stir in the garlic, basil, and peppers;
- Season to taste with salt and pepper;
- Heat oil in a non-stick 10-12" skillet;
- Dredge chicken in flour, shake off excess, then dip in egg, then breadcrumbs;
- Brown chicken, 2-4 minutes each side;
- Place chicken in a heavy casserole dish;
- Spread cheese mixture evenly over chicken;
- Sprinkle with the 2 tbsp. of bread crumbs;
- Place thinly sliced cheese evenly over top, place on baking rack in oven;
- After 45 minutes, cut into chicken to check for doneness (no pink);
- Turn oven up to 375, put casserole back in and let cook for another 15-20 min. until slightly browned on top.

297. Ritzy Chicken Casserole Recipe

Serving: 8 | Prep: | Cook: 20mins | Ready in:

Ingredients

- 8 oz. cream cheese
- 1/2 C. sour cream
- 1 (10 3/4 oz.) can cream of mushroom soup
- 1 (10 3/4 oz.) can cream of chicken soup
- 1/2 C. finely chopped onion
- 6 C. diced cooked chicken breasts
- 1 roll Ritz crackers (50 crackers)
- 1/2 C. (1 stick) melted butter

Direction

- Soften cream cheese. Add sour cream, soups, chopped onion and chicken. Pour into a 9 x 13-inch ovenproof baking dish.
- To make topping, crush crackers to make crumbs. Combine with butter. Sprinkle over chicken mixture.
- Bake uncovered at 350 degrees for 20 minutes.

298. Roasted Garlic Cream Pasta Recipe

Serving: 2 | Prep: | Cook: 45mins | Ready in:

Ingredients

- 2 brined chicken breasts, skin removed

- 3/4 cup chicken stock
- 1/2 medium onion, diced
- 1 head of garlic
- A few extra cloves of garlic, minced
- 1/2 cup milk, skim
- 1/2 cup sour cream, reduced fat or nonfat
- 1 1/2 tablespoons parmesan cheese, freshly grated
- 1/4 teaspoon ground sage
- 2-4 oz fettuccine, (cooked sometime between the beginning and last step)
- extra virgin olive oil
- salt
- pepper

Direction

- Preheat your oven to 450F. Rinse your brined chicken, and season tops with pepper (no salt), then set aside.
- Take a head of garlic and slice it through the middle of all the cloves (so that you have a top half, and the bottom half of a bundle of cloves)
- Place two halves on a sheet of foil. Drizzle with extra virgin olive oil, sprinkle with salt, and crack some fresh pepper over the halves. Put the top back on the bottom half and fold the foil into a package, all the way around the head of the garlic.
- Place on top shelf of oven for about 20-25 minutes (or until you are done with chicken, and first part of sauce).
- Meanwhile, boil water for the pasta.
- Heat about a tablespoon of olive oil in a sauté pan over high heat.
- Toss a few cloves of minced garlic in sauté pan with oil.
- Dice your onion, then sauté in pan until translucent.
- Now, lay your chicken breasts peppered side down, now season the other side. Brown first side then flip to brown other side.
- Now, pour in chicken stock. (Depending on how big your sauté pan is, the chicken should just barely be sitting in the stock.)
- Turn your heat down until you have a simmer (about medium) and cover.
- Remove the head of garlic from the oven, unwrapping foil (careful, it's HOT). Set aside to cool.
- Meanwhile, in a bowl, whisk together the sour cream, milk, chicken stock, sage, and Parmesan cheese. Set aside.
- To extract the garlic from its papery skin, take a half in your hand and gently squeeze until the cloves pop out (if the roasting was successful, this should happen pretty easily).
- You can either press this through a garlic grater or you can simply mash with a fork. Combine with the milk/sour cream mixture.
- When chicken is done, remove from sauté pan and set aside.
- Add milk/sour cream mixture to pan, then add pasta and toss together, coating pasta with sauce.
- Transfer a serving of pasta to a plate. Slice your chicken breasts on a bias, and fan across the pile of pasta to serve.
- Garnish with Italian parsley or fresh basil.

299. Rosemary Chicken Recipe

Serving: 4 | Prep: | Cook: 30mins | Ready in:

Ingredients

- 8 garlic cloves
- 4 chicken breasts
- 1 lemon
- olive oil
- dried rosemary
- salt and pepper
- Foil

Direction

- Preheat oven to 450 degrees
- Peel garlic, leave whole
- Place garlic in center of cookie sheet, put 2 tsp. olive oil over cloves
- Make a tent of foil over cloves

- Bake for 10 minutes
- MEANWHILE
- In bowl place chicken, marinating in 2 tbsp. olive oil, salt, pepper, 2 tbsp. lemon juice
- After 10 minutes take out garlic, remove foil and place chicken on garlic (spread around if necessary)
- Sprinkle with rosemary
- Bake for 30-40 minutes

300. Rotini With Chicken Asparagus And Tomatoes Recipe

Serving: 4 | Prep: | Cook: 15mins | Ready in:

Ingredients

- 8 ounces uncooked rotini (corkscrew pasta)
- cooking spray
- 1 pound skinless, boneless chicken breast, cut into 1/4-inch strips
- 1/2 teaspoon kosher salt
- 1/2 teaspoon freshly ground black pepper
- 1 cup (1-inch) slices asparagus
- 2 cups cherry tomatoes, halved
- 2 garlic cloves, minced
- 2 tablespoons chopped fresh basil
- 2 tablespoons balsamic vinegar
- 1 tablespoon extravirgin olive oil
- 1/4 cup (1 ounce) crumbled goat cheese

Direction

- Cook pasta according to package directions, omitting salt and fat.
- Heat a large nonstick skillet over medium-high heat. Coat pan with cooking spray. Sprinkle chicken with salt and pepper. Add chicken and asparagus to pan; sauté 5 minutes. Add tomatoes and garlic to pan; sauté 1 minute. Remove from heat. Stir in pasta, basil, vinegar, and oil. Arrange 2 cups pasta mixture on each of 4 plates; top each serving with 1 tablespoon cheese.

301. Sausage Stuffed Chicken Breast Recipe

Serving: 4 | Prep: | Cook: 50mins | Ready in:

Ingredients

- Ingredients
- 4-bone-in chicken breast
- 4 sausage slices
- 1/2 tsp salt
- 1 tsp fresh ground black pepper
- 1 tsp seasoned meat tenderizer
- 1/2 tsp garlic power
- 1 large onion chopped
- tomato juice or V-8 juice

Direction

- Take bones out of breast and cut a pocket in center of the meat, not to go all the way through.
- Take 1 slice of sausage roll up to fit in pocket. Sprinkle with all the seasonings (both sides) place in 9 by 12 baking dish cover with onions and tomato juice, bake at 350 degrees for 45 to 55 minute

302. Sauted Boneless Breast Of Chicken With Mushroom Sauce Recipe

Serving: 10 | Prep: | Cook: 30mins | Ready in:

Ingredients

- 2 oz clarified butter
- 10 Boneless, skinless chicken breasts
- to taste --- salt

- to taste --- white pepper
- 2 oz flour (for dredging)
- 10 oz mushrooms (white) sliced
- 1 oz lemon juice
- 2.5 cup Suprême sauce, hot (see recipe)
- ===

- For the Suprême sauce:
- 2 qt chicken velouté
- 1 pt heavy cream
- 2 oz butter
- to taste salt
- to taste white pepper
- to taste lemon juice

Direction

- Add enough clarified butter to a sauté pan to just cover the bottom with a thin film.
- Place on the range over moderate heat.
- While the pan is heating, season the chicken breasts and dredge in flour.
- Shake off excess flour.
- Place the breasts in the hot pan, presentation side (that is, the side that had the skin) down.
- Sauté over moderate heat until lightly browned and about half cooked.
- The heat must be regulated so the chicken doesn't brown too fast.
- Turn the chicken over and complete the cooking.
- Remove the chicken from the pan and place on hot dinner plates.
- Keep warm.
- Add the mushrooms to the pan and sauté briefly.
- After a few seconds, before the mushrooms start to darken, add the lemon juice.
- Toss the mushrooms in the pan as they sauté.
- For the Suprême sauce:
- Add the suprême sauce to the pan and simmer for a few minutes, until reduced to the proper consistency.
- (The juices from the mushrooms will dilute the sauce.)
- Ladle 2 oz. sauce over each portion and serve immediately.

303. Shish Taouk Chicken Kebobs Recipe

Serving: 4 | Prep: | Cook: 15mins | Ready in:

Ingredients

- 2 lbs cubed chicken breast
- 3 tablespoons lemon juice
- 1 tablespoon olive oil
- 2 cloves garlic, finely chopped
- 1/4 teaspoon cumin
- 1/2 teaspoon pepper
- 1/8 teaspoon cayenne

Direction

- In a medium bowl, combine all ingredients. Allow chicken to marinate for 2-24 hours, covered in the refrigerator.
- Place chicken on the skewers (about 5 pieces on each). Grill for 15 minutes or until done, turning every 5 minutes or so. You also can broil these in your oven.

304. Shredded Chicken Burritos With Cactus Pear Sauce Recipe

Serving: 6 | Prep: | Cook: 60mins | Ready in:

Ingredients

- For the Cactus pear Sauce
- 4 Bolivian Sweet red onions 3 whole and 1 diced
- 2 tablespoons extra virgin olive oil
- 1/2 cup Cactus pears (use Red Cactus pears) peeled purred and strained
- 1/2 cup apples (use green apples) peeled cored and pureed

- 4 tablespoons unsalted butter divided
- 1 1/2 teaspoons ground cumin
- 1 teaspoon Crushed red pepper
- 1 teaspoon ground coriander
- 1 Serrano Chiles minced
- 3 clovesPeeled garlic chopped
- 1 teaspoon lime zested
- 1/3 cup worcestershire sauce
- 1/2 cup tequila
- 1/4 cup cider vinegar
- 2 tablespoons lime juice
- 3/4 cup water
- For the Burrito
- 1 1/2 pounds Boneless and skinless chicken Breasts cubed
- 6 large flour tortillas
- 1 jar Fire roasted Sweet red bell peppers drained
- 4 1/2 cups Soy Shreds (use Cheddar Flavor)
- 1 1/4 cups sour cream
- 2 jalapeno chile diced

Direction

- Preheat oven to 350 °F.
- Coat the whole onions with the olive oil, place on a baking sheet and place in the oven. Cook until inside layers are soft, about 30-45 minutes. When cool enough to handle, peel off charred outside layers and discard. Place the onions, the cactus puree and the apple puree in a blender and mix well.
- In a saucepan, melt 1 tablespoon of the butter and caramelize the diced onion. Add the cumin and the next 5 ingredients and cook for 2 minutes. Next add the Worcestershire and the next 3 ingredients and reduce by half over medium-high heat. Stir in the cactus pear puree mix, water and salt to taste. Bring to a simmer. Remove from the heat and swirl in the remaining butter. Carefully blend the sauce until smooth.
- In a saucepan, place the chicken cubes and cover with the cactus pear sauce. Stir and bring to a simmer. Stirring occasionally, cook over low heat for about 1 hour so chicken gets very flavorful and tender. Remove from the sauce and shred the chicken using 2 forks.
- To build your burrito: reheat the chicken but be careful not to dry it out.

305. Simple Grilled Chicken Recipe

Serving: 2 | Prep: | Cook: 1hours15mins | Ready in:

Ingredients

- 2 large chicken breasts (actually, any chicken cut will do. I just like the breast because it's the meatiest)
- 1/2 lemon
- 2 tsp minced fresh parsley
- 1 tbsp honey
- 1 tbsp olive oil
- salt and pepper
- Optional Ingredients
- 1 clove garlic, minced
- 1 teaspoon of minced chili (whatever kind you like, depends on your heat tolerance

Direction

- Preparing the Chicken
- Season the chicken breasts with the salt and pepper and let it sit.
- While letting the chicken sit, mix together all the other ingredients in a separate container.
- Once thoroughly mixed, pour the marinade over the chicken. To make sure the chicken in well covered, put it in a container that's just about the same size as the chicken parts.
- Cover and put in the ref for about 15 minutes. Overnight is better.
- Cooking the Chicken
- Put the chicken and marinade in a microwave cooking safe dish and cook in the microwave oven for about 10 - 20 minutes in medium setting.

- Check if the chicken is done. If not yet, microwave it for another 5 minutes or until it's done.
- Preheat the grill pan about 5 minutes before the chicken leaves the Microwave.
- After the microwave cooking, put the chicken (leave the 'gravy' in the dish) on to the grill pan and cook it until it attains that grilled texture on the surface.
- Suggestions
- The 'gravy' left from the microwave cooking can be used as gravy for the chicken.
- This really goes well with my mashed potatoes.

306. Skillet Chicken Parmesan Recipe

Serving: 6 | Prep: | Cook: 25mins | Ready in:

Ingredients

- 6 tbsp. grated parmesan cheese
- 1 1/2 cups Prego® Traditional Italian Sauce
- vegetable cooking spray
- 6 small skinless, boneless chicken breasts (1 1/2 lb.)
- 1 1/2 cups shredded part-skim mozzarella cheese

Direction

- STIR 4 tbsp. Parmesan cheese into pasta sauce.
- SPRAY skillet with cooking spray and heat 1 min. Add chicken and cook until browned. Drain.
- POUR pasta sauce over chicken; turn breasts over to coat both sides with sauce. Cover and cook over medium heat 10 min. or until done.
- TOP with mozzarella cheese and remaining 2 tbsp. Parmesan cheese. Let stand 5 min. or until cheese is melted

307. Slow Cooker Chicken Burritos Recipe

Serving: 12 | Prep: | Cook: 8hours6mins | Ready in:

Ingredients

- 1 medium garlic clove
- 1 small red onion
- 14 1/2 ounce can diced tomatoes with chilies
- 15 ounce can kidney beans, drained
- 1/2 tsp chili powder
- 1/2 tsp table salt
- 1/4 tsp black pepper
- 1/4 tsp oregano (optional)
- 1 pound boneless, skinless chicken breast
- 12 medium whole wheat tortillas
- 3/4 cup reduced fat Mexican style shredded cheese

Direction

- Place garlic, onions, tomatoes, beans, chili powder, salt, pepper and oregano in a 3 quart slow cooker. Stir well.
- Add chicken and broth
- Cover and cook on low setting for 5 hours
- Drain of liquid.
- To serve: spoon about 1/2 cup of mixture down the middle of a tortilla and top with 1 tsp. cheese.
- Yields 1 burrito per serving
- Points: 3 Points per serving

308. Slow Cooker Chicken Taco Stew Recipe

Serving: 14 | Prep: | Cook: 210mins | Ready in:

Ingredients

- 2 16-oz can black beans
- 1 16-oz can corn (drained)
- 1 8-oz can tomato sauce

- 2 14.5-oz cans diced tomatoes w/chiles (or without if you like it mild)
- 1 1.25-oz packet taco seasoning
- 1-2 boneless skinless chicken breasts

Direction

- Mix everything together in a slow cooker except chicken
- Lay chicken on top and cover
- Cook on low for 6-8 hours or on high for 3-4 hours
- 30 minutes before serving, remove chicken and shred
- Return chicken to slow cooker, stir in, and continue cooking
- This is good eaten with cheese, sour cream, or tortilla chips.

309. Sour Cream Southern Fried Chicken Recipe

Serving: 8 | Prep: | Cook: 25mins | Ready in:

Ingredients

- 8 boneless chicken breasts, about 4 ounces each
- 3/4 cup sour cream
- 1/2 cup buttermilk
- 1 teaspoon granulated garlic
- 1 T. Hot Shot
- 1 cup tortilla chips, crushed fine (or cornflake crumbs)
- 2 tablespoons parsley, minced
- 1/2 cup potato chips, crushed fine (try changing up the flavors - cheddar & sour cream, onion, BBQ)
- 1 cup vegetable oil for frying
- salt and pepper to taste

Direction

- Pound the chicken breasts thin.
- In a large zip top plastic bag, combine the sour cream, buttermilk, granulated garlic and Hot Shot.
- Place chicken breasts in the plastic bag, squeeze out all the air and cover. Marinate in the refrigerator for at least 1 hour.
- In a medium mixing bowl, combine tortilla chip crumbs, parsley and crushed potato chips. Remove chicken from marinade and press firmly into the breading mixture, completely coating the chicken. Repeat this for each piece.
- Heat the oil in a large frying pan over medium heat until hot. Carefully place chicken in the oil and cook on each side until golden brown. This may have to be done in batches. Remove from oil and place on paper towel.
- Season lightly with salt and pepper.
- Finish cooking the chicken by placing it on a baking sheet in a preheated 375-degree oven for 8 to 10 minutes or until it reaches an internal temperature of 160 degrees.

310. Southern Marinated Maple Chicken Recipe

Serving: 6 | Prep: | Cook: 30mins | Ready in:

Ingredients

- 6 chicken breasts
- 1/2 cup maple syrup
- 1/2 cup corn oil
- 1 tablespoon garlic
- 1 teaspoon ginger
- 1 can tomato soup
- 1/2 teaspoon freshly ground black pepper

Direction

- Mix all ingredients except chicken in large mixing bowl.
- Put chicken in large plastic bag and pour marinade over top. Refrigerate overnight. Grill and serve.

311. Southwest Chicken Kiev Recipe

Serving: 6 | Prep: | Cook: 15mins | Ready in:

Ingredients

- 1 cup miniature cheese crackers, crushed
- 1-1/2 teaspoons taco seasoning
- 5 tablespoons butter, softened, divided
- 3 tablespoons shredded cheddar cheese
- 2 tablespoons canned chopped green chilies
- 2 teaspoons dried minced onion
- 1/2 teaspoon salt
- 6 boneless skinless chicken breast halves (6 ounces each)

Direction

- In a shallow bowl, combine cracker crumbs and taco seasoning; set aside. In another bowl, combine 3 tablespoons butter, cheese, chilies, onion and salt. Shape mixture into six balls.
- Flatten chicken to 1/4-in. thickness. Place a butter ball in the center of each. Roll up and secure with toothpicks. In a shallow microwave-safe bowl, melt remaining butter. Dip chicken in butter, then coat evenly with cracker mixture.
- Place seam side down in a greased shallow round 3-qt. microwave-safe dish. Microwave, uncovered, on high for 12-14 minutes or until chicken juices run clear and a meat thermometer reads 170°. Discard toothpicks.

312. Southwestern Chicken Casserole Recipe

Serving: 5 | Prep: | Cook: 30mins | Ready in:

Ingredients

- 5 or 6 large potatoes
- 4 boneless chicken breast
- 1 medium onion, chopped
- 1 can of ro-tel
- 1 can of cream of chicken
- grated cheese
- bacon bits

Direction

- Boil potatoes until they are almost done
- Cook chicken on top of stove covered in skillet with a little water, until done.
- Drain potatoes and pour them in casserole dish
- Top with cooked chicken
- Add chopped onion
- Mix ro-tel and cream of chicken together and bring to boil
- Then pour on top of potatoes, chicken and onion mixture
- Then top with grated cheese and bacon bits
- Bake for 25-30 minutes or until all liquid is gone.
- ENJOY!!!

313. Spice Rubbed Chicken Fingers With Cilantro Dipping Sauce (south Beach Diet Cookbook) Recipe

Serving: 4 | Prep: | Cook: 45mins | Ready in:

Ingredients

- 1 teaspoon chili powder
- 1 teaspoon ground cumin
- 1/4 teaspoon salt
- 1 pound chicken breast tenders
- 1/2 cup cilantro sprigs
- 1/4 cup blanched slivered almonds
- 1 clove garlic
- 1 serrano chili pepper seeded (wear plastic gloves when handling)

- 1/8 teaspoon
- 2 tablespoons lime juice
- 2 tablespoons water
- Sprig cilantro, for garnish

Direction

- Coat a grill rack o broiler-pan rack with cooking spray.
- Preheat the grill or broiler.
- In a cup, combine the chili powder, cumin, and salt.
- Cut two 1/2' deep slashes in each side of the chicken tenders.
- Rub the spice mixture over the chicken, pressing it into the slits.
- Place the chicken in a baking pan and coat completely with cooking spray.
- Let stand for 10 minutes.
- In a food processor, combine the cilantro, parsley, almonds, garlic, chili pepper and salt.
- Process until chopped.
- While processor is running, add the lime juice and oil through the feed tube, stopping the machine once or twice to scrape down the sides of the container until the sauce is smooth.
- Pour the sauce into a bowl.
- Stir in the water, cover, and chill until ready to serve.
- Place the chicken on the prepared rack and grill or broil 6" from the heat, turning several times, for 15 minutes, or until a thermometer inserted in the thickest portion registers 170 degrees F and the juices run clear.
- Serve with the sauce and garnish with the cilantro.
- Per Serving: 248 calories, 13 g fat, 2 g saturated fat, 28 g protein, 4 g carbohydrate, 1 g dietary fiber, 66 mg cholesterol, 324 mg sodium.

314. Spiced Pistachio Chicken Recipe

Serving: 6 | Prep: | Cook: 45mins | Ready in:

Ingredients

- 3 lbs boneless chicken breasts or thighs
- 1 stick butter, melted
- 4-6 cloves garlic, minced
- 1 egg
- 2T honey
- juice from 1/2 lime
- salt and pepper
- about 1 1/2 cups pistachio meats
- 1 cup Panko breadcrumbs
- 2t cayenne(to taste, of course)
- 1T dry minced onion
- 1t garlic powder
- 1/2t Old Bay Seasoning(optional)
- 1t dry mustard
- 1t celery powder(optional)
- fresh ground black pepper

Direction

- Melt butter in microwave in large glass bowl.
- Add garlic, honey, lime juice, salt and pepper and whisk together.
- Add egg and whisk again.
- Place all chicken pieces into butter mixture, turning to coat all sides.
- Let sit while preparing crust.
- Pulse pistachios in food processor to create a coarse grind.
- In large zipper style bag combine nuts, breadcrumbs, cayenne, onion, garlic powder, Old Bay, dry mustard, celery powder and pepper. Mix well.
- After chicken has rested in wash for about 10 minutes (it will get goopy and yucky looking due to the butter cooling, but don't worry :), place a few pieces at a time into zipper bag of coating ingredients and toss to coat.
- Place in baking dish or deep cookie sheet or cast iron pan (this is what I use :) Continue with remaining pieces.

- Bake at 400 for about 20-25 minutes, depending on thickness and size of pieces. Cook until juices run clear and internal temperature is 170. Do not turn chicken while baking.
- Remove from pan onto wire baking rack and let sit about 5 minutes.

315. Spicy Braised Chicken With Mushrooms And Star Anise Recipe

Serving: 4 | Prep: | Cook: 45mins | Ready in:

Ingredients

- 1 tablespoon peanut oil
- 4 chicken breast halves with skin and bones
- 12 ounces fresh shiitake mushrooms, stemmed, caps quartered
- 2 cups chopped green onions
- 2 tablespoons minced garlic
- 1 tablespoon minced peeled fresh ginger
- 2 14 1/2-ounce cans low-salt chicken broth
- 1/2 cup hoisin sauce
- 4 whole star anise
- 4 cups 3/4-inch-wide strips napa cabbage (about 1/2 small head)
- 1 tablespoon hot chili sauce (such as sambal olek or sriracha)*
- *Available at Asian markets and in the Asian foods section of some supermarkets.

Direction

- Heat peanut oil in heavy large pot over medium-high heat. Add chicken; sauté until brown, about 4 minutes per side. Transfer to bowl. Add mushrooms, 1 1/2 cups green onions, garlic and ginger to pot. Sauté until mushrooms are tender, about 5 minutes. Return chicken to pot. Add chicken broth, hoisin sauce and star anise. Bring to boil. Reduce heat, cover and simmer until chicken is cooked through, about 20 minutes.
- Remove chicken from pot; cool slightly. Remove skin and bones from chicken and discard. Cut meat crosswise into 1/2-inch-wide strips.
- Meanwhile, boil mixture in pot until reduced to 2 1/2 cups, about 20 minutes. Stir in cabbage and chili sauce. Boil until cabbage is tender, about 4 minutes. Return chicken to pot; simmer until heated through, about 2 minutes. Transfer to bowl. Discard star anise. Sprinkle with remaining 1/2 cup green onions.

316. Spicy Chicken Enchiladas Recipe

Serving: 2 | Prep: | Cook: 60mins | Ready in:

Ingredients

- 2 boneless skinless chicken breasts, cut into bite sized pieces
- 1/2 cup chopped onion
- 1/4 tsp salt
- 1/4 tsp dried oregano
- 1/8 tsp pepper
- 1/2 cup enchilada sauce
- 1 cup shredded cheddar cheese
- 1/2 cup sour cream
- 2 Tbsp chopped green chilis
- 4 8 inch flour tortillas
- lettuce
- tomato

Direction

- Preheat oven to 350.
- Spray 8 inch square glass baking dish with cooking spray.
- Heat 8 inch non-stick skillet over medium high heat. Add chicken cook 2 to 3 minutes, stirring frequently, until lightly browned.
- Stir in onion, salt, oregano and pepper.
- Cook 3 to 5 minutes, stirring frequently, until chicken is no longer pink in center.
- Cool 5 minutes.

- Meanwhile, spread 1/4 cup of enchilada sauce in baking dish.
- Stir 1/2 cup of the cheese, sour cream and chilies into the chicken mixture.
- Spoon mixture evenly down center of each tortilla; roll up and place seam side down over sauce in dish.
- Spoon remain 1/4 cup enchilada sauce over tortillas.
- Cover with foil
- Bake 30 to 40 minutes or until thoroughly heated.
- Uncover; sprinkle with remaining 1/2 cup cheese over top.
- Bake uncovered 4 to 5 minutes longer or until cheese is melted.
- Sprinkle individual servings with lettuce and tomato.

317. Spicy Chicken Pizza Recipe

Serving: 4 | Prep: | Cook: 30mins | Ready in:

Ingredients

- 2 chicken breasts cut into 1/2" cubes
- 1-1/2 cups salsa
- 1 prepared pizza crust
- 1/2 cup red pepper strips
- 1 teaspoon chopped cilantro
- 1 packet mozzarella and cheddar pizza shredded cheese

Direction

- Preheat oven to 400.
- Spray large skillet with nonstick cooking spray.
- Add chicken then cook on medium heat until chicken is cooked thoroughly.
- Stir in salsa then cook on low heat 5 minutes and spoon chicken mixture over pizza crust.
- Sprinkle with red pepper and cilantro then top with cheese and bake 15 minutes.

318. Spicy Oat Crusted Chicken With Sunshine Salsa Recipe

Serving: 4 | Prep: | Cook: 30mins | Ready in:

Ingredients

- 3/4 cup prepared salsa
- 3/4 cup coarsely chopped orange sections
- 2 tablespoons canola oil
- 1 tablespoon margarine melted
- 2 teaspoons chili powder
- 1 teaspoon garlic powder
- 1 teaspoon ground cumin
- 3/4 teaspoon salt
- 1-1/2 cups uncooked quick oats
- 1 egg lightly beaten
- 1 tablespoon water
- 4 boneless skinless chicken breast halves
- Chopped cilantro

Direction

- In small bowl combine salsa and orange sections then refrigerate until serving time.
- Preheat oven to 375.
- In flat shallow dish stir together oil, margarine, chili powder, garlic powder, cumin and salt.
- Add oats stirring until evenly moistened.
- In second flat, shallow dish beat egg and water with fork until frothy.
- Dip chicken into combined egg and water then coat in seasoned oats.
- Place chicken on foil lined baking sheet and pat any extra oat mixture onto top of chicken.
- Bake 30 minutes or until chicken is cooked through and oat coating is golden brown.
- Serve with salsa and garnish with chopped cilantro.

319. Spicy Thai Rice And Chicken Wraps Dated 1962 Recipe

Serving: 6 | Prep: | Cook: 20mins | Ready in:

Ingredients

- 6 plain flour tortillas
- 2 tablespoons vegetable oil
- 2 teaspoons minced garlic
- 1/2 cup sweet red pepper diced
- 1/2 teaspoon red pepper flakes
- 2 cups rice
- 4 cups chicken stock
- 6 cups fresh spinach leaves
- 1/4 cup chopped fresh cilantro or parsley
- 1/2 cup lime juice
- 2-1/2 tablespoons chunky peanut butter
- 1/3 cup coconut milk
- 10 ounces grilled chicken breast finely sliced

Direction

- Heat oil in large pan and sauté garlic, red pepper and red pepper flakes for 2 minutes.
- Add rice and stir until the rice is well coated then add chicken stock and bring to a boil.
- Stir then reduce heat and cover then allow to simmer 20 minutes until rice is cooked.
- Meanwhile mix cilantro, lime juice, peanut butter and coconut milk.
- Place the grilled and sliced chicken in the peanut butter sauce mixture and keep warm.
- Warm the tortilla shells slightly then cover surface of each shell with spinach leaves.
- Spread filling evenly over the spinach then roll tortilla shell up tightly and cut in half.
- Secure rolls with toothpicks and serve.

320. Spinach Chicken Pasta Recipe

Serving: 8 | Prep: | Cook: 20mins | Ready in:

Ingredients

- 4 chicken breasts
- 16 oz. chopped frozen spinach
- 16 oz. alfredo sauce
- 4 cups of any pasta noodles
- 2 tablespoons olive oil
- 2 tablespoons parsley, for decoration
- Minced garlic (optional, add as much/little as you like)
- season as desired

Direction

- Cut chicken into 2-inch pieces and sauté with olive oil and garlic in frying pan.
- Boil noodles according to package directions.
- Heat spinach.
- Combine noodles, spinach and chicken in skillet and simmer over low heat.
- Add Alfredo sauce, simmer for 15 minutes, stirring now and then.
- Garnish with parsley and serve.

321. Spinach Pasta With Alfredo And Chicken Breast Recipe

Serving: 4 | Prep: | Cook: 40mins | Ready in:

Ingredients

- 1 12 to 16 ounce bag of spinach pasta (dry or homemade)
- 4 to 6 chicken breasts
- ALFREDO:
- 1 cup milk 2%
- 1 8oz box of cream cheese
- 1 1/2 shredded Parmesean cheese

- 1 sticks butter

Direction

- Boil spinach pasta according to instructions with salted water.
- Prepare chicken the way you like; I sauté with olive oil/spices, bake with spices sprinkled on top, or actually add bread crumbs and sauté until crisp.
- After chicken is done, set aside, cut in strips or chunks for over pasta when done.
- Over LOW heat put all Alfredo ingredients into sauce pan and warm until melted and thick. Whisk or stir on low heat until blended completely. Break up the cream cheese with a food processor or smooth with a fork before heating; avoids lumps.
- When pasta is done, drain, and pour Alfredo over pasta and toss.
- Reheat chicken in sauté pan, or leave as is, and place on top of spinach pasta Alfredo. If uncut, leave on the side.
- Very simple but very YUMMY!!!

322. Stadium Salsa Chicken Rice Casserole Recipe

Serving: 6 | Prep: | Cook: 30mins | Ready in:

Ingredients

- 2 boxes Spanish rice
- 3 cups hot water
- 1 10 oz can chicken breast
- 1 jar (16 oz) Stadium salsa
- 3 cups shredded cheddar cheese

Direction

- Mix rice, contents and hot water in bowl
- Add Stadium Salsa and chicken
- Mix thoroughly
- Pour into 11 x 13 casserole dish
- Cover and bake at 350 degrees for 30 minutes
- Remove from oven and add cheese on top
- Return to oven and bake uncovered until cheese is melted
- Serve with additional Stadium Salsa on top of each serving

323. Steak Chicken And Vegetable Tacos Recipe

Serving: 6 | Prep: | Cook: 10mins | Ready in:

Ingredients

- steak
- 2 ounces pressed tamarind from a pound block, cut into 3/4-inch pieces
- . 3/4 cup hot water
- 4 unpeeled garlic cloves
- 3 scallions, chopped
- 1 1/2 teaspoons thyme leaves
- 1 tablespoon pure ancho chile powder
- 2 tablespoons extra-virgin olive oil
- 3/4 cup Coca-Cola
- salt and freshly ground pepper
- 1 1/2 pounds skirt steak, cut into 4-inch lengths
- vegetables AND chicken
- 1/2 cup extra-virgin olive oil
- 2 garlic cloves, minced
- 1 serrano chile, thinly sliced
- 2 medium zucchini, thinly sliced lengthwise
- 2 chayote—peeled, halved lengthwise, pitted and thinly sliced crosswise
- 2 large carrots, thinly sliced on a sharp angle
- 1 fennel bulb—trimmed, cored and thinly sliced
- salt and freshly ground pepper
- 4 skinless, boneless chicken breast halves, butterflied
- 36 corn tortillas, warmed
- salsa verde and pico de gallo, cilantro sprigs and sour cream, for serving

Direction

- Prepare the steak: In a microwave-safe bowl, combine the tamarind and water and microwave on high power for 2 minutes. Cover and let stand until the tamarind is softened, about 30 minutes
- .
- Meanwhile, preheat a small skillet. Add the garlic and cook over moderate heat, turning occasionally, until the cloves are blackened in spots, about 8 minutes. Peel the garlic.
- Mash the tamarind to a pulp. Strain the puree through a fine sieve into a blender. Discard the seeds and fibres. Add the roasted garlic and the scallions, thyme, chile powder and olive oil to the blender and puree until smooth. With the machine on, add the Coca-Cola in a thin stream until blended. Season generously with salt and pepper. Transfer the mixture to a shallow baking dish. Add the steak and turn to coat. Cover and refrigerate overnight.
- Prepare the vegetables and chicken: Preheat a grill pan. In a large bowl, combine the oil, garlic and Serrano chile. Add the sliced vegetables and a generous pinch each of salt and pepper and toss to coat. Grill the vegetables over high heat, turning occasionally, until tender and lightly charred, about 8 minutes. Transfer the vegetables to a cutting board and coarsely chop them.
- Brush the chicken with some of the remaining oil from the vegetable bowl and season with salt and pepper. Grill the chicken over high heat, turning once until cooked through and lightly charred, about 8 minutes. Let rest for 10 minutes, then cut into thin strips.
- Scrape most of the marinade off the steaks. Grill the steaks over high heat, turning occasionally, until charred in spots, about 10 minutes for medium-rare. Transfer the steaks to a cutting board and let rest for 10 minutes, then thinly slice across the grain.
- Mound the steak, chicken and vegetables in 3 bowls and serve with the tortillas, Salsa Verde, Pico de Gallo, cilantro and sour cream.

324. Stir Fry Chicken And Broccoli Recipe

Serving: 4 | Prep: | Cook: 10mins | Ready in:

Ingredients

- 2 boneless chicken breasts
- 1 tablespoons plus 1 teaspoon cornstarch
- 2 egg whites
- 3 broccoli stems
- 1 tablespoon sesame oil
- 1/4 cup vegetable oil
- 1 teaspoon minced garlic
- 1 teaspoon finely chopped ginger
- 1 tablespoon rice wine or dry sherry
- 1 tablespoon tamari or soy sauce
- 1 cup chicken broth

Direction

- Combine minced garlic, rice wine, tamari, chicken broth and 1 tablespoon cornstarch in a small jar with lid and shake.
- Slice chicken breasts horizontally into three strips and each of these strips into ½ inch pieces.
- Add chicken to egg whites in small bowl to tenderize and mix 1 teaspoon cornstarch with chicken and egg whites.
- Add and heat sesame oil & vegetable oil in wok when oil hot, stir-fry chicken for approximately 2 minutes or until firm.
- Transfer to colander to drain.
- Cut the stalk off a head of broccoli with sharp knife and separate florets with stems around an inch long. If the florets are large cut them in half to keep them uniform in size.
- Stir fry broccoli in oil 1 minute remove and drain.
- Heat sauce in wok add chicken and broccoli heat through stirring constantly. Remove wok from heat cover and allow to steam three minutes.
- Serve over rice

325. Stroking Chicken Recipe

Serving: 6 | Prep: | Cook: 480mins | Ready in:

Ingredients

- 6 boneless chicken breasts
- 16 oz sour cream (light or fat free work fine)
- 1 envelope onion soup mix
- 1 10 1/2 oz can cream of mushroom soup

Direction

- Combine soup mix, cream of mushroom soup and sour cream; Spread over chicken in crock pot.
- Cook on low all day-8 hours or so.

326. Stuffed Chicken Breast With Lemon Gravy Recipe

Serving: 6 | Prep: | Cook: 70mins | Ready in:

Ingredients

- 3 whole boneless, skinless chicken breasts, cut in half
- 1 box Stove Top stuffing mix
- 2 small jars Heinz roasted chicken gravy
- 1/2 pound fresh mushrooms, sliced
- 2 small lemons
- 1/2 cup warm water
- Pinch salt
- pepper to taste
- 3 tablespoons fresh parsley, chopped

Direction

- Preheat oven to 400 degrees F.
- Prepare stuffing according to package directions.
- Using a knife, make a pocket on the thick side of the breasts large enough to place a small amount of stuffing.
- **Don't overload the stuffing.
- Place stuffed breasts into a 13x9" baking pan; salt and pepper to taste.
- Mix chicken gravy with warm water and juice of one lemon.
- Pour over chicken.
- Add mushrooms to top.
- Slice lemon and place slice on each breast.
- Cover pan with foil and bake for 35 minutes.
- Uncover and bake another 35 minutes OR until chicken is tender.
- Sprinkle with parsley before serving.

327. Stuffed Greek Chicken Recipe

Serving: 4 | Prep: | Cook: 47mins | Ready in:

Ingredients

- 4 chicken breasts
- 1/2 cup crumbled feta cheese
- juice of 1/2 lemon
- 2 tsp italian seasoning
- Greek seasoning (I use Cavender's all purpose Greek seasoning)
- granulated garlic
- onion powder
- olive oil

Direction

- Preheat the oven to 350 (F). Spray a baking dish with nonstick spray.
- Slice the chicken breasts 3/4 through the center on the side, to create a pocket for stuffing and place them in the baking dish.
- Mix the feta cheese, lemon juice, Italian seasoning, about a teaspoon of the Greek seasoning, a dash each of the garlic and onion powder, and a bit of olive oil (maybe a teaspoon) together in a small bowl.
- Stuff equal amounts of the mixture inside the chicken breasts. (If the chicken breasts you are using are very small and you have stuffing

mixture left over, sprinkle it over the top. I didn't have any left after stuffing.)
- Season the tops of the chicken breasts with an additional sprinkling of Greek seasoning and garlic and drizzle with a bit of olive oil.
- Bake for about 40 minutes or until chicken is cooked through (depending on the size of the chicken breasts and your oven, more or less time may be required).
- Serve & enjoy!

328. Stuffed Santa Fe Chicken Recipe

Serving: 4 | Prep: | Cook: 30mins | Ready in:

Ingredients

- 4 boneless, skinless chicken breast
- 4 oz. shredded monterey jack cheese
- 1/2 cup melted butter
- 1/2 cup Italian style bread crumbs
- 1 tablespoon shredded parmesan cheese
- 1/2 tsp. cumin
- 1/4 tsp. salt
- 1/4 tsp. pepper
- 1 small red bell pepper
- Cheese sauce:
- 1 tbs. butter
- 1 1/2 tsp. flour
- 1 cup shredded monterey jack cheese
- 1/2 cup milk

Direction

- Pound chicken breast between sheets of wax paper. Work from the center of the chicken out until flat. Sprinkle equal amounts of Monterey cheese on each chicken breast and fold over in half.
- Combine bread crumbs, parmesan cheese, salt cumin and pepper. Holding the open end closed drench chicken breast in butter and them in bread crumb mixture. Place chicken in 9x13 baking dish. Drizzle a little bit of the

melted butter over the chicken. Refrigerated for 1 hour. Bake in a preheated 375 degree oven for 30 minutes or until chicken is done.
- While chicken is cooking make a roux with the butter and flour. Add milk. Bring to a simmer. Add cheese and lower heat, constantly stirring so cheese won't burn. Add extra milk if needed to thin out sauce.
- Dice bell pepper and cook in a small pan with some butter until tender.
- When chicken is done, pour some cheese sauce over top and sprinkle with peppers. :)

329. Sunday Chicken And Rice Casserole Recipe

Serving: 46 | Prep: | Cook: 5121mins | Ready in:

Ingredients

- 1/2 - 1 stick of margarine
- 6 chicken breast (can take skin off)
- 1 - 1 1/2 c uncooked rice
- 1 can beef consomme soup
- 1 can French onion soup

Direction

- Preheat oven to 250 degrees.
- Melt margarine in casserole dish.
- Pour rice evenly over melted margarine.
- Pour beef consommé over rice.
- Put chicken breast over rice.
- Pour French onion soup over chicken breast.
- Cover casserole dish with aluminum foil and bake.

330. Super Easy Chicken Manicotti Recipe

Serving: 7 | Prep: | Cook: 65mins | Ready in:

Ingredients

- 1 jar (32oz) marinara sauce, or use homemade
- 1/2 to 3/4 cup water
- 1 teaspoon garlic salt
- 1 1/2 lbs (about 14 tenders) chicken breast tenders, not breaded
- 14 uncooked manicotti shells (8 oz)
- 2 cups shredded mozzarella cheese
- Chopped fresh basil leaves

Direction

- Heat oven to 350
- Mix marinara sauce with water in medium bowl
- Spread about 1/3 of the sauce into a 13x9 inch baking dish sprayed with non-stick spray
- Sprinkle garlic on chicken
- Insert chicken into uncooked manicotti shells, stuffing the tender from end to end
- Place stuffed shells on sauce in baking dish
- Pour remaining sauce over shells, covering completely
- Cover with foil and bake about 1 hour or until shells are tender
- Sprinkle with cheese and bake uncovered about 5 more minutes until cheese is melted
- Sprinkle with basil leaves

331. Sweet And Sour Chicken Recipe

Serving: 5 | Prep: | Cook: 60mins | Ready in:

Ingredients

- * 3 whole Boneless, skinless chicken Breasts
- * salt And pepper
- * 1 cup cornstarch
- * 2 whole eggs, Lightly Beaten
- * ¼ cups canola oil
- * FOR THE SAUCE:
- * ¾ cups sugar
- * 4 Tablespoons ketchup
- * ½ cups vinegar
- * 1 Tablespoon soy sauce
- * 1 teaspoon garlic salt

Direction

- Cut chicken breasts into chunks.
- Season with salt and pepper.
- Dip chicken in cornstarch and then in egg (yes, this will be messy but it will be worth it, I promise!).
- Fry in a little oil until browned on all sides but not cooked through.
- Place in a single layer in a baking dish.
- Mix sauce ingredients together and pour over chicken.
- Bake for one hour at 325 degrees F.
- Turn chicken every 15 minutes.
- If you like extra sauce, make another batch of sauce and bring it to a boil on the stovetop.
- Stir constantly and let cook over medium heat until thickened and reduced, about 6 to 8 minutes.

332. Szechuan Chicken Recipe

Serving: 12 | Prep: | Cook: 30mins | Ready in:

Ingredients

- 7 green bellpeppers
- 2 broccoli stalks
- 12 green onions
- 2-3 Tbsp. ginger(fresh)
- 7 chicken breasts
- 8 dried arbol chilies(or other small spicy chile)
- 2 Tbsp. black bean Garlic Sauce
- 3 Tbsp. hoisin sauce
- 2 Tbsp. plum sauce
- cornstarch
- peanut oil
- sesame oil(optional)

Direction

- Dice bell peppers and broccoli into bite size pieces, and cut the green onions into 1 1/2 inch lengths.
- Dice chicken into bite size pieces, and put into a bowl of cold water mixed with 3 Tbsp. cornstarch. It should be high enough to cover all the chicken. Soak for 15 minutes.
- Grate the ginger with the skins shaved off, and grate into a small bowl. Reserve.
- Soak the chilies in hot water to re-hydrate while you work.
- Drain most of the water from the chicken, leave about a couple teaspoons of water left. Mix in more cornstarch until it's a paste that covers the chicken (will help make a nice sauce). Mix together thoroughly.
- Add peanut oil to your wok, enough to cover the bottom and sides. Add a drizzle of sesame oil for flavour, and heat till when a drop of water is thrown in, it sizzles.
- Add chicken to heated wok and add salt and pepper to taste. Brown the chicken. Reserve in a bowl when cooked.
- Add a little more oil to the bottom of the wok and heat.
- Dice the chilies fast and small, and add to the heated oil. Stir for 30 seconds or so.
- Add ginger and cook for another 30 seconds.
- Add green onions in, and another 30 seconds.
- Add the broccoli pieces, and cook for a minute to two.
- Add the bell peppers, and cook for another minute.
- Add the chicken, and then the sauces right after. Add more of each sauce in equal parts if not enough.
- Serve over hot rice.

333. TEX MEX CHICKEN Recipe

Serving: 6 | Prep: | Cook: 10mins | Ready in:

Ingredients

- 4-6 BONELESS chicken breasts
- 1/2 CUP Miracle Whip
- 1/4 CUP hot salsa
- 1 TSP chili powder

Direction

- MIX MIRACLE WHIP, SALSA AND CHILI POWDER
- STIR IN BREASTS TO COAT
- BROIL 5 MINUTES ON FIRST SIDE
- BROIL 5 MINUTES ON SECOND SIDE
- EAT

334. Tasty Apricot Chicken Recipe

Serving: 8 | Prep: | Cook: 45mins | Ready in:

Ingredients

- 8 boneless skinless chicken breasts
- sea salt and fresh ground pepper to taste
- granulated garlic to taste
- 8 oz jar apricot preserves
- 6 oz (1/2 bottle) Russian dressing
- 1 pkg dry onion soup mix

Direction

- Heat oven to 350F
- Season chicken well with sea salt, pepper and granulated garlic
- Place in a 13x9 in casserole dish
- Mix together the apricot preserves, Russian dressing and onion soup mix
- Pour over chicken
- Bake for 45 minutes or until tender

335. Teriyaki Chicken Salad Recipe

Serving: 4 | Prep: | Cook: 1hours | Ready in:

Ingredients

- 2 boneless, skinless chicken breasts
- Marinade
- ¼ cup light soy sauce
- ½ tsp prepared mustard
- ¼ tsp ginger
- 1/8 tsp garlic powder
- 8 ounces rottini pasta
- Oil
- Salt
- Dressing
- 4 TBSP vinegar
- 1/2 cup extra virgin olive oil
- 6 TBSP sugar
- 1/2 tsp garlic powder
- 1/2 tsp salt
- 1/4 tsp pepper
- Romaine or baby spinach
- ½ cup feta cheese - more if you are feta freaks like us
- 1/3 cup sliced black olives
- Chopped pimento

Direction

- Marinate chicken breasts for at least 20 minutes.
- Bake at 350* for approximately 30 minutes, brushing with marinade every 10 minutes, or grill if desired. Cool and slice.
- Cook pasta till al dente, drain, and cool.
- Coat pasta with ½ of dressing, reserving other half.
- Arrange greens on dinner plates.
- Top with the pasta and sliced chicken.
- Sprinkle feta, olives and pimentos on top and drizzle with remaining dressing.

336. Thai Chicken Patties Recipe

Serving: 4 | Prep: | Cook: 30mins | Ready in:

Ingredients

- 1 small onion, roughly chopped
- 1 clove garlic
- 2 tsp fresh grated ginger
- 1 green chili or jalapeno, seeded
- 4 (1-3/4 lbs total) boneless, skinless chicken breasts, cut in pieces
- 1/3 c cilantro leaves
- 2 TB low-sodium fish sauce
- 2 egg whites 1.2 c plain bread crumbs
- sweet chili sauce
- lime wedges

Direction

- Combine onion, garlic, ginger, and chili in food processor and pulse till finely chopped. Add chicken, cilantro and fish sauce and pulse until well blended but not quite pureed. Transfer to a bowl and stir in egg whites and bread crumbs.
- Heat broiler to high with rack 4" from heat. Line 2 baking sheets with foil and lightly coat with cooking spray. Coat hands with cooking spray and shape 24 patties, about an inch thick; place on baking sheets.
- Broil each batch until patties are lightly browned, about 4 mins. Then turn patties over and broil 4 mins more. Serve with chili sauce and lime.

337. Thai Green Curry With Chicken Winter Squash And Fresh Basil Recipe

Serving: 4 | Prep: | Cook: 30mins | Ready in:

Ingredients

- 1 lb boneless skinless chicken breast
- 3 cups low fat coconut milk, divided in half
- 1 - 2 Tbsp green curry paste
- 3 - 2 inch pieces of lemon grass stalks, bruised with the bak of a nkif or 1 tsp dryed lemon grass
- 2 Tbsp fish sauce
- 1/4 tsp slat
- 3 Tbsp sugar
- 1/2 tsp tumeric
- 3/4 lb butternut squash, cut into 1/4 inch dice (about 2 1/2 cups)
- 3 kaffir lime leaves, cut into strips
- 2 tomatoes, cut in wedges
- 1/2 c frozen peas
- 1 small red chili pepper, seeded and chopped
- 1/2 cup fresh Thai basil or Italian basil leaves, coarsely chopped

Direction

- Sauté chicken in oil until cooked through.
- Put aside
- Heat wok over med- high heat for 1 min
- Add 1/2 cup of coconut milk. Add curry paste and allow mix to sizzle for 1-2 minutes, stirring constantly.
- Add remaining coconut milk, lemon grass, fish sauce, salt, sugar and turmeric. Increase heat to high and bring to boil, stirring frequently.
- Add squash and cook 4 min or until slightly softened, stirring frequently.
- Add the chicken, lime leaves, tomatoes, peas, chili pepper and basil leaves; cook 1 minute.
- Serve with rice.

338. The Best Homemade Sweet And Sour Chicken You'll Ever Have!! Recipe

Serving: 0 | Prep: | Cook: 2hours | Ready in:

Ingredients

- 1 lb boneless, skinless chicken breast
- 1 1/2 cups corn starch
- 2 eggs
- salt/pepper to taste
- 3/4 cups sugar
- 4 tbsp ketchup
- 1/2 cup white vinegar
- 1 tbsp soy sauce
- 1 tbsp garlic powder
- 1 tbsp duck sauce
- 1 tsp red pepper flakes

Direction

- Preheat oven to 325 degrees...
- Make the sweet and sour sauce:
- Whisk sugar, ketchup, vinegar, garlic powder, soy sauce, duck sauce, and red pepper until completely combined and set aside.
- Cube chicken breasts and season with salt and pepper. Beat eggs in separate dish, season lightly with salt and pepper. Heat a large skillet with oil to medium heat. Dredge chicken in corn starch and dip in eggs. Place chicken in skillet and cook until browned, but not cooked thoroughly.
- Grease a 9 by 13 (or whatever you have on hand) pan and add chicken after browning into pan. Once all pieces of chicken are browned, top with sweet and sour sauce ensuring all chicken is covered with sauce. Place pan in oven and every 15-20 minutes remove from oven and stir to ensure even coverage. Repeat this process 3 to 4 times (cook no longer than an hour and 20 minutes). Serve over rice and Asian veggies.
- I guarantee you will never order sweet and sour chicken from your Chinese restaurant ever again.

339. Tippin Family Fajitas Recipe

Serving: 4 | Prep: | Cook: 20mins | Ready in:

Ingredients

- 2 lbs. chicken breasts or chicken tenders, sliced into strips
- flour tortillas (we used flavored tortillas, like sun dried tomato and spinach)
- 3 onions, chopped medium (each onion is prepared differently)
- 1 jar D. L. Jardine's Fajita marinade sauce (or any marinade you prefer)
- Grated cheddar cheese
- olive oil
- fresh basil and oregano, chopped
- For the Special Sauce:
- 1/2 cup Cabernet Sauvignon (or any red wine)
- 2 tablespoons worcestershire sauce
- 1/4 to 1/2 cup white vinegar
- 2 tablespoons liquid smoke (optional)

Direction

- Marinate chicken strips in marinade sauce for about an hour
- Grill marinated chicken strips until seared on both sides. (The Tippins use an outdoor grill because they like the taste, but you can also grill stove top).
- While the chicken is grilling, stir fry three rounds of onion in olive oil. The first round is cooked until they are almost black. Add the second onion right on top of the blackened onion and cook until they are just translucent. Add the third chopped onion to the same pan, and barely cook it. (The three variations of cooked onions add a marvelous depth of flavor.)
- Break the cooked chicken into pieces and add it to the pan of onions
- In a small bowl, combine Special Sauce ingredients and add to the chicken and onions. Season with basil and/or oregano. The Tippins like to use both. Cover and let the flavors blend for a few minutes.
- Place the fajita mixture on tortillas with grated cheese and roll them up. You can serve this with any of your favorite side items, like sour cream, salsa, guacamole, refried beans, etc.

340. Top Ka Gai Chicken Coconut Soup Recipe

Serving: 3 | Prep: | Cook: 45mins | Ready in:

Ingredients

- 2 cups coconut milk
- 1 cup chicken stock or water
- 5 piece of fresh or dry galangal (peeled & sliced)
- 3 chicken breast fillets thinly sliced
- 1-2 tsp finely chopped chillies or dried red pepper
- 1 tbsp fish sauce
- 1 celery 1/2 inch long
- 1/2 cup fresh cilantro leaves
- extra cilantro leaves for garnish
- 1 lemon grass cust in long pieces
- 4 hole leaves of lemon leaves
- 2 green onion chop into small cubes
- 2 lage tomatoes
- 1/2 can of straw mushroom or fresh
- pinch of dried roasted crushed pepper for topping (optional)

Direction

- Combine coconut milk, chicken stock and galangal in a pan, lemon grass, lemon leaves, tomatoes and coriander root and celery. Bring to boil and simmer over low heat for 10 minutes, stirring occasionally.
- Add chicken pieces, simmer for another 10 minutes or till chicken are cook though.
- Stir in fish sauce, lemon juice, green onion and chilli. When done pour in a serving bowl, top with cilantro and red roasted pepper and it ready to serve can be serve with rice or as soup.

341. Torikatsu Chicken Cutlets With Hot Sauce Recipe

Serving: 6 | Prep: | Cook: 20mins | Ready in:

Ingredients

- Ingredients:
- 2 lb   chicken breasts
- 1 teaspoon   salt
- 1/2 cup   flour
- 2   eggs, beaten
- 2 cups   panko
- 1 quart   salad oil for frying
- 1/3 cup   A-1 Sauce
- 2 teaspoons   catsup
- 1 teaspoon   soy sauce
- 1 teaspoon   sugar
- Dash   pepper
- Dash   hot pepper sauce

Direction

- Preparation:
- Remove skin and bones from chicken breasts; sprinkle chicken with salt. Dredge in flour, dip in eggs, and coat with panko. Heat oil in electric skillet to 375 degrees F. Fry chicken until golden brown; drain on absorbent paper.
- Combine remaining ingredients. Serve with chicken.

342. Tortilla Crusted Chicken With Salsa Recipe

Serving: 8 | Prep: | Cook: 30mins | Ready in:

Ingredients

- 8 boneless skinless chicken breast halves
- Marinade:
- 3/4 cup tequila
- 1/2 cup fresh lime juice
- 1 tablespoon honey
- 1/2 cup grated lime zest
- 1/2 cup fresh cilantro leaves minced
- 1/4 cup corn oil
- 1 tablespoon dried tarragon
- 1 tablespoon minced garlic
- 1/4 cup hot pepper sauce
- 1/2 teaspoon salt
- Crust:
- 2 cups all purpose flour
- 1 teaspoon seasoned salt
- 3 large eggs
- 1/2 cup club soda
- 1 tablespoon hot pepper sauce
- 1 teaspoon seasoned salt
- 4 cups lightly salted corn tortilla chip crumbs
- Salsa:
- 4 cups cooked fresh or frozen corn kernels
- 1 cup finely diced pineapple
- 3/4 cup finely diced purple onion
- 1/2 cup finely diced red bell pepper
- 1/4 cup finely diced green bell pepper
- 1/3 cup finely chopped fresh cilantro leaves
- 2 teaspoons finely minced fresh garlic
- 1/4 cup tequila
- 1 tablespoon hot pepper sauce
- Reserved reduced marinade

Direction

- Combine all marinade ingredients then put half in plastic bag with chicken at marinate 2 hours.
- Put remaining marinade in pot and cook over medium heat until reduced by half then reserve.
- To prepare crust remove chicken breasts from marinade.
- Add seasoned salt to flour then dredge chicken in flour shaking off most leaving light coating.
- Whisk together eggs, club soda, pepper sauce and seasoned salt.
- Dip each chicken breast into egg wash to coat then shake off excess.
- Coat each evenly with tortilla chip crumbs then sauté chicken in 2 tablespoons oil until golden.

- Combine all salsa ingredients including reduced marinade then mix gently.
- Place each chicken breast on a serving plate and top with 1/2 cup salsa and garnish with cilantro.

343. Turkish Rice Pilaf With Chicken Recipe

Serving: 2 | Prep: | Cook: 18mins | Ready in:

Ingredients

- 1 Cooked chicken breast ,cutted
- 3 tbl olive oil
- 1 cup long grain rice
- 1 ½ cup chicken broth
- 1 1/4 tsp salt

Direction

- In a small pot, sauté the washed rice in olive oil until glazed, about 2-3 minutes.
- Add the boiling chicken broth and chicken breast and the salt and allow it to boil for about 1 minute.
- Reduce the heat to low and simmer, covered, until the liquid is absorbed, about 18 minutes.
- Place a folded paper towel over the rice, cover the pot and let rest, with the heat turned off for about 10 minutes before serving

344. Tuscan Chicken Recipe

Serving: 4 | Prep: | Cook: 40mins | Ready in:

Ingredients

- 4 large chicken breasts
- crushed garlic
- 2 tbsp. oil
- 2 tbsp. butter
- chopped onions (more or less, depending on your tastes)
- 6 sprigs fresh rosemary
- 2 tbsp. flour
- 1 C. wine
- 1 can beef broth

Direction

- Brown chicken pieces (3.5 lbs. of thighs and breasts) in pan with crushed garlic and a little oil.
- Remove chicken and garlic, add a 2 tablespoons butter, chopped onions, and 6 sprigs of fresh rosemary.
- Add a couple of tablespoons of flour to make a little roux.
- Add 1 cup of wine and then 2 cups beef broth; return chicken to the pot and simmer until chicken is cooked through (7-8 minutes).

345. Twenty Minute Chicken Creole Recipe

Serving: 4 | Prep: | Cook: 20mins | Ready in:

Ingredients

- nonstick cooking spray as needed
- 4 medium chicken breast halves skinned boned and cut into 1" strips
- 14 ounce can tomatoes cut up with juice
- 1 cup chili sauce
- 1-1/2 cups green peppers chopped
- 1-1/2 cups celery chopped
- 1/4 cup white onion chopped
- 2 cloves minced garlic
- 1 tablespoon fresh basil
- 1 tablespoon fresh parsley
- 1/4 teaspoon crushed red pepper
- 1/4 teaspoon salt

Direction

- Spray deep skillet with nonstick spray coating then preheat pan over high heat.
- Cook chicken in hot skillet stirring 5 minutes then reduce heat.
- Add tomatoes, chili sauce, pepper, celery, onion, garlic, basil, parsley, red pepper and salt.
- Bring to boiling then reduce heat and simmer covered for 10 minutes.
- Serve over hot cooked rice or whole wheat pasta.

346. Two Soup Chicken Recipe

Serving: 6 | Prep: | Cook: 45mins | Ready in:

Ingredients

- 6 boneless skinless chicken breasts
- 1 box long grain wild rice
- 1 can cream of mushroom soup
- 1 can cream of asparagus soup
- 3/4 soup can milk

Direction

- Mix uncooked rice with seasoning packet together with soups and milk.
- Pour small portion in bottom of a rectangular glass baking dish.
- Add chicken breasts then cover with remaining mixture.
- Cook uncovered at 350 for 45 minutes then serve immediately.

347. Unbelievable Chicken Recipe

Serving: 6 | Prep: | Cook: 20mins | Ready in:

Ingredients

- 1/4 cup cider vinegar
- 3 tablespoons prepared coarse-ground mustard
- 3 cloves garlic, peeled and minced
- 1 lime, juiced
- 1/2 lemon, juiced
- 1/2 cup brown sugar
- 1 1/2 teaspoons salt
- ground black pepper to taste
- 6 tablespoons olive oil
- 6 skinless, boneless chicken breast halves

Direction

- In a large glass bowl, mix the cider vinegar, mustard, garlic, lime juice, lemon juice, brown sugar, salt, and pepper. Whisk in the olive oil. Place chicken in the mixture. Cover, and marinate 8 hours, or overnight.
- Preheat an outdoor grill for high heat.
- Lightly oil the grill grate. Place chicken on the prepared grill, and cook 6 to 8 minutes per side, until juices run clear. Discard marinade.
- Note: total time taken is 9 hrs.
- The nutrition data for this recipe includes information for the full amount of the marinade ingredients. Depending on marinating time, ingredients, cook time, etc., the actual amount of the marinade consumed will vary.

348. Utica Chicken Riggies Recipe

Serving: 0 | Prep: | Cook: 50mins | Ready in:

Ingredients

- 4 tablespoons butter
- 2 1/2 lbs chicken breasts (I usually use three to four chicken breasts)
- 3 oz baby portabella mushrooms, sliced
- 1 green pepper, chopped
- 1 red pepper, chopped
- 2 large garlic cloves, minced

- 2 -3 cherry peppers, chopped. Add ½ - 1 oz of the juice also.
- 1 red onion, chopped
- 3/4 cup white wine
- 1/4 cup chicken stock
- 1 1/2 cup vodka sauce
- 1/2 pint heavy cream
- 1 teaspoon smoked paprika
- 1 teaspoon cayenne pepper
- 1 teaspoon parsley
- 1 teaspoon basil (finely chopped)
- salt and black pepper
- flour to thicken sauce if necessary (preference)
- crushed red pepper flakes (if you want it hot)
- 2 lbs rigatoni pasta, cooked and drained

Direction

- In a large pot melt butter and then add chicken.
- Cook chicken over medium heat just until they begin to turn white.
- Add mushrooms to chicken and cook for 5 minutes.
- Add peppers and onions cook 5-7 minutes (I usually season the veggies and chicken with salt and pepper at this point).
- Add wine, stock, vodka sauce, heavy cream, and spices.
- Simmer for 20 min, stirring occasionally.
- If it is runny, add flour or let stand to thicken.
- Stir in cooked pasta and serve immediately, sprinkling each serving with shaved or shredded Parmesan cheese.

349. Velveeta Cheesy Pasta Casserole Recipe

Serving: 8 | Prep: | Cook: 40mins | Ready in:

Ingredients

- What you need!
- 1-1/2 lb. boneless skinless chicken breast, cut into 1-inch pieces
- 4 cups cooked rotini pasta
- 1 pkg. (1 lb.) frozen Italian-style vegetable combination, thawed
- 1 cup (10 oz.) RO TEL diced tomatoes & green chilies, undrained
- 3/4 lb. (12 oz.) Velveeta Pasteurized Prepared cheese Product, cut into 1/2-inch cubes

Direction

- Make it!
- Heat oven to 400 degrees F.
- Combine ingredients in 13x9-inch baking dish, cover with foil.
- Bake 40 minutes.
- Let stand 5 min.; stir.
- Total: 55 min.
- Makes 8 servings

350. Waikiki Beach Chicken Or Pork Recipe

Serving: 8 | Prep: | Cook: 45mins | Ready in:

Ingredients

- 3 pounds boneless chicken breast or thighs
- (boneless pork works, too)
- 1/2 C flour
- salt and ground pepper
- 4 T oil
- 1 Can (20 oz) crushed pineapple in juice
- 1 C tangy barbeque sauce
- 2 T cornstarch
- 2 T brown sugar (dark or light)
- 1 t dry mustard
- green pepper rings (optional)
- sweetened coconut (optional)

Direction

- Cut boneless chicken or pork into nugget-sized pieces. Trim all visible fat from chicken thighs.
- Blend flour, salt and pepper. Dredge chicken/pork pieces to coat thoroughly.
- Brown chicken in hot oil over medium heat - I usually brown in 2 batches. (Hint, oil is too hot if it "spits" when you add chicken.) Chicken should be golden, but not brown on both sides.
- Combine undrained pineapple, BBQ sauce, cornstarch, brown sugar and dry mustard.
- Return all chicken to skillet and pour sauce over, mixing thoroughly. Cover and cook over low flame for approximately 35 minutes turning chicken pieces about half way through. Uncover and cook 10 more minutes.
- Garnish with green pepper rings and sprinkled coconut if desired.

351. Way To Go Dad Chicken Recipe

Serving: 4 | Prep: | Cook: 30mins | Ready in:

Ingredients

- 4-6 boneless chicken breasts
- 1(10 3/4 oz) can cream of chicken soup
- 1(8oz.) sour cream
- 1c crushed frosted flakes
- 1 stick butter, melted

Direction

- In a sauté pan, boil chicken breasts in water (save broth for another time)
- Tear chicken in small pieces and put back in pan. Mix soup and sour cream, pour over chicken. Put frosted flakes on top, pour melted butter over the crumbs. Bake at 350 for 30 mins
- Best if you have oven-proof pan so you don't have to use 2 pans.

352. Wheat Free Chicken Nuggets You Cant Stop Eating Recipe

Serving: 4 | Prep: | Cook: 25mins | Ready in:

Ingredients

- chicken breasts
- rice cakes
- yogurt (I prefer Stonyfield vanilla)
- dry basil
- egg whites
- Grated romano cheese (You can use Parmesean - I stay off of cow's milk - Romano is Sheep milk)

Direction

- Spray lined cookie sheet with butter or olive oil spray
- Cut chicken into nuggets and set aside
- Take one large bowl and crumble up rice cakes into smallish pieces
- Add Romano cheese but don't mix too much because it will fall to bottom
- Add Basil to taste
- Add any salt and pepper to taste
- Set aside rice cake bowl
- In another bowl scoop yogurt and add some egg white and mix.
- Dip chicken in Yogurt/egg mixture and then into rice cake mixture and put onto cookie sheet. Keep doing this until finished
- Bake in oven at 325F until done.
- You can make any kind of dip if you want. I love Trader Joe's Mesquite Honey mixed with Trader Joe's Dijon with White Wine.
- Enjoy! And let me know what you think!!!

353. Worcestershire And Lemon Baked Chicken Recipe

Serving: 4 | Prep: | Cook: 1hours15mins | Ready in:

Ingredients

- 4 large bone-in chicken breasts
- olive oil
- paprika
- garlic powder
- black pepper
- juice of one half lemon
- 1/4 cup worcestershire sauce

Direction

- Place chicken breasts in lightly greased 13x9 baking dish.
- Pour a small amount of olive oil over each chicken piece, sprinkle with paprika, garlic powder, and black pepper to taste. Rub into chicken.
- Pour lemon juice and Worcestershire over the chicken, cover dish with aluminum foil and allow to soak while oven is preheating.
- Bake in a 350 degree oven for 45 minutes. Uncover, baste with the cooking juices and continue baking uncovered for about 10-15 more minutes or until done.

354. Yakisoba Chicken Recipe

Serving: 6 | Prep: | Cook: 10mins | Ready in:

Ingredients

- 1/2 teaspoon sesame oil
- 1 tablespoon canola oil
- 2 tablespoons chile paste
- 2 cloves garlic, chopped
- 4 skinless, boneless chicken breast halves - cut into 1 inch cubes
- 1/2 cup soy sauce
- 1 onion, sliced lengthwise into eighths
- 1/2 medium head cabbage, coarsely chopped
- 2 carrots, coarsely chopped
- 8 ounces soba noodles, cooked and drained

Direction

- In a large skillet combine sesame oil, canola oil and chili paste.
- Stir fry 30 seconds.
- Add garlic and stir fry an additional 30 seconds.
- Add chicken and 1/4 cup of the soy sauce and stir fry until chicken is no longer pink.
- Remove mixture from pan, set aside and keep warm.
- In the emptied pan combine the onion, cabbage and carrots.
- Stir fry until cabbage begins to wilt.
- Stir in the remaining soy sauce, cooked noodles and the chicken mixture to pan and mix to blend.

355. Zesty Apricot Chicken Recipe

Serving: 4 | Prep: | Cook: 45mins | Ready in:

Ingredients

- 4 skinless chicken breasts
- 1 large red chili pepper-finely chopped
- 1/2 jar apricot preserves
- chili powder
- Fresh cracked black pepper

Direction

- Heat oven to 375 degrees. Place chicken breasts in a glass baking dish. In a skillet mix apricot preserves, chopped chili pepper, and cracked pepper--heat until warmed through. Sprinkle chicken with chili powder and baste with a light coating of apricot sauce. Bake for 35 minutes. Coat chicken with the rest of the sauce and bake for an additional 10 minutes or until chicken is done.

356. Asian Spiced Chicken With Vanilla Apricot Sauce Recipe

Serving: 2 | Prep: | Cook: 10mins | Ready in:

Ingredients

- 1# boneless, skinless chicken breasts, cut in 1/2" cubes
- 1 cup finely minced onions
- 2 Tbs. soy sauce
- 1 tsp. lemon juice
- 2 Tbs. olive oil
- 1 tsp. dried basil
- 3/4 tsp. ground ginger
- 1 tsp. ground cumin
- 1/2 tsp. black pepper
- 1 cup of fresh spinach, cut into thin strips
- >
- >
- vanilla apricot sauce;
- 1/2 cup apricot jam
- 1 Tbs. orange juice
- 1 tsp. vanilla extract
- 1/4 tsp. ground ginger
- 1/8 tsp. pumpkin pie spice

Direction

- Combine chicken, onion, soy sauce, lemon juice, olive oil and spices in a bowl, mix well and refrigerate, covered, for 15 minutes
- Heat a large skillet over medium-high heat.
- Add chicken mixture and marinade and cook 7-10 minutes, or until chicken is done
- Drain liquid from pan
- Serve over rice
- >
- >

- To prepare sauce; combine all ingredients in a small microwavable bowl and cook for 25 seconds (until sauce is warm)
- Serve on the side or over the chicken

357. Baked Chicken Breasts To Perfection Recipe

Serving: 4 | Prep: | Cook: 35mins | Ready in:

Ingredients

- 2 1 1/2# whole chicken breasts with skin, rinced and dried
- 2 Tbs. soft butter
- 1/2 tsp. salt
- pepper as needed
- 3 Tbs. vegetable oil

Direction

- Preheat oven to 450F.
- Line bottom of broiler pan with heavy foil
- Place broiler rack on top
- In a small bowl mix salt and butter
- Gently free skin an both sides of breasts and with a small spoon insert 1/4 of the mixture to the center of each breast and smooth it around, coating the breasts under the skin
- Oil outside of breasts with 1 1/2 tsp. oil each
- Salt and pepper underside of chicken
- Use only pepper on top
- Spread ribs apart so breast rests on the ribs and they don't fold under.
- Bake 35-40 minutes till done
- The following is why this is a veritable recipe:
- Add 1 Tbs. chopped kalamata olives-2 tsp. chopped parsley and 1 tsp. lemon zest to butter-follow above recipe
- Add: 2 tsp. chopped chipotle in adobe sauce, 1 tsp. ground cumin and 2 tsp. chopped cilantro to butter mix
- Add: 2 cloves of minced garlic, 2 tsp. fresh rosemary, minced and 1 tsp. lemon zest etc.

- Add: 2 Tbs. dried porcini mushrooms, reconstrued with boiling water, drained and chopped finely and 1 tsp. each fresh thyme and rosemary to butter etc.

358. Creamy Baked Chicken Breast Recipe

Serving: 8 | Prep: | Cook: 50mins | Ready in:

Ingredients

- 8 boneless, skinless chicken breast{I use walmarts already boneless chicken breast)
- 8 slices{4 inch} swiss cheese{or other mild cheese}
- 1 {10 3/4 oz.}cream of chicken soup {undiluted}
- 1/4 cup dry white wine
- 1 cup herb stuffing mix crushed
- 1/4 cup butter

Direction

- Arrange chicken in a lightly greased 13x9 x2 inch Baking dish
- Top with cheese slices
- Combined soup and wine stir well
- Spoon over chicken
- Sprinkle with stuffing mix
- Drizzle butter over crumbs
- Bake at 350 degrees for 45-55 minutes

359. Easy Baked Ranch Chicken Recipe

Serving: 5 | Prep: | Cook: 50mins | Ready in:

Ingredients

- 1/1/2 cups of corn flakes
- 1 pack of hidden valley ranch dip mix.
- 1 tbs. of parmesan cheese..
- 5 large boneless skinless chicken breasts.
- 1 freezer size ziploc bag

Direction

- Preheat oven to 350*
- Put corn flakes, cheese, and ranch dip mix in the freezer bag and crush them all by hand.
- After you feel that the cereal pieces are small enough put a chicken breast in it and cover it,
- Set on an ungreased pan and bake for 50-60 min

360. Fiesta Chicken Recipe

Serving: 6 | Prep: | Cook: 45mins | Ready in:

Ingredients

- fiesta chicken
- 1/4 cup all purpose flour
- 1/4 teas. salt
- 1/4 teas. pepper
- 6 skinless-boneless-chicken breasts
- 1 tbl. veg oil for browning
- 2 cans 10 oz mexican festival rotell with liquid
- 4 green onions sliced
- 1 can 2 1/4 oz olives drained
- 1 pkg. 16 oz yellow rice- prepare according to directions
- sour cream
- shredded cheddar cheese
- cilantro

Direction

- Combine flour and salt and pepper, roll chicken in flour
- Put in preheated cast iron large skillet
- Brown the breasts over med heat
- Add tomatoes, onions and olives
- Heat to a boil then reduce the heat and simmer for 20 minutes or till sauce has thickened

- Serve over the yellow rice, top with cheese, then sour cream
- Then sprinkle with the cilantro

361. Lemon Chicken Recipe

Serving: 2 | Prep: | Cook: 30mins | Ready in:

Ingredients

- 1 tablespoon butter
- 1 tablespoon olive oil
- 2 boneless chicken breast halves
- 4 garlic cloves, chopped
- 8 slices lemon
- 2 tablespoons fresh lemon juice
- Chopped fresh parsley

Direction

- Melt butter with olive oil in heavy medium skillet over high heat. Add chicken to skillet and sauté until brown, about 2 minutes per side. Overlap 4 lemon slices on each piece of chicken. Pour lemon juice around chicken. Simmer until chicken is cooked through, about 5 minutes

362. Potato Chip Chicken Recipe

Serving: 4 | Prep: | Cook: 30mins | Ready in:

Ingredients

- 4 skinless boneless chicken breasts
- 1/2 cup yogurt (or sour cream)
- potato chips (any flavor you want)

Direction

- Preheat oven to 350 degrees F.
- Put potato chips into ziplock bag and thoroughly crush them with a rolling pin
- Dredge chicken breasts in yogurt
- Roll in potato chips
- Place chicken breasts in greased baking dish
- Bake for 30 min., serve hot

363. Sour Cream And White Wine Chicken Recipe

Serving: 4 | Prep: | Cook: 60mins | Ready in:

Ingredients

- 1 cup low fat sour cream
- 1 can of condensed cream of chicken soup
- 1/3 cup dry white wine
- 4 boneless skinless chicken breasts
- 1 medium red onion chopped
- 2 cups small mushrooms quartered

Direction

- Preheat oven to 350 F
- Combine sour cream, soup and wine, mix well with a whisk. Add mushrooms and onion, stir.
- Put chicken in a 9X13 inch baking dish. Pour sour cream mix over the chicken. Bake in the preheated oven for an hour till chicken is cooked through.

364. Tuscan Chicken Recipe

Serving: 4 | Prep: | Cook: 60mins | Ready in:

Ingredients

- 6 roma tomatoes (about 1 pound)
- 3 medium zucchini (about 1/2 pound each)
- 1 bulb fennel
- 3 tablespoons oil, divided
- 3/4 teaspoons salt, divided

- 4 cloves garlic, finely minced
- 1 teaspoon lemon zest
- 1 tablespoon lemon juice
- 4 chicken breast halves skinless, bone-in (about 2 1/2 pounds)
- Freshly ground black pepper
- 1 tablespoon fresh chopped rosemary leaves or 1 teaspoon dried

Direction

- Preheat the oven to 375 degrees F.
- Cut the tomatoes lengthwise into quarters and remove the seeds.
- Trim the zucchini and cut it in half crosswise and then cut each piece in half lengthwise once if the piece is thin and twice if it is thicker, so that the pieces are relatively uniform.
- Remove the outermost layer of the fennel bulb and discard.
- Cut the bulb in half so that each half retains part of the stem end.
- Cut each half into 8 thin wedges so each wedge is held together by a little piece of stem.
- Put the vegetables into a large baking pan.
- Toss them with 2 tablespoons oil and 1/4 teaspoon of salt.
- Arrange the chicken pieces in the pan with the vegetables.
- In a small bowl combine 1 tablespoon of oil,
- 1/2 teaspoon of salt, the garlic, lemon zest and lemon juice.
- Rub the mixture into the chicken in the pan.
- Season with a few turns of pepper.
- Roast in the oven for 30 minutes, then give the vegetables a stir and add the rosemary.
- Cook for about 20 to 30 minutes more until the chicken is done and the vegetable are tender and beginning to brown.

365. Zucchini Stuffed Chicken Breasts Recipe

Serving: 4 | Prep: | Cook: 30mins | Ready in:

Ingredients

- 1 medium onion chopped
- 3 garlic cloves minced
- 2 tablespoons olive oil divided
- 2 cups diced zucchini
- 1 cup diced sweet red pepper
- 1/3 cup grated parmesan cheesed
- 1 tablepoon minced fresh basil or 1 teaspoon dried
- 1/2 teaspoon salt
- 1/4 teaspoon pepper
- 4 bone in chicken breast halves with skin

Direction

- In a large ovenproof skillet sauté onion and garlic in 1 tablespoon oil for 3 minutes. Add zucchini and red pepper, sauté for 3 minutes. Remove from heat, stir in parmesan cheese, basil, salt and pepper.
- Carefully loosen the skin of each chicken breast on one side to for a pocket; stuff with vegetable mixture. In the same skillet, brown chicken skin side down, in remaining oil. Turn chicken. Bake uncovered at 375 F for 25 - 30 minutes or until chicken juices run clear.

Index

A

Almond 3,5,13,78,104

Anise 7,154

Apple 3,14

Apricot 3,6,7,8,11,14,15,122,162,171,172

Artichoke 3,16,20

Asparagus 3,4,7,17,37,41,67,147

Avocado 6,125

B

Bacon 3,5,6,18,19,55,84,88,105

Baking 173

Balsamic vinegar 128

Basil 6,7,136,163,170

Bay leaf 62

Beef 3,4,22,69

Beer 3,22

Bread 4,6,45,55,112

Brioche 90

Broccoli 5,6,7,72,91,132,158

Burger 6,136

Butter 3,6,26,86,124,126,127,129

C

Cayenne pepper 55

Champ 5,75

Chard 89

Cheddar 55,87,142,149

Cheese 3,4,5,33,34,36,37,39,45,68,69,73,87,160

Cherry 3,19

Chicken 1,3,4,5,6,7,8,9,10,11,12,13,14,15,16,17,18,19,20,21,22,23,24,25,26,29,30,31,32,33,34,35,36,37,38,39,40,41,42,43,44,45,46,47,48,49,50,51,52,53,54,55,56,57,58,59,60,61,62,63,64,65,66,67,68,69,70,71,72,73,74,75,76,77,78,79,80,81,82,83,84,85,86,87,88,89,90,91,92,93,94,95,96,97,99,100,101,102,103,104,105,106,107,108,109,110,111,112,113,114,115,116,117,119,120,121,122,123,124,125,126,127,128,129,130,131,132,133,134,135,136,137,138,139,140,142,143,144,145,146,147,148,149,150,151,152,153,154,155,156,157,158,159,160,161,162,163,164,165,166,167,168,169,170,171,172,173,174,175

Chipotle 5,79

Chorizo 3,4,18,45

Chutney 4,44

Cinnamon 3,12

Cloves 99

Coconut 3,5,7,15,80,83,165

Cola 157,158

Cranberry 5,82

Cream 3,4,5,6,7,8,15,16,35,37,44,45,46,51,75,76,83,84,85,87,115,133,142,145,151,173,174

Crumble 54,104,143

Cucumber 4,58

Cumin 5,6,90,107,122

Curry 4,5,6,7,53,80,85,104,106,112,163

D

Date 7,156

Dijon mustard 42,47,57,134,139,144

Dill 50,51

Dumplings 3,5,26,94,95

E

Egg 55

F

Fat 29,59,103

Fettuccine 5,81

Fish 5,79

Focaccia 5,95

Fontina cheese 27

Fruit 90

G

Garlic 3,4,5,7,10,23,37,41,43,45,55,86,99,100,101,145,161

Ghee 58

Gin 4,5,6,44,101,135

Gorgonzola 4,50

Grapes 4,70

Gravy 4,5,7,63,89,159

H

Ham 4,69,86

Harissa 6,108,109

Honey 5,6,91,110,138,170

J

Jam 6,31,32,114

Jus 129

K

Ketchup 109

L

Leek 3,22

Lemon 4,6,7,8,70,107,122,159,171,174

Lentils 6,128

Lime 3,4,6,22,69,106,123,124

Ling 92

M

Macaroni 3,13

Madeira 44,45

Mango 6,124

Mayonnaise 128

Meat 130

Milk 127

Mince 53,76,156

Mozzarella 36,45,142

Mushroom 3,4,5,6,7,20,37,41,61,70,71,72,75,84,89,106,131,147,154

Mustard 6,130,138

N

Naan bread 113

Noodles 5,43,79,92

Nut 74,81,97,99,121

O

Oil 4,37,43,86,90,92,113,114,144,163,172

Olive 37,86,114

Onion 23,86,102

Orange 4,6,44,110,134,135

Oregano 3,21

P

Paella 3,18

Pandan leaves 16

Paprika 4,56

Parmesan 6,7,12,14,22,23,25,29,37,39,49,50,55,58,72,88,99,101,112,113,126,127,131,137,138,146,150,169

Parsley 86

Pasta 3,4,5,6,7,14,27,37,45,47,50,57,81,100,103,118,145,156,169

Pastry 61

Peach 3,6,24,138

Peanut oil 120

Pear 7,148

Peas 131

Pecan 4,5,6,7,58,99,138,139

Peel 56,68,146,149,158

Pepper 3,4,5,6,21,23,37,71,82,101,106

Pesto 5,75

Pie 4,5,6,40,43,55,59,60,67,85,128,130

Pineapple 4,59

Pistachio 7,153

Pizza 3,4,5,7,17,59,81,155

Plain flour 109

Plum 5,104,105

Polenta 88

Pork 6,7,116,169

Port 3,4,6,10,16,71,106,121

Potato 3,5,8,31,35,71,86,88,174

Pulse 99,153

R

Rice 3,4,6,7,23,34,35,36,39,62,68,87,112,140,141,156,157,160,167

Ricotta 7,145

Roquefort 4,63,64

Rosemary 7,146

S

Salad 4,5,6,7,47,103,125,129,143,163

Salsa 3,4,7,31,32,34,66,155,157,158,166

Salt 22,23,30,37,45,76,86,101,163,172

Sausage 7,147

Savory 5,104

Sea salt 55

Seasoning 101,153

Sherry 5,72

Soup 3,4,5,7,9,35,46,83,87,102,165,168

Spaghetti 3,35

Spinach 5,7,74,115,142,156

Squash 7,163

Steak 7,157

Stew 5,7,87,150

Stuffing 4,65

Sugar 97

T

Tabasco 123

Taco 4,6,7,66,106,150,157

Tagliatelle 5,72

Tapenade 6,125

Tea 46,68,170

Tequila 5,6,81,123

Teriyaki 7,15,163

Thai basil 164

Thyme 6,107

Tomatillo 6,107

Tomato 3,4,5,7,19,23,38,53,71,127,147

Tortellini 4,67,68

V

Vegetables 6,52,108

W

White pepper 55

White wine 101

Wine 8,86,170,174

Wraps 7,156

Z

Zest 8,171

L

lasagna 45,53,60,118

Conclusion

Thank you again for downloading this book!

I hope you enjoyed reading about my book!

If you enjoyed this book, please take the time to share your thoughts and post a review on Amazon. It'd be greatly appreciated!

Write me an honest review about the book – I truly value your opinion and thoughts and I will incorporate them into my next book, which is already underway.

Thank you!

If you have any questions, **feel free to contact at:** author@friesrecipes.com

Laura Mueller

friesrecipes.com

Made in the USA
Monee, IL
01 February 2025